TURKEY'S DEMOCRACY SAGA

TURKEY'S DEMOCRACY SAGA

The Struggle against Interventionist Politics

Ali Bulaç

NEW JERSEY • LONDON • FRANKFURT • CAIRO • JAKARTA

BLUE DOME

NEW YORK

Published by Blue Dome Press
244 5th Avenue, Suite D-149
New York, NY 10001, USA

www.bluedomepress.com

Library of Congress Cataloging-in-Publication Data Available

ISBN: 978-1-935295-78-5

Back flap photo: A mass peaceful protest outside Istanbul's Çağlayan Courthouse in December 2014. Thousands of people gathered at courthouses and town squares throughout the country to show support for the detained journalists and police officials, the latest victims of the Erdoğan administration's witch hunt.

Printed by
İmak Ofset, Istanbul - Turkey

Contents

Introduction

I t's difficult to comprehend the complicated socio-political events of the Middle East. In the last few years, protests have rocked the Muslim world from North Africa to Central Asia. Local conflicts in Libya and Syria have become full blown global wars while Israel and Palestine continue their seemingly endless struggle. Low level disputes across the Gulf region threaten to shake up the global economy. And the West continues to make inroads into places, as always.

At the center of it all is Turkey: once the region's biggest empire, then its "model" democracy—and always the bridge between the Middle East and Europe. As uneasy alliances have shifted and battles have threatened its borders, Turkey has remained one of the region's most vibrant economies and a melting pot of traditional wisdom and Western reforms—a volatile mix that has often times boiled over. Since the introduction of multi-party democracy after WWII, Turkish society has proven that it possesses a dynamic internal force for change and a strong will for more democratic reforms. At the same time, it has also shown a strong resistance when the "state-center" imposes top-down secularist modernity as reforms upon the "social-center."

In 2008, the country was shaken by two watershed moments—the Ergenekon trials which (seemingly) shook out the military-bureaucratic "state-center" and the ruling AK Party's narrow survival in a constitutional court case. Since then, the country has undergone a dramatic political reorganization. In 2011, the AKP led by the then Prime Minister Recep Tayyip Erdoğan secured a record 50% of the vote in parliamentary elections. Upon victory, the Prime Minister declared that his party had gone through their apprenticeship stages to reach "mastery."

What was supposed to be the AKP's "mastery" phase has instead been marked by unprecedented turmoil—some of it from within, and plenty from without. As the Arab Spring protests in places like Syria and Libya spiraled into global conflicts, Turkey experienced its own unrest. The Gezi Park Protests of 2013 shook the foundations of the country's political order, leading to the groundbreaking corruption charges launched against the oligarchic cadre at the helm of the Erdoğan government and the government's subsequent strikes against journalists, free speech, and the rule of law—in an attempt to cover up the massive government corruption.

In this collection of essays, Ali Bulaç eruditely addresses issues as diverse as Turkey's relationship with the global powers, the Kurdish issue, and the Turkish State's roots in the Ottoman Empire. Bulaç leverages a wealth of knowledge to dissect Turkey's vital role in the ongoing conflicts in Syria, Iraq, and Israel, and he uses his position as a government outsider to examine Turkey's internal dynamics from a fresh perspective. In his honest, direct analysis, he boldly challenges the status quo, such as Turkey's one-way relationship to the West, the supposed "end" of military-bureaucratic tutelage, the AK Party's image as a "religious" party, and the transformation of former Islamists into Muslims' monster.

The essays, originally published in *Today's Zaman*—Turkey's no1 English language daily and close sibling to *Zaman*, Turkey's largest daily and one of the papers most impacted by the Erdoğan administration's crackdowns on free speech—cover the years from 2008 until the present moment, charting Turkey's changing role within the larger Muslim and global communities as developments, both expected and surprising, have altered perceptions about the country.

Starting with a comprehensive analysis of the historical account of the social-center's uphill battle for democracy against the interventionist politics of the state-center, this collection of essays provides a deep insight into the most important developments of the last decade. Its focus begins on the internal dynamics within Turkey, from the democratization efforts the AKP initially undertook, to the landmark Ergenekon trials, up through the tumultuous events of the recent years which have been characterized by the reversal of democratic progress and curtailment of human rights and freedom. It sheds light on the bigger picture beyond the current AKP-Hizmet row, tracing the telltale signs of how the old state-center restores itself through the ruling party, thus explaining the reasons for the once-reform government undoing hard-fought reforms and its insatiable desire for power, carried out through witch hunts and policies of polarization.

In its later chapters, the book takes a close—and oftentimes critical—look at Turkey's relationships with the US, Europe, Israel, and the Gulf States. In addition, it expands its view to take the pulse of the wider Middle Eastern region as it tries to stake a claim for its own identity after centuries of Western interventions. It tackles some of the most relevant issues of our time, such as the Israel-Palestine conflict, the Arab Spring, and the war in Syria, from a perspective too often overlooked in the West—the perspective of an ardent Islamist, a defender of human rights and peace, and a proponent of dialogue and engagement. At times critical and at others hopeful, the essays both identify the root causes of the Middle East's and Turkey's seemingly intractable problems and offers common-sense, faith-inspired solutions to them.

Just as they identify problems, these essays also pose questions. Where can the West and the Islamic world find common ground on human rights? Why has Turkey struggled mightily to reconcile its perception as a model democracy to the reality on the ground? How could the situation in Syria have been solved before it devolved into full blown war? And above all, the book asks: how will the Muslim world, of which Turkey is a vital part, confront the ambivalent West which adopts a policy of double standard?

It is hoped that this book will encourage conversations and further reading. Instead of blindly assuming that Western concepts of nation-state, class-based society, materialist economy, secular-oriented reforms, and modernity are the only options to the Middle East's conflicts, these essays emphasize the fact that there are internal dynamics and a plethora of homegrown ideas to which one can and should have recourse in solving all major problems in the region—and that what has led to the present conflicts has been a radical break away from the traditional values and modes of thought.

In short, with his unprecedented insight and profound intellect, Ali Bulaç has given in these essays an ideal introduction to the socio-cultural and political canvas of both Turkey and the Middle East.

Chapter 1

Turkish Modernization Project

The Roots of Tension[1]

It is possible to argue that what distinguishes the Turkish modernization project from other similar endeavors is based on three major elements: "Westernization," "state-centrism," and "secularization."

The social repercussions of Turkish Westernization were an imposition of modernization or reformation attempts by state elites without considering the cultural internalization of its core values by the peripheral actors and the subsequent tension associated with this move. This is most likely the primary reason for the tension that has existed between the society and the state throughout the last two centuries. This tension still exists with its own dynamics in a number of fields, including in the political, cultural, and social spheres.

Institutions which the Ottoman State had created and which had functioned properly for a long time became ineffective (especially in the late Ottoman period); they proved to be inadequate vis-à-vis new developments and the needs of the age. Undoubtedly, there was a need for dramatic reformation. With the exception of the scholastic class, which supported maintaining traditions because of its historical role within the state, all other actors agreed change was necessary.

It could be said that both the state and the society were aware of this need for reform; we would not be struggling with the current ten-

---

1   First appeared in *Today's Zaman* daily on Mar. 11, 2008

sions if a broad consensus had been achieved to acknowledge the primary reasons for this need, based on sound dialogue between the state and the society. However, because the Ottoman rulers and administrators tended to regard subjects as members of a class to be ruled rather than active actors who should be consulted about the implementation of social practices and general politics, they did not consider maintaining dialogue with civil powers and actors. Ottoman statesmen simply held that the subjects were impotent; they had to yield to the state authority and nothing else.

The Republican elites who assumed office and administrative control from the Ottoman dynasty also adhered to this basic approach to society. They resorted to authoritarian, radical, and rigid policies to make society undergo a thorough transformation to attain Western standards.

At the beginning, the primary objective of reformation was the attainment of a contemporary level of civilization. But when reformation was defined as Westernization and the latter was interpreted as secularization, which excludes religion, it came to be perceived as outside the realm of what would be beneficial for the government and society as a whole.

Like the Islamic world, people living in Turkey believed that material and institutional reforms were needed. No one praised poverty, illiteracy, and weakness. But when the reformation process was imposed by the state as an agent of secularization and Westernization, Muslims felt threatened by this approach, which sought to undermine their beliefs that connected them to the universe and to life; subsequently, Muslims detached themselves from this world and became alienated from the political regime and the state in an attempt to preserve their existence in the world and in history.

This detachment from the world and the state did not bother the pro-Western power elites; on the contrary, they were pleased with it simply because they found the rationale to forcefully implement the radical secularist modernization project in the absence of public consent.

Is Modernism Limited to Reforms Alone?[2]

Due to the fact that the architects of the change sold to us, since the 19th century, as "modernization" are Westerners, they have determined the criteria and models of this change. Our intellectuals, scientists, and ruling elite have settled for simply translating this modernism, the framework of which was drawn up in certain Western capitals. They chose to become the consumers of modernism. We should accept that we have not made any contributions to the development of modern processes other than with our God-given natural resources, raw materials, and our status of being a mere market. The "Turkish heroes" exalted in the last two centuries have been found praiseworthy on account of their success in establishing the Western modernism in Turkey.

Universities, educational institutions, curricula, state institutions, and the media operate to serve the modernization policy. The degree to which we have understood and internalized the Western mindset, approached the Western institutions, and of course the extent to which we have become disconnected from the traditional understanding and institutions that belong to our own past are considered the criteria for our ability to change and participate in modern life. This process is unquestionable; even attempting to take a critical approach to it, let alone opposing it, is enough to have your most fundamental rights and freedoms limited, and to be branded as a "bigot," "obsolete," or a "religious extremist."

But in reality there are questions to which no complete answers have yet been provided: Are Islamic societies really unwilling to change? Are they so perfectly content with their current conditions? Are they taking a critical approach to modernity because they want to repeat the history and already lived experiences just as before, because everything in their past was "extraordinarily good and perfect"? We have to answer these questions very prudently.

The change that occurs in the world of creation is realized when a desire and force emerge, manifesting themselves in the form of a demand. Social change depends on the same laws. When a desire and a will appear

---

[2] First appeared in *Today's Zaman* daily on Jun. 20, 2008

in the internal dynamics of a society, they turn into power and the change occurs. Therefore, what is essential is the manifestation of a desire and a will. A society that wants change will manifest this through a will. This is the indispensable condition for change.

Considering we take this to be an accurate conclusion, we can state this: As the project of change that came from the West (modernism or modernization) is outwardly mechanical and peremptory, it is cut off from internal dynamics. And perhaps for this reason, society has viewed the processes of change dubiously and acted reluctantly toward participation in the development and improvement of policies imposed by the state, because initially, the Ottoman ruling elite, namely the palace, had participated in modern life since the time of Sultan Mahmud II (reigned 1808-1839). When making this decision, they did not feel the need to consult with their people. Because of this, Turkish modernization is authoritarian by nature—closed to democratic discussion and civil participation.

The second parameter of Turkish modernization is that it defines itself as non-religious. Since the 19th century, it has been claimed, through right or wrong analogies between Islam and Christianity and Islamic and European history, that the religion in this land has been an "obstacle" preventing us from developing. According to this claim, since Europe achieved its development by "getting out of religion," even by adopting a stance against religion, as seen in the example of France, our modernization should also have been formulated in a non-religious fashion and even by assuming a stance against Islam. If it is "not possible to take religion completely out of the cultural and social bounds"—which is another formula—then let's make reforms in the religion and "protestantize" Islam. Those who purported this idea had a basis: Max Weber's thesis that the Protestant ethics constituted the spirit of capitalism and motivated development and progress in Europe. But Weber's thesis was wrong from its foundation, because Protestantism formed after capitalism; in other words, it was not Protestantism that created capitalism, but capitalism that gave birth to Protestantism.

Formalism and Mimicry[3]

Turkish modernization is a movement based on copying, mimicking, and translation, and has taken Europe as such a lodestar that it has come to regard participation in modern life as "Westernization." For this reason, the proponents of this movement tended to attach great importance to form and apparel. For instance, the reforms introduced during the reign of (the late Ottoman period) Sultan Mahmud II included replacing the traditional Ottoman military marching band of Mehterhane with the polyphonic Mızıka-i Hümayun, Persian with the French language, the traditional army apparel with French army uniforms, and adopting the Western style in male and female clothing. Later on, allowing alcoholic drinks to be consumed at official ceremonies and the headscarf issue also have their roots in these reforms.

In a nutshell, the three parameters of Turkish modernization can be defined as the "state's preference," formulation of "the secular," and "Westernization." This is one of the most important reasons why the Muslim community tends to view modernity and "development programs" associated with modernity with skepticism.

There is also another, more profound reason: the incompatibility of the fundamental philosophical assumptions of modernity as posited by the power elites with the Islamic world's conception of existence, life, humanity, and its cultural codes. In this framework, modernity—a product of the Enlightenment—is based on three basic assumptions: (a) individualism, (b) secularization and (c) the nation-state. What do these three foundational parameters of modernity mean?

It should be noted that these three parameters are problematic with respect to ancient sacred traditions, divine religions, and Islamic perspective. Religions teach man how to worship God and submit to divine will. On the other hand, "individualism" rejects not only monarchs and masters as the symbols of absolutist rule, but also all forms of authority over man, including God's intervention with nature, history, and life. Individualism does not mean having a "personality" in the simple and desired manner or using one's reason against the captivat-

---

[3] First appeared in *Today's Zaman* daily on Jun. 24, 2008

ing temptations of feelings or learning how to be self-responsible, which is the primary goal of every Muslim. Being an "individual" implies being autonomous, free and independent vis-à-vis God—and Muslims have failed to find a way to find a compromise between this implication and their faith.

When you tend to see "secularization" as "laicism" in the simplest manner, everyone agrees to the need to protect everyone's freedom of religion and personal freedom. The public sphere or state and adminis-tration should not be under the control or influence of the clergy or the church in their organization. Everyone's freedom of religion and con-science should be protected and at the same time, there should be no pressure on the religious life of individuals. In other words, democracy should be protected against absolutism, and secularism against theoc-racy. Muslims have no problem with respect to these points.

Secularism as indoctrinated by the Enlightenment seeks to remove religion from the minds, life, social relations and institutions of individ-uals, isolate beings from the sacred, and reject the idea of the unseen world or life after death—the Hereafter—by suggesting that everything belongs to the "here and now."

This form of secularism functions as an ideological formation that prevents the people from participating in modern life. There are groups who want to impose this view, as they believe that the participation of the people in the modernization process—by making contributions and getting a great share in the national income—threatens their privileges. The principle of "statism," implemented in Turkey since 1929, provides for collecting resources from the nation and transferring them to wealthy groups. As the ordinary people become richer and get more involved in the modernization process, the privileges of the administrative center will be weakened and the ordinary people will get a chance to develop their own lifestyles. This runs against the second function expected from "statism." According to the power elites who seek to impose an authoritarian form of modernization on society, the rich groups sup-ported and funded by the state will be the driving force of development and at the same time, they will be the pioneers of modern lifestyles. This is because modernization is Westernization, decided by the state, and requires secular forms. The sui generis forms of modernization developed by the power elites—i.e., centripetal forces—are not acceptable.

Is Non-Western Modernization Possible?[4]

Many researchers agree that Islamist movements, which have been making inroads into Turkey's cultural and intellectual arenas since 1856, have "assumed a modern and modernizing mission." These movements can hardly be said to be "Western" or "Westernizing."

The authenticity of the difference between "modern" and "Western" is a big question, but according to the concept adopted by these Islamist movements at the very beginning, the Muslim world had to modernize and become part of the contemporary age. Otherwise, it would be pushed aside, left behind, and destroyed. At that time, Muslims (the Ottomans) were facing defeats in wars and losing land and they feared they might have to leave Anatolia and return to the depths of Asia. They feared the tragic experience of Andalusian Muslims might be repeated. Perhaps it was this fear that urged Ziya Pasha to write a history of Andalusia at the time.

A century after the emergence of the first Islamist movements, certain concepts and relationships among them started to become clear. For instance, objections were raised against modernism as a form of Westernization. The set of existing religious values, part of the Muslim world's historical traditions, and its real search and capacity for harmony, paved the way for many Islamists to believe that modernism can be reproduced in any human or cultural crucible using the appropriate forms and methods. In this context, famous sociologist Peter Berger argues, "Religions are not against modernity, but against secularization." For him, Europe has never been as religious as it is now. Other religions, too, can become more widespread and more social thanks to modernity. This means: in the West, modernity necessarily engaged in tension and clashes with religion, but this religion was a specifically institutionalized religion, i.e., the church and its dogmas, as well as the hegemony of the Christian clergy over the state apparatus. Neverthe-

---

[4]   First appeared in *Today's Zaman* daily on Jan. 28, 2013

less, the development of modernity ensured the democratization of religion. Communication, education, and greater mobility afforded by modernity ensured greater socialization of religion. It follows, then, that religions do not clash with modernity, but with secularization. In the final analysis, secularization has evolved into a sort of nihilism. A world dominated by nihilism needs religion as much as and even more than it needs modernization.

According to Islamist movements, one of three major factors that prevented the development of modernity and society's modernization during both the late Ottoman and Republican eras was that modernity had been imposed on the public through imperative, top-down, state-formulated policies. Secondly, modernity was defined as Westernization and this set the guidelines for modernization. This was modernism as an ideological concept which didn't play well with the traditional culture of the society. However, modernity is not an ideology, but a human condition; so it must be defined in this manner and it must respond to this condition.

This human condition cannot be ignored, but is Westernization the only way to internalize it? Those who advocate the thesis of non-Western modernization attach a great deal of importance to this question. For them, non-Western modernity should be possible, at least on a theoretical basis.

The third factor is that, perhaps in connection with the other two factors, modernity has emerged as a non-religion, i.e., a secular process under the profound influence of 19th century positivism. This has come to be translated as laicism in Turkish politics, and unlike its implementation in Europe or in other Muslim countries, this laicism has created significant problems in Turkey's specific historical and political circumstances.

Turkey: A Unique Example[5]

Ernest Gellner says that Turkey is a unique example in both the Islamic world and in non-Western societies of a country that belatedly joined the process of modernization.

---

[5]   First appeared in *Today's Zaman* daily on Dec. 16, 2013

Turkey is unique because its Islamism did not totally surrender to modernity. Turkey is also unique because of its secularism, which has been alive since the first quarter of the 20th century. According to Gellner, these two cases make Turkey a country with a double-layered reality.

Gellner also views Islam's attitude, compared to other religions, of standing against the modern world as a miracle in itself. Turkey is the most notable and remarkable example of this within the Islamic world. There are some factors that led to Gellner making such an assessment on Turkey. First, let us consider the attitude and response to modernity by the other major religions.

Independent of the ongoing dispute over Palestinian lands, Judaism has been subjected to some sort of a liberal change and transformation in the US. If you ask Meryem Cemile, who converted to Islam from Judaism, modernity has radically changed Judaism; she argues that the transformation was so huge that they abandoned their original religious premises and arguments. This can be explained by migration to the US. The history of the Jews is a history of migration, exodus and Diaspora—but their migration to the heart of the modern world is different. The initial observable result of this is the tendency among the subscribers of this religion to practice some vague liberal interpretations of their faith in their daily lives.

Muslims also migrated to the West, particularly to western European countries. But unlike Jewish migrants, they placed greater emphasis on their religious identity and traditional habits; they developed autonomous spheres in certain centers of the modern world, spheres that are against integration. However, everybody upheld that Turkish people who moved from the rural areas of Anatolia to Europe as laborers would leave their traditional customs and ties and go through a major process of transformation, of melting themselves into modern life.

The outcome is obvious for Christianity, which had encountered modernity head on. A British history professor in comparative religion, Robert Charles Zaehner, best explains this. He explains that Christianity threw something out of the boat in the face of a demand by modernity. Later on, there was nothing left to throw out of the boat because Christianity had nothing left.

A quick look at the geography where Islam was dominant historically reveals that this land was at some point under colonial rule. Only Turkey, Iran, and Afghanistan did not experience this. Is it possible that this is one of the reasons for the transformation of tension into a crisis in these three countries in reference to modernity (i.e., the Islamic revolution in Iran, the Taliban's role in Afghanistan and the secularism debate in Turkey)? Even so, why is Turkey a unique case in this area and in non-Western societies because of its own understanding of religion and secularism?

In addition to Turkey, South Africa, India, and Mexico have provisions on secularisms in their constitutions. However, the issues of religion, state and secularism have features and characters that go beyond the constitutional definition and framework. The primary factor that blocks the making of a new civic Constitution in Turkey is the definition of the constitutional provisions on secularism as irrevocable and unchangeable.

İsmet İnönü, who after Mustafa Kemal Atatürk became Turkey's strongest and most powerful leader, said in 1942: "By 1950, religion will be no longer a matter of debate in this country." A long time has passed since then. Turkey is still discussing the issues of religion, state and secularism.

State–Religion Relations[6]

The relationship between state and religion is one of the most important discussions carried out on the grounds of laicism in Turkey. Those who are familiar with political and social life in Turkey assume that the country always has a secret agenda.

This is one of the major problems that this country needs to resolve. Like many others, this problem may only be resolved through a method that we can call the "politics of negotiation." However, as far as laicism is concerned, democratic participation or politics of negotiation is simply set aside. Moreover, this issue comes to the forefront in times of military coup, anti-democratic intervention, or the eruption of tensions.

---

[6]   First appeared in *Today's Zaman* daily on Nov. 17, 2009

Unless the issue of laicism is clarified, it will take a long time for Turkey to become a real democratic state.

The most visible characteristic of Turkish laicism is that it still remains undefined. There is no generally accepted definition for this term in the Constitution or other relevant legislation. This is one of the issues that we need to focus on. If something is undefined, it is used by anybody from their perspective. However, because of inequality between the strength and power of the relevant actors, the privileged circles will have the right to impose their own definition. If there is no generally acceptable definition, the terms may become subject to exploitation and abuse.

From this perspective, we may argue that laicism does not have a legal, philosophical, or cultural framework in Turkey. Because of this problem, the term laicism is assessed as a functional value subject to change depending on the circumstances and conditions. In other words, laicism may take different forms and definitions depending on varying assumptions, the new initiatives intervening the on-going process, and the positions of those pursuing them, especially the state elites' particular interests and advantages.

Secondly, laicism does not assume a concrete and historical model as a reference point in Turkey. This refers to a lack of criterion. Ernest Gellner relates this to Turkish modernization, adding that this is a unique case and example. It should be noted that this is an important point.

Foreign scholars working on Turkish-style laicism fail to make a comparison between this version and secularism as followed in European countries by considering the historical grounds and the cultural and religious dichotomy during its emergence in the continent. They do not run a critical approach vis-à-vis the existing state-religion relations. What they are mostly doing is defining the state position as a value that should be inherently proper by neglecting many democratic values.

A number of scholars attempting to explain the crisis stemming from the application of laicism and social tension caused by this crisis view this as some sort of disharmony problem. They hold that the state's attitude has been proper since the beginning. They believe that the Muslim people fail to adapt to conditions created by the secular order. In short, the subject itself is troublesome and problematic, and this problem points to a pathological case. If a patient who needs treatment is taken to you, you make your own assessment based on your knowledge and expertise; in such a case, you do not have to hear his complaints. This is the basic point of departure held by the intellectual despotism relying on 19th century philosophy. Constitutionally, laicism is not a matter of discussion or negotiation; it is a foundation of the legal hierarchy that cannot be amended. The fact that it still remains undefined facilitates the job of the effective actors in the system to use the term in accordance with their wishes and needs. This is the primary reason for the controversy over the term.

This makes European institutions indifferent to the complaints and violations of rights of the people eager to observe their religious duties freely; in such cases, these institutions adopt a double-standard approach. In consideration of this indifference and lack of a generally acceptable definition, the state elite and holders of power claim a right to intervene in religion and religious precepts.

Demand for Good Governance[7]

The influential actors of Turkish modernization have been the "military-civilian bureaucracy," "the class with big capital"—which actually flourished with state support—and "the class of intellectuals,"—which replaced the Ottoman class of scholars (*ulama*). These actors serve to forcefully change the people and further monitor the process of change. They hold that people cannot be trusted because of their cultural references and for historical reasons; people can only be enlightened, and what the people are supposed to do is comply with what they are instructed to do. Despite universal precursors of democracy, the initiative that the people are allowed to enjoy in politics, administration, and even in their individual domain is limited to the project framework determined by power elites who devise plans to ensure social transformation in reliance on the state apparatus.

However, as recent history has shown, this project was not successful. At the current stage, it is obvious that we have to undergo a thor-

---

7   First appeared in *Today's Zaman* daily on Mar. 15, 2008

ough reform process. The problem is that the military-civilian bureau-cracy, the state-backed capital class, and intellectuals still rely on their old-fashioned methods, further excluding public opinion in the creation of this new project. They still hold that regardless of developments in the world, the probable project should remain state-oriented and rely on secularizing principles. Their understanding of secularization also requires protection of their privileges. For this reason, while secularism is supposed to guarantee freedom of religion and conscience, their version creates tension between the state and the people.

It is not plausible to seek a legitimate base by making references to an alleged threat of backwardness; such an approach simply ignores the visible impact of a multiparty democracy and enhanced standards of human rights on the domestic legal order, as well as a reduced role of the state in the economic sphere following the failure of communism. It is now obvious that no one in this country wishes to take Turkey backward; all in this country simply want Turkey to overcome its serious problems, which include illiteracy and poverty. They also hold that the proposed project by the elites creates problems for this country and undermines its image in the international arena.

All who are defined by the law as "equal citizens" are entitled to be involved in politics with equal opportunities and without having to compromise their identities. They are entitled to a share in the economy, trade, education, and health; this demand is now being voiced more loudly by the masses. Religion is one of the most important factors that affect political and social life in Turkey; this is also the case in the entire Middle East region. The rights of people to freely perform their religious duties and to freely express their beliefs (as long as they do not infringe upon others' freedoms) are fundamental rights.

All of these are legitimate demands and requests. Repression of social demands via coercion will resolve nothing, and will only exacerbate the current problems; this will eventually weaken the social and political unity in the country, further threatening social peace and harmony. Years ago, Bediüzzaman Said Nursi noted that people may not be forced to comply with certain rules and instructed people to observe the bans and strict rules; he said that our age required mutual dialogue to deal with the problems. This is what civilized men and women should do.

Those who have been relying on a policy of coercion should review what they have done; what have they resolved? They should also consider the repercussions of coercive policies. Good governance makes people enjoy life; it does not make life unbearable for them.

Can the Turkish Model Be a Source of Inspiration?[8]

Unlike the commonly held view, the modernization that Turkey experienced and the democratic model it is based on does not rely on a sui generis doctrine where Islam is reconciled with secularism.

The argument that Islam has been reconciled with secularism in the processes where democratic institutions operate in Turkey should be questioned because religious people and groups in Turkey have not acquired the rights granting them full autonomy in the social and public realm and to live according to their beliefs in their civilian life.

Even though this seems a little theoretical, it has come to the fore as a source of tension between religious communities and the political administration. The eagerness of the political administration to restrict these communities and groups in recent times is relevant to politics, democratic theory, and political sociology rather than a power struggle between two different poles.

It is inherently difficult for social elements and groups whose spheres of service and expertise are different to have a working division of labor and to work together smoothly. The division of labor or motivation for offering services turns into a competition or a mortal conflict in the modern sense, and a race of benevolence in an Islamic framework. Secularized politics does not recognize a criterion above it; its ultimate goal is pure success. For this reason, competition constitutes its dynamism. Muslims, on the other hand, are obligated to vie in benevolence regardless of their sectarian or ideological affiliations. Ethical legitimacy is the primary element that motivates the political and social movement of Muslims; this has to correspond to social good.

---

[8]   First appeared in *Today's Zaman* daily on Oct. 22, 2012

From the perspective of Turkey's modern history, we could argue that social Islam, whose sphere of service and activity is to support society in ethical and material terms, has been alienated from political movements whose goal is political utility—which we could call political Islam—due to improper modernization policies. Our socio-political issues include the removal of this state of alienation and the establishment of solidarity, and a division of labor by keeping each on their natural track and course. Sometimes, it is observed that the social is blended with the political and that there are political attempts to put pressure on the social. However, in a world where democracies are emerging as working processes, similar issues and tensions are observed everywhere between political society and civil society. The issue is relevant to the nature of the modern mode of political and social organization and this is a problem everywhere. We could resolve this problem by following the developments in the modern world carefully with reference to our religious references and historic experiences. We have to do this because, as usual, religion determines the civilian sphere of Muslim society. This demonstrates that while it has emerged in a secular character in the West, civil society bears a religious character in the Muslim world and it is a sphere regulated and protected by the religion vis-à-vis the state. In the Ottoman model, public law protected the state while Sharia law protected society vis-à-vis the state.

We cannot risk wasting two major developments in our near history: the overlap between external pressures and the encouragement of a process of change and domestic demands for social change—I am not referring to the EU or US projects; I am referring to the course of regional and global events—and the emergence of a religious and social Islam in connection with a political move in the relevant fields over the last decade. If we are able to address the problems and the tensions that could be removed by past experiences without hurting this historic connection, it could be possible for us to develop a model in the new era that could serve as a source of inspiration for the Muslim world.

The Turkish Model: Breaking the Spirit of Authoritarianism[9]

If you ask me what the "Turkish model" is, my answer will be "the experience Turkish society has gained in its attempt to civilianize or tame the authoritarian political regime."

A great number of local and foreign observers tell us that the Turkish model is a "compromise between Islam and secularism." There clearly has not been an experience of such a compromise. Our ruling elites have come to perceive secularism not as the state's attitude towards religions and beliefs but as the ideology of an authoritarian practice.

In the Middle East regimes are autocratic, monarchic, or dictatorial. It goes without saying that Turkey, with its single-party regime between 1923 and 1950, was not a democracy. Under pressure from the outside world, Turkey made the transition to the multiparty democratic system, but what made this democratic regime survive two violent and three bloodless military interventions was people's prudence, patience, and, in a general sense, self-preservation. The part the political parties that sprung from the National View (Milli Görüş) movement and the Islamist intellectuals played in this cannot be denied. Thus, the vast majority of Islamists here lent support to the Islamic revolution in Iran, but we did not ignore the fact that this method would be ineffective in Turkey. Our heritage of political culture and our experiences in the 20th century urged us to pursue other methods. And we sought other means, and, eventually, we arrived at the current workable and meaningful result. Even our "most radical" Islamic movements and groups refrain from violence, terror, or armed struggle.

There are a number of reasons why the political regimes in the Middle East need be overthrown through armed conflict. This should be discussed separately. However, today we see that such attempts are not effective or cost too many lives and at the price of great destruction as in the case of Syria or Libya.

The Turkish model has two parameters:

---

[9] First appeared in *Today's Zaman* daily on Sept. 12, 2011

- the social development of the political regime and the Islamically motivated and legitimate change in social culture.

- granting diverse religious, sectarian and ethnic groups the right of representation and expression along with the main body of Muslims without denying their existence or assimilating them. This can only be done today by firmly established political parties.

The West invaded Muslim countries under the pretext of introducing democracy and freedoms to those countries and with the hidden agenda of plundering their resources. Turkey cannot and should not impose its own model or a self-styled leadership on the region.

Of course, we have great responsibilities toward the region. But just as Iran's attempt to export its revolution and sectarian beliefs to other countries is met with disapproval, our efforts to promote our model or a Turkey-centered strategy will be disliked as well. The region should be rebuilt with participation from all sides.

For Turkey to actively cooperate with other countries in the region and play an active role, it should do the following:

It should solve the ongoing Kurdish issue and make Kurds the principal actors of a grand strategy to this end. It should mobilize all Kurds living in the region, but first it should settle its own Kurdish issue.

Our economy is not yet fully protected against sudden shocks. We are able to handle our current account deficit and foreign loans, but everything may be turned upside down if the flow of money is disrupted. In addition, we are seriously troubled with how to ensure an equitable distribution of income.

Turkey is dependent on foreign countries for defense and weapons technology. We need to develop our own weapons technology, at least in some fields, like Iran. How can Turkey, a NATO member and part of the Western alliance, attempt to play a leadership role in the region, making decisions independently? Someone should analyze this matter and provide a logical explanation for this. Let us discuss which intellectual, political, or moral values we will take to the region. What material do we have other than the bad copies of the West's established values as marketed in Turkish TV series?

Concerning the prime minister's visit to Tunisia and Egypt, The Wall Street Journal reported that Prime Minister Erdoğan's chief adviser, İbrahim Kalın, said, "We have always made clear that we do not have imperial intentions, but there are demands from Arabs to this end." I don't think Kalın made such a remark, but some people (both within and without the government) may really be nurturing such motives. Some people are trying to push us into adventure by triggering these motives. We must be alert!

Sui Generis "Model of Secularism"![10]

Can Turkey's authoritarian secularism, enshrined in its Constitution since 1937, be a model for Middle Eastern countries? This has been one of the most frequently asked questions recently.

A couple of problematic points should be brought to the fore in any discussion on secularism in Turkey. Some describe secularism as "undefined." I agree with this description. This is one of the points that we must deal with. If something is undefined, then everyone can use it arbitrarily, trying to redefine it according to their subjective perspectives. Yet, as not all groups have equal powers or status, those who are more powerful can make their definition a generally accepted one. If a definition cannot be agreed on by everyone, then it is prone to being abused.

From this perspective, it is clear that in Turkey, secularism does not have a framework that is defined by philosophical, cultural or legal perspectives. This allows secularism to be treated as a functional value that changes depending on the situation and conditions. In other words, secularism can be defined differently depending on the conjecture, the initiatives involved, the elites who are concerned about their own advantages, positions, and status, and the bureaucratic forces that control the center. When then-Parliament Speaker Bülent Arınç said in 2006 that secularism should be defined, this led to outrage. An undefined concept can be stuffed with anything one desires and it can be easily abused.

The second important point is that in Turkey, secularism does not rest on any concrete or historical model. This implies a loss of criteria.

10　First appeared in *Today's Zaman* daily on Feb. 22, 2011

Ernest Gellner associates this with Turkish modernization, describing it as a "unique example." How can a unique form of secularism be a model for other countries?

Foreign scholars who study Turkey's secularism practices carefully avoid drawing comparisons between secularism as it emerged in Europe, with its historical background and cultural and religious dilemmas, and the Turkish form of secularism. They do not criticize the current relations between religion and the state—in particular, with respect to how they are implemented in the West. What they do, instead, is accept the state's position as the correct value by ignoring many democratic values. This is what politicians and jurists in the West and Turkey categorically do as they study secularism. Of course, there have recently been considerable changes in the perceptions of secularism. For instance, there is a major difference in the viewpoints of today and those of 50 years ago. However, these changes have not yet influenced the official view on secularism.

Many scholars and researchers who try of explain the deep crisis that emerged along with secularism and the social tension that feeds on it see this as a sort of incompatibility. For them, the reason for the deep crisis and social tension is Muslim subjects' failure to adapt to secularism and their pathological mindset. Accordingly, the state has always adopted the correct and ideal attitude, while Muslim people have failed to adapt to secularism. In short, the subject is problematic and this indicates a pathological case. If a patient that needs treatment is referred to a physician, the physician will take no notice of his ranting and administer the medicine which he believes the patient needs. Thus, the patient cannot democratically raise objections to the exact science of medicine. This is the departing point of intellectual despotism that rests on positivism and the 19th century philosophy. Constitutionally, secularism is both a disputed matter and is enshrined in the Constitution as an unchangeable article. Actually, no one intends to change it, but the problem is what should be its definition on which everyone reaches a consensus.

Due to this, European institutions tend to turn a deaf ear to the human rights violations Muslim groups in Turkey suffer, and they automatically adopt double standards. The current conceptual framework allows the state and the ruling elites to meddle with religion, its philosophy, ontological visions, and sacred references.

Ultra-Secularism vs. Democratic Secularism[11]

Secularism is one of the controversial issues that may potentially create tension in Turkey. This tension is most times misinterpreted by the outside world—particularly the West and Europe. Those who use secularism as a political tool within the domestic political landscape refer to segments of society eager to perform their religious duties in compliance with the laws as a "threat" to the secular regime. Foreign actors unfamiliar with Turkey's domestic structure get convinced by this simple propaganda and subsequently come to the conclusion that religious people disrespect the lifestyles of others and are involved in conspiracies to introduce a new system that would take the country to the level of medieval Europe. They even stress that the religion itself is the primary reason for remaining underdeveloped; it should be noted that this is not the case.

I sincerely believe that people who take their religion seriously have no problem with secularism vis-à-vis the issues of the protection of freedom of religious belief and conscience for all. Nor do religious people have a problem with the prohibition of the introduction of a system based on religion that would make a group of clerics privileged and dominant over the rest of the society and forcing members of other religions or faiths to adopt their own beliefs; in their actions and constructive behavior, religious people do not feel any obligation to hide their original ideas and beliefs and seek the best time to execute their conspiracies. There is no sign that they will have any troubles at all with secularism in the future.

Islamic history clearly shows that Muslims have paid utmost attention—even in times of their dominance—to the preservation of religious freedoms of non-Muslims. Currently, non-Muslims freely observe their religious beliefs and duties in predominantly Muslim countries. In present-day Turkey, there is some pressure on their particular liberties —i.e.,

---

[11] First appeared in *Today's Zaman* daily on May 27, 2008

the failure to reopen a seminary on Heybeliada Island off the coast of Istanbul and restrictions on foundations of non-Muslims, but these problems stem from secular circles rather than pious people.

The view that a positivist and materialist world and lifestyle is intended in secular design and that anything with a religious dimension is inherently bad and should be declared harmful is a philosophical approach that has nothing to do with secularism. This approach turns the lives of Muslims and members of other religions into hell in Turkey.

For a long time now, those who limit secularism to a perspective of materialism and positivism and seek to strip daily life of the influences of Islam have been known as supporters of real modernity and a modern lifestyle. For this reason, they have undeservedly received the greatest attention and support. However, events throughout Turkey's EU bid showed that this was actually a legend. EU authorities and some intellectuals have realized this. European Commission President José Manuel Barroso's frequent reference to democratic secularism is one indicator of this new tendency.

No doubt secularism is a byproduct of the experience of European history. Of course, Europe has not given up on the secularism it exported to the world; however, it stresses that the secularism as observed in Turkey, considered an important partner for the future of Europe, is not democratic. According to EU Enlargement Commissioner Olli Rehn, the ongoing tension will be effectively handled only if a truly democratic secularism is adopted. The EU holds that large religious masses do not pose any threat to the secular character of the country. In this case, there is no option other than making attempts to make the ultra-secularists adopt a democratic republic and secularism. The EU is obviously not fond of religious people and secularists for no reason. In the final analysis, it views Turkey as a dynamic actor that will play an active role in the global world and for this reason pays attention to the probable role of the religious segment of Turkish society. Certain ultra-secularists who view modernity as nudity and obscenity and freedom to have alcoholic beverages at a restaurant in a fairly conservative small Anatolian town are not what the Europeans, who seek real secularists, intend. The EU is simply asking Turkey to undergo dramatic reforms for the sake of maximizing its own interests.

The Democratization of Secularism[12]

The negative effects of the absence of a "church against the state" in the Muslim world and the gravitation of the state toward a rhetoric that religion is against it is much deeper than assumed. (This issue has been the leading critical obstacle in Turkey's EU bid since the mid-1990s.) If the end result of Turkish modernization is reaching a "level of contemporary civilization," which according to Mustafa Kemal Atatürk it is, then the secularism viewpoint in question makes the contemporary civilization ideal invalid and makes the crucial institutions of contemporary civilization almost ineffective.

When we say contemporary civilization today, we don't mean industrial development, soccer stadiums, big airports, sea ports, highways, and expressways. We mean human rights, freedom of conscience and religion, the protection of individual rights and freedom, minority rights, recognizing differences, pluralistic democracy, participation, the influence the governed have on the decision process, and the rule of law. But the state's evaluation of secularism within this conceptual framework causes a huge chasm between these ideals and the state.

The state's adoption of an anti-religion stance is the result of its exalting a particular ideology. "Laicism" is a concept that expresses the Turkish elites' understanding of secularism.

The first person to express this was Şükrü Kaya, who served as interior minister in 1937. Malatya Deputy İsmet İnönü and his three friends made a legislative proposal to incorporate laicism into the constitution. Speaking on behalf of the government when the bill was being discussed in Parliament, Kaya said:

"This country has suffered great harm because the consciences of seers and irresponsible people were effective and because they were involved in state and national affairs. Since we were determinists in history and since we are materialists in practice now, we must (take an action and) prepare our own laws. With the kind of freedom and secularism we plan, we want to ensure that religion is not effective and in charge in state affairs. This is our framework and limit for laicism. We

---

12   First appeared in *Today's Zaman* daily on Nov. 24, 2009

want religion to stay in the consciences and houses of worship. We don't want it to interfere in material life and worldly affairs, and we will not allow it to."

In 1937 the Ministry of Interior spoke about being "determinist" and "materialist." He was trying to impose determinism and materialism on the people and "laicism" on the state.

Without any doubt, this is an anachronistic view, at least from the perspective of the current valid viewpoint. It is a very striking situation for a state which has assumed responsibility of public affairs to identify as determinist, positivist, and materialist, and to adopt an anti-religion stance because of an understanding of modernization it formulated due to, perhaps, historical reasons. This situation is one of the main causes of tension experienced during the 20th century and it continues today.

Of course this situation also led to the intervention in and definition of religion. One of the leading causes of religion and Islam becoming politicized is the state's interference in religion and attempt to decide what people should believe in and how they should live their lives. On the one hand, the state tried to teach citizens the kind of religion they should believe; on the other, it tried to remove religion from individual, social, and public life because of its ideological modernization mission.

This fact gave the state an "eternal" authoritarian and totalitarian-strained attribute that was in conflict with religion and religious people. It was said that this concept could "last for a thousand years" if necessary. It is for this reason that the problem today is not a problem between religion and the state. Religious people do not have any objection to "secularism where the state is fair to all religions." The state is supposed to protect the freedom of religion and conscience through laws by adopting a neutral stance. It must treat beliefs and sects equally; it must prevent one religion or sect from oppressing other religions or religious groups. But it must not inhibit any religion from being visible in the public sphere nor inhibit it from coexisting in line with the "unity in plurality" principle. Religious people in Turkey desire secularism within this kind of framework. Just like the state, secularism needs to be democratized as well.

Transcending Modernity[13]

The Muslim world has revised its socio-political system in order to help overcome problems inherited from the recent past and has opened relatively more liberal spaces for Muslims.

However, this should lead us to make a critical, selective, and conscious decision on what we should take from the outside world, because failing to do so could cause a radical change in our essential goals without us even being aware of it.

Even if the participation of Muslims—against whom there has been a strenuous effort over the past century to exclude not only from the political sphere, but also from the social and public space—in current institutional structures (the economy, politics, education, culture, arts, and so on) is "beneficial," failing to ask how, how much, and why we should participate could lead to great damage that could be hard to compensate for in the future. Therefore, we should always be conscious of the issue. When we say, "let's focus on material life (disregarding the spiritual and otherworldly dimensions)," we may unknowingly "take part in the system (of the 'modern' world) and become a piece—with the identity and image of Islam—of the given world."

There are two drawbacks to the issue. The first is the belief in a separate and autonomous phenomenon that can exist independently from the Muslim world and community while dealing with the problems in the nation state and downgrading Islam only to a nation-state's geographic, economic, and political issues. The other drawback is secularizing, materializing, and nationalizing Islam as a result of the former wrongful conviction. This situation could force us to adopt one of two attitudes in the face of the modern world, which can be seen as either our rival or our goal. These two unhealthy attitudes are known as "conflictive Islam" and "compatible Islam." These two concepts are different from the "radical Islam" and "moderate Islam" dilemma that the media have recently been emphasizing. "Conflicting Islam" and "compatible Islam" look different, but are essentially the same. Both perceive the given world—in other words, modernity—as the whole of correct and man-

---

[13] First appeared in *Today's Zaman* daily on Aug. 20, 2010

datory values that need to be acquired and can be partially modified to fit Islamic principles.

The only difference between "Iran's radical Islamists," who are committed to challenging the West in the areas of military, technology, economics, science, and politics, and Malaysia's "conciliatory Islamists," who argue that one can become a military, technological, economic, scientific, and political power by becoming a sub-component of the great world system, is the form and methods they use. There is no difference between them in nature.

But the main problem facing mankind, including Muslims, is the problem of "overcoming the modern world," which is based on concentrating power in those fields mentioned above. A religion, especially if this religion is Islam, should not be expected to define itself according to its rival or to look like it and use its means and methods. Instead, it should be expected to point to the horizons of a new world using its own unique goals and authentic means and methods. Christianity suffered great pains in its first 300 years. But then it emulated its oppressor, the Roman Empire, and evolved into a Romanized church. Islam should not go through the same tragic experience. Therefore, it is a top priority for Muslims who develop good-intentioned but naïve ideas about the modern world to crystallize their goals and plans.

In this respect I think they need to make clear suggestions on the following topics:

1. The humanization and liberation of people after witnessing the death of the individual

2. Determining the genuine meaning and purpose of life, which has lost meaning and purpose through the process of secularization

3. Ending the conflict between people and nature, and people and life

4. Recommending a new model of organization and a new art of living together peacefully with other people who are losing the desire as well as the experience and skills to do so.

What needs to be overcome is modernity and its basic assumptions, such as individualism, secularization, and the nation-state. This is possible by turning to that which transcends modernity, not by emulating and repeating the modern world.

Muslims, whether they adhere to "conflicting Islam" or "compatible Islam," cannot create the individual in the name of Islam. They cannot attempt to regulate worldly life by disregarding the spiritual and otherworldly dimensions of religion and the divine love, and they cannot ignore the reality of the global Muslim community and deal solely with the problems that occur within their national borders.

Chapter 2

Relations between the Center
and the Periphery

The Periphery's Attempts to Integrate with the Center[14]

To better understand the basic codes of politics in Turkey, we can use the concepts of the "center" and the "periphery." Turkey adopted a multiparty system in 1946; before this, elections were held according to the anti-democratic principle of "open ballot, secret counting"! In the 1950 elections, the Democrat Party (DP) won 53.3 percent of the vote and 416 seats in Parliament, while the Republican People's Party (CHP) won 39.9 percent of the vote and 69 seats in Parliament. The DP's votes did not come solely from a homogenous section of society, but rather included the votes of Sunnis, Alevis, Turks, Kurds, villagers, townsmen, devoutly-religious people, slightly religious people, and practicing Muslims as well as those who are "culturally" Muslim. All these groups came together under the DP's banner.

In 1954, the DP increased its votes, winning a total of 505 seats in Parliament while the CHP won only 31 seats in Parliament. In the 1957 elections, the DP won 424 seats in Parliament while the CHP won 178 seats. In 1960, a coup d'état was staged on May 27.

The post-coup elections held in 1961 were very interesting because the CHP won 173 seats in Parliament and became the interim ruling party. In the 1965 elections, the Justice Party (AP), the DP's successor, won 53 percent of the vote and 240 seats in Parliament while the CHP

14   First appeared in *Today's Zaman* daily on Jul. 24, 2009

won 134 seats. In the 1969 elections, the AP won 256 seats, and the CHP won 143 seats.

The Republican People's Party (CHP) became the majority party for the first time in the multiparty system in the 1973 elections, winning 33 percent of the vote and 185 seats in Parliament. This was the Bülent Ecevit period. There were three important factors that made Ecevit and the CHP the leading party:

a) The removal of the second president of the Republic of Turkey, İsmet İnönü, from the political scene. This was fairly important because it not only marked İnönü losing his party's leadership race to Ecevit, but was also the removal of a single-party system icon.

b) The CHP's opposition of the March military memorandum, with Ecevit calling it "an attack against myself and democracy." These words showed Ecevit was against military intervention in politics.

c) The impression during this period that Ecevit was a man of the "people," earning him the nickname "Karaoğlan" after a heroic cartoon character of a soldier.

The periphery, or the centrifugal powers that came together in the 1950, 1954, 1965, and 1969 elections, gathered around Ecevit in 1973. They then gathered around Turgut Özal in 1983. The biggest reason for this was the push by Kenan Evren, the powerful general who plotted the Sept. 12, 1980 coup, to elect another general, Turgut Sunalp, in the elections. But to Evren's dismay the public voted for Özal, bringing his Motherland Party (ANAP) into ruling power.

The 1995 elections are another political process that should be analyzed within this frame. The Welfare Party (RP), led by Necmettin Erbakan, whose political parties have been dissolved several times by the military, won 21.8 percent of the vote and became the leading party. Then finally, the same periphery forces brought Recep Tayyip Erdoğan's Justice and Development Party (AK Party) into power on Nov. 3, 2002 and again on July 22, 2007.

In short, during every period, the periphery makes a democratic attack on the state center, and they bring into power whoever the military and bureaucracy oppose. This is the real story of politics in Turkey. Surely during this period, the central power does not just stand idly by, but stages operations to set back the periphery. In this model, which we can describe as the "Turkey Model," there is a tide between the central and the centrifugal powers, or more precisely, there is a tide between the "bureaucratic center" and the "societal center."

The problem is the same across the Muslim world. Muslim populations are increasing in major cities. Literacy rates are increasing, and better relations are being formed between the East and West owing to communication, transportation, education, the economy, trade, and tourism. Technology and globalization make this inevitable.

If you ask anyone, from Morocco to Indonesia, what the one thing they want is, their response will be "political representation, democratic participation, freedom of religion and conscience, freedom of speech, the right to association, the rule of law, better health care and more education, and city services." Large crowds have innocent and legitimate demands. The problem, however, is the military-civil bureaucracy, the huge capital of people that have made full use of the state resources to become rich, and higher education institutions, all of which guard this ideology—in other words the state center isn't meeting these demands.

The Codes of Turkish Politics[15]

Parties in Turkey, whether they are right or left wing, differ from the parties in the West which have emerged out of the criteria of social class. They conduct politics taking into consideration political identities which have arisen from the class structure. There is a certain pathology inherent in this.

The second important issue is that when parties conduct politics with an identity based on class criteria in a society that does not have classes they end up belonging to the center or the state. These parties may appear to be conducting politics for the people; however, these parties, in reality, can't help but conduct politics on behalf of the state.

---

[15] First appeared in *Today's Zaman* daily on Jun. 21, 2009

In Turkey, the center and the core of the center is made up of the following factors: the military, civilian bureaucracy, the judiciary, super rich people holding a majority of the capital, and academia and intellectuals. These five elements, which combined create the core of Turkey's center, are almost like an atomic nucleus. The center, however, is made up of centrifugal forces and showcases the desire to conduct politics based on religion.

Although unspoken, in Turkey and the Islamic world, only Islamist movements and parties conduct politics based on values. The others, let us take the nationalists as an example, conduct politics based on race, ethnicity, class, clan, and family. There is a paradoxical situation taking place here; politics based on values encompass all classes and ensures that all owners of rights, including the rich, are given their rights. It is based on justice and principle. For example, according to Marxist theory, the bourgeoisie never improve; they commit suicide. There is a suicide of class in Marxism. According to the Islamic perspective, everyone can attain value. And the highest value in politics is justice.

There is another issue as well: Neither the Ottomans nor the Islamic world experienced the Industrial Revolution, which took place in 1750. Therefore, there is no bourgeoisie class. When there is no bourgeoisie, there exists no corresponding politics or thoughts from liberal politics. There was also no feudalism in our history, either. The "sipahireaya" relationship, being the relationship between the military representative of the governor—in charge of cultivating the land and training soldiers—with the people, was never the same as the relations between "sires and serfdom." In the end, because there was no industrial revolution, there was no working class. Certainly there was a demographic that worked; however, they didn't carry an awareness of themselves as proletarian or an awareness of class structure. They did not experience a conflict based on class. They don't look at the world from a historic, materialist perspective. A working person is a Muslim and a workman. In a 1968 study in Turkey, workers were asked the question "Which one of the following defines you?" and workers answered with the following definitions in this order: "Muslim," "their hometown," "Turkish," and finally "workers."

This tells us that there is a different situation from that of the West. So in a place where there is no working class, or awareness of a proletariat, there can be no socialist or communist party—and even if they did exist, they cannot represent a given class. Similarly, because there is no class of industrialists, liberals, or bourgeoisie, there is no meaning in a conservative, liberal or nationalist party, because there is no equivalent of these political identities in society.

One of the factors which has become entrenched within the state and exists within the nucleus is the big capital. The wealthy, who make up 20 percent of the population, take 46 percent of the national income. While 60 percent of the population takes 50 percent of the national income, the remaining 20 percent of the population takes 4 percent of the income. Therefore, 80 percent of the population is disadvantaged (while those who live a privileged life make up 20 percent of the population); however, this disadvantage is not limited to finance alone; receiving 46 percent of the national income also translates to entertainment, housing, and living a humane life. Now if parties based on class and politics cannot represent this disadvantaged crowd, surely "values" will.

The perception of Islam is not the same among the Western public and the dominant media and the people. The West usually presents Islam as an authoritarian and totalitarian religion. Undoubtedly, Islam calls upon people to have high morals, cover themselves with neat and loose fitting garments, pray five times a day and observe the lawful and unlawful; however, it does not force anyone to do so. When we say "people" in Turkey, this includes devoutly religious, slightly religious, Turkish, Kurdish, Arab, Circassian, Pomak, Sunni, Alevi, villagers and city-dwellers, farmers, workers, civil servants and retirees; these people convene at different times and take part in democratic moves against the center.

Sociocultural Roots[16]

There is a fundamental reason for each of the problems that Turkey has been experiencing. The reason behind the problems stems from the lack of compatibility, and thus conflict, between "traditional and modern."

---

[16] First appeared in *Today's Zaman* daily on Jul. 17, 2009

When the notion of the modern state entered Turkish politics along with the era of Tanzimat ("Reforms" in the late Ottoman period), there became a need to build a community and create an identity. Thus the political tradition of the Ottomans was gradually abandoned; the role of those who were behind the political steering wheel changed accordingly, as well.

There were three arms to the Ottoman administration: soldiers, bureaucrats and the *ulama* (Islamic scholars). Both the soldiers and bureaucrats changed their worldview following the shift to modern history, and the *ulama* were eliminated. The equivalent of the Ottoman bureaucrats (court officials) in modern Turkey is the civil service (Mülkiye); the administrative civilian bureaucrats created especially by the Ottoman Imperial High Schools (*Sultanis*), such as Galatasaray High School, and various other political science faculties are a continuation of the Ottoman bureaucrats.

When we look at the three classical and modern administrative classes (of bureaucracy, military, and academia), we see that not much in the way of their roles has changed in terms of their special status within the state. Traditionally, the Ottoman bureaucrats were trained in the palace institution of Enderun (literally "the inner section of the sultan's palace") within the Ottoman palace. A large portion of those taken into the Enderun were recruited via the *devshirme* method—the practice by which the Ottoman Empire conscripted boys, predominantly from the rural Christian population of the Balkans. They were trained from a young age, taught the beliefs and practices of Islam and thoroughly educated (in various fields, including the law, sciences, sports, and administrative skills) to become either civil bureaucrats or soldiers. The military has been continuing along its way with its effective status since the Ottoman times. As for the third arm of the administrative classes, universities replaced the religious and cultural İlmiye institutions after the reforms that took place in the 19th century, while the *ulama* (from this İlmiye class) were replaced with the laic intellectuals.

During the initial years of the 20th century—in the 1910s—the emergence of İttihat and Terakki, or the Committee of Union and Progress (CUP), as the leading power caused a dramatic shift in politics. So much so that one of the most important factors determining Turkish politics today is still dominated by the tradition brought on by the "Unionist" (*Ittihatçı*) politics.

Sait Halim Pasha, one of the intellectuals of the late Ottoman period, pondered upon this effect, saying that there is a fundamental cultural difference between Islam and the West. In the West, the roots of culture are "socioeconomic," while in Islam they are "sociocultural." He also noted that the division of people in the West is based on the notion of class. In Islam and for the Ottomans, classes emerged based on the notions of "religion and identities." In the *Millet* (nation) system of the Ottoman Empire, people existed within the communities based on their religious identities: the Islamic society, the Jewish society, the Slavic Orthodox society, the Armenian Orthodox society, or the Protestant society. There are, however, classes in the West such as the bourgeoisie, the working class, the aristocracy, and so on. Sait Halim Pasha would say, "If we want to understand the politics of the Ottomans of the modern Islamic world, we need to take into consideration these basic criteria."

In Turkey, we see that financial classification does not play a role in the behavior or preferences of voters. In order for a social layer or group to be defined as a "class," it needs to have three attributes. Firstly, the financial income difference that it possesses needs to provide it with the privileges of political and legal support. Secondly, it needs to come from a tradition. If a group like this emerges suddenly, then it's not considered a class. In order for it to be a class, it has to be traditionally continuing within society, having followed a historic course. Thirdly, the transition between classes needs to be very difficult. This is not possible in Turkey as there is transition and mobility between social classes.

Furthermore, people in Turkey don't value the class difference between people very much, and this ensures a natural sense of justice in society; there is this fairness, for instance, in the way people from all walks of life stand shoulder to shoulder in congregational prayers. Therefore, you can easily see a boss and a worker praying alongside one another during the Friday Prayers. Indeed, justice is the key to "politics based on value and ethics." Justice is the delivery of rights to each rightful owner of rights. As such, the Messenger of God, peace and blessings be upon him, described justice as the union of the owner of rights with their rights; for them to take possession of their rights. Similarly, following the implementation of a multi-party system in Turkey right after WWII, words such as "rights and justice" began being highlighted by leading parties: Bülent Ecevit's "Equitable order" of the Republican People's Party (CHP), Süleyman Demirel's Justice Party (AP), Necmettin Erbakan's "Just order"—the central program of his Welfare Party (RP), and Recep Tayyip Erdoğan's Justice and Development Party (AK Party).

The "Other" Factor in Politics[17]

Typical politics regulates power relations within a context that is inclined to making certain definitions. Hence, politics and politicians have always needed the "other." The "other" is the instrument of legitimizing the opposite pole. When necessary, its image is rebuilt and reedited. What the "other" means according to its own realities is not important at all; what matters is how we perceive it and the image we accordingly attribute to it as a result. A rationalizing formula has been discovered for this process: "What you say is not important; how you are perceived and understood is important." This is exactly what Orientalism is all about. This is the real message: "If I perceive you in a certain way, then you are exactly that; you should also perceive yourself that way."

Dialogue or the desire to establish a relationship with the "other" by getting to know it harms those in power because "one is the enemy of what one doesn't know." Keeping the enemy alive, or always having an enemy, is tantamount to consolidating our power. The never rectified error in the process of "othering" is that one never endeavors to get to know and understand the perceived enemy in terms of its intrinsic content or reality.

Ensuring that the "other" lives in an isolated ghetto in its own neighborhood is possible by building "thick walls" between neighborhoods. Information exchange and mutual visits, in this sense, damage the usual power relations. New railroad and bus lines should be prevented from being set up between such neighborhoods at all costs, (or

---

[17] First appeared in *Today's Zaman* daily on Jan. 22, 2008

symbolically speaking, there should be no ferry lines set up between the isles of prejudice.)

The "other" should also be prevented from expressing its thoughts about our common problems, and the rest of "us" should thus be prevented from knowing what sort of stance the other takes in regard to those problems. The defining politics and the political power which this defining politics gives to interest or pressure groups encompasses an approach that looks less than fondly on new and different pieces of information. As Aristotle put it, knowledge itself is power, or at least has the power to open up new power zones. We already know what the other thinks (or we assume we do), and have already been informing the residents of our neighborhood of its thoughts using our own rhetoric. What we expect from the residents in return is that they should perceive the other the way we do and eventually take sides with us in the struggle for political power.

Just like the industrial policies that are based on the replacement of the locally made with the imported, thus disabling homegrown goods and services to participate in free competition, such forms of politics prevent different ideas and information from becoming a part of the free competition of thoughts. The political elites (the central bureaucracy, and interest and pressure groups) that will benefit from this situation will always tell us that they are not against us, but against the "other"—that is, our enemy—and will thus further consolidate their political power.

In order to make the conflict an everlasting one, a new threat definition should be made every day and according to every situation, and new policies that are in line with the old ones should be made in accordance with the new "threat" definition; consequently, the hawks will always be in power as long as this vicious circle persists. If you ask me whether hawks or doves are stronger, I would say with no hesitation that doves have a much greater advantage. The hawks of politics feed on conflict; this is for sure. So where will the doves find their power? In conciliatory politics; or to put it another way, in the words supported by a sound moral foundation, and in the power of the words' sincerity.

Conciliatory politics is the art of solving every social problem by using the possibilities of politics, expecting a solution from politics, and basing politics on respect, mutual visits, maintaining dialogue, negotiation, discussion, and intellectual exchanges. The modern theories of democracy haven't quite reached the moral and harmonizing references of conciliatory politics with regard to their intellectual resources. However, there is a very conscientious ongoing search throughout the world for such politics. When we view Islam and its historical references from this perspective, it is apparent that it has very rich philosophical resources that will help current democracies prosper. The fundamental problem lies in the intrigue of "othering," although we may accept those who have the right to regulate political power relations. When we surmount this problem, we will reach the moral aim of conciliatory politics.

To Be Able to Reconcile with the System or Not[18]

When we look back upon our painful history of democratization, which started in the 1950s, we can see that two leading social actors, religious people and the peasants, have reconciled with the system, whereas three groups—the Kurds, Alevis, and the non-Muslim minorities—have not yet been able to do so. It is also safe to say that the ongoing political crisis is attributable to their failure to reconcile with the system.

When the Turkish Republic was founded as a modern nation-state in 1923, the state chose the peasants, religious people, the Kurds, and minorities to be "others." Let us take a look at how the state wanted to position these social groups:

The peasants would be modernized by top-to-down policies. The religious would not be allowed to convey religion to social life; instead, they would be able to practice their religion to the extent the state granted permission. Even though they were praised by the new regime, the Alevis would not privy to the Sunni-Hanafi services to be provided by the Religious Affairs Directorate and they would have to keep their Alevi identity in a fairly narrow sphere. The non-Muslim minorities, on the

---

[18] First appeared in *Today's Zaman* daily on Jun. 16, 2011

other hand, would have to agree to the minimal rights recognized under the Treaty of Lausanne as they were considered a potential threat.

This suggests that the republican regime not only failed to include these social groups in the system but also subjected them to its own definitions; if they agreed to this definition, the state regarded them as safe and confident. But of course, these groups did not endorse these definitions and, as they raised objections, they were subjected to increasing "othering" and "alienation." As expected, these excluded groups' relations with the state and powerful elites became a fundamental crisis in the administrative and political system. The real and fundamental problem since the foundation of the Turkish Republic has been around these groups' integration with the system.

After the coming of the Democrat Party (DP) to power in 1950, the peasants who were neglected during the single-party era (1923-1950) were brought to the center. In bringing them forward, the political administration made sure they had contact with the administrative and bureaucratic center. This was late Prime Minister Adnan Menderes' greatest achievement. Former President Turgut Özal did something similar with the religious in 1983; the integration of the religious groups with the system was further reinforced in 1994 when the pro-Islamic Welfare Party (RP) won the mayoral elections. Religious people enjoyed the benefits of staying in power in this period, which was during the rule of Özal and RP-held municipalities. In the same period, they also realized that holding on to power was more functional than clashing with the system and trying to transform it to one based on the principles of fairness and justice.

Having preserved the intervention tradition of Turkey's 1910 Committee of Union and Progress (CUP), the bureaucratic center took over power through a military coup in 1960 by provoking the army. According to Süleyman Soylu, who knows well the Democrat Party experience, the 1960 coup was "the Karbala of politics," in reference to the ruthless massacre of the Noble Prophet's grandson Husayn and his company in the city of Karbala. The coup interrupted this integration process (which started with the coming of the multi-party system in Turkey after WWII). The military not only interfered with politics but also did great harm to the political traditions so that intraparty democracy did not take root. The Democrat Party (DP), which came to power with the 1950 elections, revived a strong tradition from the pre-1923 (i.e. the Ottoman) era. For instance, during parliamentary negotiations over a draft bill, the deputies who thought that their views were not adequately represented or heard would ask for the resignation of Prime Minister Menderes. Today, it is not possible to find a member of parliament who would raise objections to his leader, let alone ask for the resignation of a party chair or the prime minister. Soylu underlines that Menderes' tolerance could be called "democratic anarchism" and that Turkey needs this anarchism today.

At the current stage, the republic's troubles are caused by its failure to integrate the Kurds, the Alevis, and the religious minorities into the system. Their non-integration with the system has led to a political crisis. Menderes, Özal, Erbakan, and Erdoğan waged a war to integrate the peasants and religious people with the system and save them from becoming "others." The June 12, 2011 elections can be, in a way, seen that this integration has been fulfilled for these two social groups. However, the problem with the Kurds, Alevis, and non-Muslim minorities continues.

June 12, 2011 Elections and the Faint Hope for More Democracy[19]

The July 22, 2007 general elections in Turkey bestowed great opportunities on the Justice and Development Party (AK Party) in a number of arenas. Attaining 47 percent of the vote, the generally high voter turnout and representation of 86 percent of the political spectrum in Turkish Parliament gave the AK Party a great amount of legitimacy and strength, especially when compared to the period following the 2002 general elections.

Part of what went into creating this victory was not only a great rise in the percentage of vote obtained, but also its winning over of various social factions within the mainstream. As in other regions of Turkey, the AK Party also managed to double the number of votes it received in the Southeast. What this really meant was that the majority of Kurd-

---

[19] First appeared in *Today's Zaman* daily on Jun. 02, 2011

ish citizens perceived a possible solution to Kurdish problems under the umbrella provided by the AK Party, as votes dwindled for the Democratic Society Party (DTP). Many people, until seeing for themselves the results of the 2007 elections, had believed that the Kurds had already broken away from the system. But on seeing these 2007 election results, they realized that actually the Kurds were right in the middle of things. What's more, Alevi members of society also showed a leaning towards the AK Party in the 2007 elections. In the end, the mainstream of society wound up casting their votes in favor of lawful and valid politics, choosing the AK Party to fix problems and find solutions.

In essence, the political profile that has emerged ever since the 1994 elections following the lines of the National View has begun to represent more of a "societal center" and speaks more loudly to a wider swath of society itself. When you look at all of the tense political events that have marked our recent history as a nation, you can note that the main characteristic of these events is tension between the "societal center" and the "bureaucratic center." The bureaucratic center is composed of a tough shell, with solidarity and cooperation in its inner ranks, while the societal center is what we call a wide swath of society which is marked by its religious, ethnic, and class similarities and differences.

The AK Party entered the scene with the assertion that it in fact represented the center. In the past, parties such as the Democrat Party (DP), the Justice Party (AP), and the Motherland Party (ANAP) had been partially able to do this, although there is no question that representing what you allege to be the center of society is not all that easy either. In the elections of 1950 and 1954, the DP was able to achieve this sort of success. This was repeated in 1965 by the AP and in 1983 by ANAP. But it should also be noted that this sort of success can be exploited. One should recognize that in fact the "center" is not a neutral spot. Differing from the societal center, the "center" actually means the "state."

When those who represent society in politics start working in close concert with factors at the "center" of the state, such as the military, the traditional bureaucracy or the forces of big capital, they will be punished by the people of this society. The faith society has in certain ideologies or leaders is not infinite. If the AK Party were to forget that its mission was to represent mainstream society, it would be relegated to the same fate experienced in the past by the AP and ANAP. In fact, this is the greatest danger awaiting the AK Party. In a sense then, the upcoming June 12, 2011 general elections will make it clearer for all to see just how much the AK Party has managed to represent the interests of the societal center.

Over its past eight-and-a-half-years in power, the AK Party has signed off on a number of significant achievements; to say it was not successful would be completely unfair. But at the same time, some of the problems still left unsolved from this period include the Kurdish problem, poverty and unemployment, unfair wages, increasing social violence, and signs that families are falling apart.

Of course, great steps have been taken in the arena of foreign policy. And some significant steps have been taken with respect to the Kurdish problem, with an important initiative started up in 2009, with a new state television channel broadcasting in Kurdish and with religious talks being given in Kurdish at mosques. While economic discipline was tightly adhered to, it was not sufficiently recognized that the social dimensions of this program were weak. This can be seen by the serious complaints about the merciless subcontracting of workers as practiced by local municipalities, as well as the difficulties faced by local merchants as the result of malls being built everywhere, not to mention complaints from the retired. When there are various weaknesses and problems being witnessed in family units in a nation where conservative-religious people are in power, the reasons for this should not be ignored. Just as all this means we need to review our entire educational system and policies, it should also be enough to give us an idea of the weak cultural foundations that our conservative-democratic politics are based upon.

The First Elections of the Post-Kemalist Era and the Hardest Time Yet to Come[20]

The June 12 general elections, as expected, have placed an even heavier load on the shoulders of the Justice and Development Party (AK Party), which won power for a third term. The main problem of this new term in power lies in the failure of the correct interpretation of

---

[20]   First appeared in *Today's Zaman* daily on Jun. 13, 2011

problems as Turkey transitions from Kemalism to post-Kemalism, and the protection of social peace and political stability as the country tries to find rational solutions to various problems. Though the Republican People's Party (CHP) was the key party in these elections, it was not able to play a key role.

The 16 elections that have taken place since the death of Mustafa Kemal have been marked by struggles characteristic of the "Kemalist period" represented by the CHP. Throughout the past, it was always the CHP and the "others." I refer to the word "others" in the sociological political sense that "those that have been otherized." Included in these "others" were the Democratic Party (DP), the Justice Party (AP), and the True Path Party (DYP) of the "center right;" the Motherland Party (ANAVATAN) of the "right conservatives;" the political parties engaging in politics along "the National View" (Milli Görüş) lines; the Nationalist Movement Party (MHP) of the "rightist nationalists;" and then, of course, the AK Party, which is a "conservative democrat" party. The Democratic Left Party (DSP) and similar others on the left took specific opposition to the CHP, and in doing so became parties of the center to the degree that other parties were closer to the CHP. The "others" of the social bedrock of parties, which carried out politics based on "Kurdish nationalism," were actually not too distant from the CHP mentality in terms of their ideological stance; in fact, we could call them "Kurdish Kemalists."

The CHP is the political representative of a tough inner shell of bureaucracy in Turkey. The main components of this tough shell are the military, the civilian bureaucracy, big capital, the judiciary, higher education institutions, civilian state institutions, and their extensions within the media and the artistic world. It was only ever Bülent Ecevit who tried to break the CHP away from its historical position and allegations; these efforts of his were reflected in the 33.3 percent of votes he got in 1973, and then the 41.3 percent he got in 1977. The efforts to distance Ecevit from the CHP were the results of the policies he had developed with the "others" in mind.

During "normal" times when the military guardian regime cannot be directly influential, the CHP represents the "civilian guardianship."

When we look at the previous 16 elections, we see that the votes are split by the CHP as the state's Kemalist ideological party and the other parties, as a reflection of an unending struggle between the "administrative-bureaucratic center" and the "societal center."

The key party for these elections was the CHP. Had the new CHP leader and his spokespeople been actually able to carry out deep-rooted reforms as they had talked about, Turkey's democratization would be much easier today. Instead, the CHP chose to continue its mission as the party of the bureaucratic center—the party that founded the state and the party which now sees large masses of Turkish people running away from it. There are many reasons that we could list for its choice. But in the wake of the elimination of Deniz Baykal—who was the former representative of politics from the previous generation—the new CHP did give off strong signals that it might in fact be a pro-reform party perfect for the post-Kemalist era. In fact, many political science observers became very hopeful about the CHP in this regard; in the end though, the CHP was resolute in continuing with its traditional reflexes.

Why were the June 12, 2011 elections the first elections of the "post-Kemalist" era? Turkey, in a social, economic, administrative and political sense, is no longer able to put on its old clothes. After all, these are clothes which were cut and sewn for the first quarter of the last century. And of course, the tailor responsible for these clothes was the CHP.

For the first time ever, the CHP was divided into two main groups; but this was no classic schism. One group was busy defending the idea of passing up on Kemalism; able to read the dynamics of social change correctly, this group perceived that if the CHP was going to undergo its own reforms, it would have to give up on the Kemalist ideology and open the way forward for the democratization of the republic. As for the other group, it simply defended the idea that putting some new make-up on old Kemalism was enough for now.

What the June 12 general elections did reveal was that the CHP did not make the expected deep-rooted reforms, and that it is still searching for its real identity somewhere in Kemalism. The heavy load in this coming post-Kemalist period thus once again lies on the shoulders of the AK Party. However, a difficult period has begun for both the AK Party and Turkey, as it will be a period that calls for the necessity of shared intelligence, common ground, and a search for dialogue.

Nothing Has Changed in the State Center's Ideology: "Reactionaryism" Out; "Abuse of Religion" In![21]

The National Security Policy Document, or the Red Book in popular parlance, which used to be considered the "secret constitution" of Turkey, has recently changed, and for the first time, no reference was made to "reactionaryism" (*irtica*) as a threat in it. The international world does not know what reactionaryism really is in Turkey.[22]

Since 1908, reactionaryism has been part of the official rhetoric in Turkey. Philosophically, it is based on 19th century positivism and scientism—the idea that science is the sole guide and savior for humankind—and on the belief that history progresses toward better days.

None of these assumptions today bears any truthfulness. The positivist paradigm has now been replaced with relativism, postmodern indifference, and the anything-goes mentality. The majority of Turkish intellectuals still insist on investing faith in the Newtonian mechanical universe, but the theory of relativity is what is currently accepted in physics. This theory may be replaced by another in the future. Scientism has come to be perceived in the world as a childish belief, and the conviction that humanity is continuously advancing in the company of technology and economy, as two major dynamics of Western civilization, has been shaken as well. Our typical pro-Enlightenment Jacobin intellectuals are either not aware of these developments or falsely think that they can withstand the strongly flowing river of time that sweeps away everything in its path. Everyone is free to sleep soundly in this deep dogmatic sleep. We can do nothing for them except to say "good night."

---

[21] First appeared in *Today's Zaman* daily on Nov. 26, 2010

[22] Secularist state elites have long used the opprobrious epithet of "irtica" (returning to the dark, olden times) as a veiled reference to the so-called "reactionaryism" or "backwardness" of practicing Muslims, thus accusing them of being "religious reactionaries" and trying to obstruct their access to the public sphere. (ed.)

Although the paradigm itself failed, reactionaryism continued to be a useful tool for domestic politics for about a century. This indicates the anachronistic character of the Turkish Enlightenment. Reactionaryism is only paranoia, a manufactured delusion and an effective tool for politics. It does not have any philosophical or intellectual depth. It is just used to prevent emerging and growing peripheral social forces from flowing to the center. It is true that there is a certain class twist to the matter at hand. The fact that the small and influential groups who do not want to lose their economic, bureaucratic, and political advantages or privileges—we call them the White Turks—are exerting pressures on society in the name of an archaic ideology is not important. They do not have the courage to advertise these archaic and old intellectual materials in the international arena, and they already choose to exist within the narrow boundaries of the domestic world. This is the reason why their neo-nationalism has no counterpart around the globe.

Some suggest the term "extremism" in lieu of reactionaryism, thereby proposing to allow social groups that they label as extremists to "get to the center" in this way and "without" discrimination, but this is the very ground on which tension sits. There is a simple oddity to all this. They assume that the problems can be solved by allowing some marginal/extremist groups that they imply are spiritually and mentally underdeveloped, thus "getting them to the center." But who is letting whom to the center? Who are the broad social groups that have been supporting the center-right and National View (Milli Görüş) parties, bringing them to power since 1950? Has the center, i.e., the political/economic center, accepted these social groups as part of itself? Who is at the heart of the problem: the center or the periphery? Have groups that used to be socially and culturally isolated and that were denied their share in the national income been allowed to take their place among the core elements of the center—the military, the civilian bureaucracy, the big capitalists, and academia as the intellectual driving force of the center's ideology and the intellectuals who are their extensions in the media? No.

Since 1950, all parties except the Republican People's Party (CHP) have been centrifugal forces; they get to the center and promise to do politics in the name of the periphery, and they are either bought by the center or have to turn their backs to the periphery upon intimidation by the center. And then, the periphery stops supporting them.

The system in Turkey is centralized, hierarchical, and actually purely totalitarian. The system's center of gravity has a hard core that has organic bonds to its elements. Since the 1950s, there has been a conflict between the broad masses of people, i.e., the civilian (pluralistic and productive periphery) and the core at the center that exploits the periphery and sits on unearned positions. Reactionaryism is the name given to this conflict. Reactionaryism is removed from the secret constitution as a threat, but is replaced with "politics based on the abuse of religion." So reactionaryism is out and abuse of religion is in.

Chapter 3

Politics of Intervention

Tracing Telltale Signs of Interventionist Politics[23]

T urkish politics were rocked by a memorandum on April 27, 2007. There was no physical intervention that took place; however, the tremors of that day still continue. The international community and the domestic community ponder, "Could there be a new coup in Turkey?"

This is the distance we have traveled on a road paved by the military coup of May 27, 1960. There have been two military coups in Turkey: one took place on May 27, 1960, while the other was the coup of Sept. 12, 1980. In each of these coups, Parliament was dissolved, and the military took over the leadership of the country. Furthermore, in the May 27, 1960 coup, then-Prime Minister Adnan Menderes and the ministers of finance and foreign affairs received the death penalty. Similarly, in the 1980 coup, many people were given capital punishment.

A "memorandum," which entered the Turkish political vocabulary on March 12, 1971, was a powerful warning, and following this 1971 memorandum, the direction of Turkish politics took a turn in a different direction. Another important intervention which was not an open military coup took place on Feb. 28, 1997. There were different methods utilized in this event;[24] however, it changed the course of politics in

---

[23] First appeared in *Today's Zaman* daily on Jul. 14, 2009

[24] In the 1997 post-modern intervention, the military held the political reins indirectly by working through the National Security Council (MGK) and brought down the government without dissolving the Parliament. (ed.)

terms of its outcome. Feb. 28 cost Turkey $54 billion as the economy reeled from the political intrigue. The latest controversial statement, posted on the chief of general staff's Web site on April 27, 2007, was also in this regard a memorandum.

The controversy arose mainly over the nomination of Abdullah Gül, who had Islamic leanings, for the 2007 presidential election. The general election was set to take place on Nov. 4 of the same year, as the government had announced; however, it was moved to an earlier date because a snap general election had to be called to overcome the parliamentary deadlock. The president was to be chosen, but due the obstructionist tactics to prevent the selection of Abdullah Gül, this didn't happen, either. Meanwhile, relations between the central right and central left parties warmed up—some unions, forced marriages, and engagements took place between them.[25] The elections were moved to July 22, 2007. Later, then-Chief of General Staff Gen. Yaşar Büyükanıt admitted that he personally penned the memorandum. All of this shows us that politics don't flow in their own natural channel. There is a major struggle taking place between civilians and those looking to intervene in politics. And this struggle is so important that it determines not just Turkey's, but also the Middle East's political future.

It might be beneficial to look behind the surface of the matter because there is more to this picture than what meets the eye. In order to understand the dynamics and real factors that create this picture, we need to examine the far and near future. Turkey is a country that is more complicated than most imagine.

It is possible to attribute the politics in Turkey to a few sources. First, we can attribute it to the tradition of politics that existed in the Ottoman state after the *Tanzimat Fermanı* (Imperial Edict of Reorganization), whose administrative reforms had far-reaching effects. The Ottoman

---

[25] The central left parties of the Republican People's Party (CHP) and the Social Democratic People's Party (SHP) made an election alliance with the Democratic Left Party (DSP) in May 2007. Similarly, the central right parties of the True Path Party (DYP) and the Motherland Party (ANAP) was to merge into the Democratic Party (DP). However, shortly before the elections, the DYP went back on the promise it made in the unification protocol. (ed.)

politics came to a breaking point with these administrative reforms in 1839. In a way, the Ottomans broke away from their traditional politics after this date and stepped into modern politics. Of course, this didn't mean a complete parting of ways with Ottoman traditions.

The Tanzimat, in addition to being a breakaway from the old Ottoman traditions to some extent, was a period in which Western-influenced politics began to be practiced. This Tanzimat (Reformations) era began in 1839 and ended in 1908 with the Young Turk Revolution,[26] which also marked the onset of the Second Constitutional Era and the take-over of the Committee of Union and Progress (CUP). All this culminated in a political style peculiar to Turkey, which is called the "Young Turks," or more commonly known as the "Unionist" (İttihatçı) style.

The Ottoman tradition of statehood and politics comprised four main pillars. In addition to this, the Ottoman period should be divided into two because up until Fatih Sultan Mehmet, the Ottomans were a state of (mostly Turcoman) tribes. It is not possible to speak of a full state when examining the periods of Osman Ghazi—the founder of the Ottoman (or Osmanlı in Turkish) State—and Orhan Ghazi. During this period, people engaged in conquests with the spirit of *jihad* (striving on the way of God). Their political methods were very different. With Fatih Sultan Mehmed II, the Ottoman state was redesigned as an empire.

Sultan Fatih (the Conqueror) was affected by four main factors when designing the empire: The first was from the Mughal State tradition. The second was the Yassa, or customary law, of Genghis Khan. Thirdly, the Arabic right to the sword; and fourthly, the palace and empire traditions, as well as the church-state relationship, of the Byzantines influ-

---

[26] Deriving from French "Les Jeunes Turcs" ("Jön Türkler" in Turkish), "the Young Turks" was a secret society that led a rebellion against the absolute rule of Sultan Abdülhamid II, replacing the traditional Ottoman monarchy with a constitutional monarchy in 1908. Following this Young Turk Revolution in 1908, the Committee of Union and Progress (CUP) became the secretive Young Turks' umbrella political party that gained de facto rule over the Ottoman state after the 1913 coup d'etat (aka "the Raid on the Sublime Porte"). This raid on the Ottoman government was led by Talat Pasha, Enver Pasha, and Ahmed Cemal Pasha—"the Three Pashas" (or "dictatorial triumvirate"), of the Committee of Union and Progress. (ed.)

enced Fatih's re-envisioned empire. The first thing that pops into mind in relation to the Ottoman politics is "the politics of fighting to the death" (*qital*) because someone who wanted to engage in politics was someone who was ready to fight to the death.

Naturally, this does not mean that lawlessness and arbitrariness reigned supreme during the Ottoman era. But it was understood that Ottoman politics was "a method of administration and manners." And the leading modern Turkish elite continue to see politics in this light. They refuse to see politics as a common ground for discussion to maintain the relationship between the powers that be.

The Feb. 28, 1997 Postmodern Coup and Its Hard-hitting Consequences[27]

We know little more about the Feb. 28, 1997 postmodern military coup despite all the years that have gone by. Necmettin Erbakan, a victim of the coup and the prime minister at the time, died on Feb. 27, 2011—a day before the fourteenth anniversary of the coup. He perhaps took many secrets with him. There are a series of questions that need to be answered. One such question is: Who was not happy with the then-ruling Welfare Party (RP) government?

Several groups were apparently provoking and trumpeting the idea that the "fundamental characteristics of the Turkish Republic" were being undermined. Their propaganda relied completely on the assumption that the fundamental character of the republic was under threat, and they suggested "something be done to prevent this." Was there a real "threat" to "the fundamental characteristics of the republic," as they argued, or did they have other goals in their mind, such as camouflaged abuse?

Let me give you an example of how Mustafa Kemal Atatürk was abused. I personally listened to this story from former Kayseri Mayor Şükrü Karatepe, who was victimized during the Feb. 28 postmodern coup. "In the run-up to [the military coup of] Sept. 12 [1980], it was decided

---

27 First appeared in *Today's Zaman* daily on Mar. 01, 2011

that three gas stations should be demolished in Kayseri because they posed a threat to the life and property of the city's inhabitants. As the municipality was trying to demolish these stations, the military overthrew the government on Sept. 12. This came as a golden opportunity for these stations' owners. They quickly erected a huge statue of Atatürk at the very center of the city—which still triggers debates about its aesthetics—and, in this way, the three stations were saved from being demolished. In every coup, Atatürk is exploited to the full extent because Kemalism is used as a basis for granting legitimacy to coup plots and military interventions."[28]

The groups that openly voiced support for a military intervention on Feb. 28 mainly comprised people who accumulated wealth by exploiting public resources. These groups later engaged in large-scale fraud at banks they owned and the losses these banks suffered were reimbursed by the state.

When we look at the international dimension of the issue, the stance of the larger world over the Feb. 28 coup was interesting. Though the global powers used to lend indirect support to coups, they did not openly give a "green light" to a military coup at the time. European countries in particular even made it obvious that they were "cold" toward such a coup. It was quite meaningful that one day after the infamous meeting of the National Security Council (MGK) on Feb. 28, 1997, German Chancellor Helmut Kohl scheduled a meeting with Erbakan for Sept. 30. The statements made by US officials to lend support to the Feb. 28 coup, accompanied by the rhetoric of the "sanctity of secularism," were seen as third rate, given the US administration at the time. The masterminds behind "the Feb. 28 process" had failed to take this into consideration.

The military had formerly taken full initiative in the military coups of May 27, 1960, Mar. 12, 1971, and Sept. 12, 1980. Although in each case

---

[28] The official ideology of the state was termed Kemalism (from Atatürk's given name of Kemal). Kemalist laicism, which is one of the Six Arrows (or fundamental pillars) of Kemalism, has become an instrument for control and supervision of Islam by the state, and has been used as a pretext in all the military interventions that marred democratic development in Turkey from 1960 on. (ed.)

it was certain civilian segments who would incite the military to carry out a military coup—as this was frequently stressed by the Commanders Muhsin Batur and Kenan Evren—the military would make their plans and implement them on their own.

But, this time, there was a fundamental change in the manner the intervention was conducted. There were "foul odors" in the air. Civilian groups fulfilled their duty to incite the military into action; in particular, the media exerted great efforts to make a military intervention seem "reasonable and necessary." Yet, one could still get the strong impression that certain interest groups which wanted to overthrow the government through anti-democratic methods and the opponent civilian politicians who acted in coordination with them were actually trying to attain their own political goals "through non-political methods" and to "indoctrinate the military along these lines."

The Feb. 28, 1997 meeting produced difficult-to-implement decisions and, once again, "the fear of the military" affected social life in a profound manner; the military became the subject matter of speculations; financial and stock markets fluctuated considerably. Politicians whose political careers suffered and who were suspicious about their social support but were still fearful of reviewing their performances saw it as a golden opportunity to prefer the political power offered by the postmodern coup of Feb. 28 to democracy.

The majority of secular intellectuals and media figures did nothing but applaud the process. But the Feb. 28 coup had an unexpected benefit: It caused the main body of the nation to feel disappointment and resentment towards the military's influence in politics. It is this resentment that facilitated the discovery and litigation of recent coup attempts in Turkey. Thus, we can conclude that sometimes "sufferings or tribulations are bliss."

Will the Military Ghost Rise Again?[29]

The postmodern military coup process of Feb. 28, 1997, which overthrew the coalition government of the Welfare Party (RP) and the True

---

[29]　First appeared in *Today's Zaman* daily on Jul. 07, 2009

Path Party (DYP), was said to "last for 1,000 years." It was former Chief of General Staff Gen. Hüseyin Kıvrıkoğlu who made this assertion.

A period of 1,000 years is a long span of time, but it is obvious that there are people who want to keep this "intervention process of Feb. 28" going. The leading players of the direct coup of Sept. 12, 1980 and the indirect coup of Feb. 28 are alive and kicking. The main players of the intervention process of Feb. 28 from the media are still "at work." Occasional confessions made by some of the media figures who played their part in this intervention process are staggering. Such confessions have been made a number of times by Dinç Bilgin, the former owner of the *Sabah* daily, who is a leading Feb. 28 figure. Despite the fact that their boss has gone, some leading journalists are still active, doing their job of coup provocation. Columnists, editors-in-chief, and Ankara representatives are all there.

The document designed as an action plan to terminate democracy, as disclosed by the *Taraf* newspaper on June 12, 2009, has been prepared with the same mentality. This document lists horrendous, provocative actions.[30] Now, the same players from the Feb. 28 process are rushing to claim that the document is not connected with the coup attempt. They uttered many things similar to this nonsense during the Feb. 28 process: fabricated news stories about "Qur'an training courses," headlines about "hair-raising oaths" or "the fight until a theological state is established," or "the Çankaya government," or "unarmed forces" and much more. The current "action plan" document was intended to stoke horrific activities. The document, undersigned by a colonel working at the headquarters of the General Staff, serving in the army's psychological warfare unit, has now turned into a litmus test for the democratic sentiments of civilians and the military. Ironically, the groups that have never paid respect to freedom of expression are now saying that "planning a coup or advocating a coup is not a thought crime." But

---

[30] This action plan document, which was originally called "Action Plan against Religious Fundamentalism," details plots to sow violence in the country and create the conditions for a military takeover in order to get rid of both the Hizmet Movement and the then-reform government of the AK Party that were treated as threats to the official ideology of the state. (ed.)

a party—the Welfare Party (RP)—that had secured the votes of about 6.1 million people was closed down just because it disclosed its opinions and tens of thousands of people were victimized.

Today, such victimization still continues. During the Feb. 28 process, the same columnists and editors-in-chief set off a witch hunt.

In 1997, I was a columnist at the *Yeni Şafak* newspaper, and I recalled that I had written: "We should prepare a page called the 'Feb. 28 page' in which we should quote the articles of leading journalists. This will provide a good archive for those who will write about these days in future. Perhaps, we will soon have the opportunity to provide these articles as proof of disgraceful acts by these columnists."

What gave the Nationalist Movement Party (MHP)[31] governmental office after the coalition government of the RP and the DYP was forced to step down in 1997 and the Justice and Development Party (AK Party) governmental office in 2002 was the rage the electorate felt against the military's meddling with civilian politics on Feb. 28, 1997.

Turkish people are, however, disappointed once again. This time, they are deceived by the "consensus doctrine" of the AK Party government. When they were told, "We will reach a consensus with three big powers and assume governmental office and stay there," they thought that this was a new political tactic. Today, it has become evident that this was just a fancy idea.

In Turkey, radical reforms are needed, and in particular, European Union standards concerning the administrative structure must be implemented. What will bring good days to Turkey is not the formula of a "civilian-military alliance or consensus," but making sure that the military does not intervene in the will of civilian politicians and that they contain their interest to their specific area of activity. Today, it is clear that the military-civilian doctrine has proved to be false. Actually, everything was obvious from the start. The mentality of the Feb. 28 process could not live in the social and political life of Turkey, and those who imposed this military-civilian alliance doctrine on the minds of conservative pol-

---

31   The Nationalist Movement Party (MHP) became the second largest party, and thus was dubbed "the second winner" of the 1999 general elections. (ed.)

iticians were forcing them to flog a dead horse. Even without this doctrine, the same politicians would have made the same achievements in politics.

In the 2002 general elections, the possibility of any of the center-right or center-left parties assuming governmental office was not even one in 1,000.[32] A political movement profile was created (for a new party) out of deception, and this new movement has misperceived that to reject its Islamic origins and traditions is to "truly perceive the change." The most important factor that has brought such complicated circumstances to the existing AK Party government was its failure to keep up with the reform process started in 2005, thinking that it could maintain its power by establishing an alliance with the central forces holding the state power. However, Turkish society now believes that politics must be left to civilians only. We have reached the end of the tradition of coups.

Coups Cannot Always Be Repeated[33]

Barely a decade has passed since the postmodern coup on Feb. 28, 1997. There are still questions that need to be clarified. Today we have strong evidence that links the Feb. 28 postmodern coup to the Ergenekon crime gang. The aim was to banish the Welfare Party (RP), which had secured 21 percent of the national vote in the 1995 elections, from the political arena. Question: Who was not happy with the RP government?

Several groups were trumpeting that "fundamental characteristics of the Turkish Republic" were being undermined and that something should be done to prevent this. Was there a real threat to "the fundamental characteristics of the republic," as they argued, or did they have other goals in mind? The groups who openly voiced support for mili-

---

[32] The 2002 general election was held during a grievous economic crisis which resulted in a deep resentment of the governments of the center-right or center-left parties which had governed the country since the 1980 military coup. Dissatisfied with the policies of the coalition governments of the center-right and center-left parties, the voters protested all of the center-right and center-left parties and elected the AK Party as a political newcomer, which was founded barely a year before the 2002 elections. (ed.)

[33] First appeared in *Today's Zaman* daily on Aug. 12, 2008

tary intervention in the Feb. 28 process consisted mainly of people who had accumulated wealth through exploiting public resources. Later these groups would commit large-scale frauds in the banks they owned, and the losses these banks suffered would be reimbursed by the state. It is estimated that the Feb. 28 coup cost Turkey $74 billion.

There is a famous argument that has stood since the May 27, 1960 coup: No military coup is possible in Turkey without foreign support. The rest of the world's stance toward the Feb. 28 process was interesting. The world did not openly give a "green light" to a military coup. In particular, European countries even made it obvious that they were "cold" toward such a coup. It was meaningful that just one day after the National Security Council's (MGK) famous meeting on Feb. 28, German Chancellor Helmut Kohl set up a meeting with [then Prime Minister Necmettin] Erbakan for Sept. 30. The statements made by US officials supporting the Feb. 28 process, accompanied by rhetoric on the sanctity of secularism, were seen as gratuitous. The masterminds behind the Feb. 28 process had failed to take this into consideration.

Formerly, the military had taken full initiative in the coups of 1960, 1971, 1980. Although in each case it had been civilians who encouraged the military coup—as was frequently stressed by Muhsin Batur and Kenan Evren—the military would make their plans and implement them on their own. But this time there was a fundamental change in the manner in which the intervention was conducted. There were "bad odors" in the air. The civilian groups did fulfill their duties for inciting the military into action; in particular, the media exerted great efforts to make a military intervention seem "reasonable and necessary." Yet one could still get the strong impression that certain interest groups who wanted to overthrow the government through anti-democratic methods and the civilian politicians who acted in coordination with them were actually trying to achieve their own political goals "through non-political methods" and to "indoctrinate the military along these lines." The Feb. 28 process produced decisions that were difficult to implement. Once again "the fear of the military" profoundly affected social life. The military became the subject matter of speculation; markets fluctuated considerably. Politicians who were unsure about their level of support from the people but who were still fearful of evaluating their own political performance saw the coup as a golden opportunity to take political power. The majority of secular intellectuals and media figures did nothing but applaud the Feb. 28 process. Today, there are some who want to employ the same tactics to grab political power. The coup attempt, which surfaced along with proof of the clandestine Ergenekon organization's existence, was an attempt to re-launch something similar to the Feb. 28 coup.

Their tactics designed to force the military into action included triggering a Turkish-Kurdish conflict, serial murders and shocking assassinations. If this had been successful, they would have derailed Turkey from the Western axis and pushed it toward the Russian-Chinese axis. But they failed to do it.

The Ergenekon Case: The Ontological, Essential, and Historical Correlations[34]

The indictment prepared by the Istanbul chief prosecutor for the Ergenekon case has been admitted by the court. The court hearings will begin on Oct. 20, 2008. From this stage on, we may say that a big struggle will be initiated over the law—and not on legal grounds. In fact, there has already been such a struggle, since the first day the issue came to the agenda. Now, this struggle will be carried on in a different form and via different methods.

A segment of the media in Turkey has so far tended to ignore this issue, expending great efforts to belittle the accusations, allegations, grave charges, and news and reports on the issue. But it has become evident that the magnitude of the case is no longer concealable; attempts to conceal it will only be harmful to those trying to cover it up.

The first objection staged following the indictment's filing was that the document was full of "abstract" thoughts and accusations. In particular, the main opposition Republican People's Party (CHP) still seeks to disseminate the view that the case does not rest on solid ground. CHP

---

[34] First appeared in *Today's Zaman* daily on Jul. 28, 2008

leader Deniz Baykal even asserted that he is the "defender" and attorney of those arrested in connection with the case.

It is interesting that some renowned lawyers have also raised this objection. For instance, a retired chief prosecutor from the Supreme Court of Appeals is among them; according to this retired prosecutor, Turkey has entered "a fascist era" by carrying out these operations. It appears that this case is very complicated—its extensions into politics, the business world, and media have not yet been revealed.

First, there is an "entity" out there. This is a very complicated entity, whose relations are intricate. While it is loosely organized, the actors of this entity seem to focus on the same goal and target.

Second, the illegal entity called "Ergenekon" has a goal, and its members have undergone a process of preparations to achieve this goal. As part of these preparations, they have held meetings, prepared plans and programs, and devised a division of labor based on a certain hierarchy, order, and chain of command. In connection with these preparations, they adopted goals to render the government non-operational, incite the public against the government, and probably expend efforts to create an environment suitable for a coup.

Third, plans were put into action. To this end, the indictment references the attacks against the Council of State and the *Cumhuriyet* daily and the grenades and bombs[35] seized in Ümraniye and Eskişehir.

More importantly, some important assassinations and murders committed since the 1990s are associated with this case. The file also mentions incidents in Istanbul's Gazi district that terrified all of Turkey in 1995. The indictment asserts that the Ergenekon organization sought opportunities for infiltration within the Turkish Armed Forces (TSK). It is also asserted in the indictment that assassinations have been planned against the members of some judicial institutions, including the Council of State and the Supreme Court of Appeals, some journalists, three

---

[35] The Ergenekon investigation was actually launched upon the discovery of a number of grenades in a shanty house in the Ümraniye district of Istanbul in June 2007. The grenades were traced to a retired military officer. Subsequent investigations led to the discovery of other weapons throughout the country as well as assassination plans, and clues to political murders in Turkey's recent history. (ed.)

renowned politicians from the Democratic Society Party (DTP), and even the current chief of the Turkish General Staff, who will retire in three months. Moreover, the indictment further underlines that this illegal entity was eager to exert influence on the Kurdish issue, which is about to become gangrenous to Turkey.

Of course, the allegations need to be proven by the alleger. Unless a court concludes after a fair trial that a crime has been committed, each suspect is a defendant; in other words, he or she is still innocent and is only under suspicion. This is the case. It is essential to remain respectful of this golden rule of law and to not violate the fundamental rights and honor of the accused. While this is a general principle that needs to be observed by all, it is also necessary to wait for the trial process and take the indictment seriously, because the allegations are grave. Even if only one-tenth of the accusations are true, this is truly terrifying. It seems that shedding light on Turkey's near history depends partially on the healthy conclusion of this case.

Domestic and International Dimensions of the Ergenekon Case[36]

According to the indictment prepared by the Istanbul chief prosecutor with regard to the Ergenekon coup plot case, "The assassination plans aimed to incite provocations. They included Fener Patriarch Bartholomew, Armenian Patriarch Mutafyan, and Jewish businessman Ishak Alaton. Some other names were also included." If the allegations are true, the goal of the clandestine Ergenekon organization was to ensure a civil war broke out. The plan of *Cumhuriyet* publisher and columnist İlhan Selçuk, who is charged with serving as the civilian administrator of the Ergenekon organization, was to "let the fights grow so that the military will have to intervene."[37] The clandestine Ergenekon organization seeks to topple the government. Because they are convinced that this will not happen through democratic means, former Istanbul University Rector Kemal Alemdaroğlu says, "This job cannot be done through democracy."

---

[36] First appeared in *Today's Zaman* daily on Aug. 08, 2008
[37] *Zaman* daily, Aug. 4, 2008

When elections and democracy are discarded, the old method left from the Unionist (İttihatçı) leaders is naturally considered—and this is a coup! The point that needs to be underlined is that the existence of the entity called Ergenekon was verified by the National Intelligence Organization (MİT); in addition, just like the General Staff, MİT also asserts that they have no connection or relation to this organization or entity. Of course this does not necessarily mean that Ergenekon was not organized within the army and that it does not have extensions in it. But the army itself has nothing to do with this as an institution; in other words, Ergenekon attempted to do something inside the army. It would not be an exaggeration to say that this "something" was a coup attempt. Therefore, it is possible that the upcoming supplemental indictment is related to this.

This picture can be drawn when these two points are combined: There is an entity outside of the institutional identity of the Turkish Armed Forces (TSK); the goal of the entity is to cause turmoil and chaos and force the TSK to stage a coup in this chaotic environment. We can call this the creation of a suitable environment for a military coup.

Apparently the strategy was to stage a coup. The tactics were prepared based on a pretty simple logic: As noted by İlhan Selçuk, it was based on forcing the military to stage a coup with a fait accompli. First, the relevant external attempts would be made and the military would necessarily follow. Such horrible and terrorizing provocations would be carried out, and such shocking assassinations would be committed, leaving the military no choice but to intervene because when internal safety is at stake and the government is paralyzed or unable to maintain law and order, interference by the military would be inevitable.

This is one side of the coin. Of course, when the murders and assassinations committed in the near past are considered, the conclusion of this case is deeply important for helping to illuminate the near past; some circles—especially religious—were blamed for the murders and assassinations, the perpetrators of which were never identified. They were accused of crimes they did not commit and other circles polarized the society to obtain political advantage.

Undoubtedly, the Ergenekon case is not all about this. In other words, there is one dimension of this operation that concerns foreign policy and is not discussed adequately. As is known, a National Security Council (MGK) secretary said a while ago that Turkey would draw a new road map that would exclude the US and the EU and that it might get closer to Russia, Iran, and China. At the same time, a speech by then-Russian President Vladimir Putin was posted on the General Staff's Web site while the chief of general staff was on an official visit to the US.

All this led to the emergence of a view that a group inside the state which may be considered an important actor—and not the state itself—was eager to move Turkey from its Western orientation to the axis of Russia-Iran-China. As the operations become more conclusive and deeper, it becomes apparent that the entity called Ergenekon was really inclined toward Russia and that those who executed this operation were called "Eurasianists."

Considering all this, one cannot help but ask: Did the operations not seek to eliminate this group in addition to destroying their internal extensions? If so, it may be said that the US should be pretty content with these operations.

The Sledgehammer Coup Plot[38]

The 10th High Criminal Court ordered the arrest of 102 suspects, including 25 generals, in the investigation into the Sledgehammer Coup Plan in mid-July, 2010. Some of those to be arrested are still in their posts.

Although a week has passed since the court order, none of the suspects have turned themselves in. According to one claim, under the guidance of General Staff lawyers, the military officers are trying to buy time. During a funeral ceremony in Adana of four police officers (who were killed in Hatay), Interior Minister Beşir Atalay and 6th Army Corps Commander Gen. Nejat Bek, for whom the court issued an arrest warrant, were standing in the same row. It seemed like they

---

[38] First appeared in *Today's Zaman* daily on Jul. 30, 2010

were trying to say, "Yes everyone is equal before the law, but some people are more equal."[39]

The charges that the military officers are facing are quite scandalous: Attempting to overthrow the constitutional order by force, fomenting chaos to overthrow the government, detonating a bomb at two historical mosques (Fatih Mosque and Beyazit Mosque) in Istanbul during crowded hours, shooting down a Turkish plane and then blaming Greece to spark a crisis between the two countries, arresting thousands of people and gathering them at stadiums, and assassinating 19 intellectuals, writers, and journalists, including myself.

Certainly these allegations alone deserve to be investigated. But not only do the military officers refuse to surrender, but they can't be removed from their positions, either. The Supreme Military Council (YAŞ), which convenes every August, has been dismissing dozens of people on grounds that they engaged in "reactionary activities" since 1997. A reactionary activity includes a military officer performing the daily prayers or his wife wearing a headscarf.

Those who speak on behalf of the army say people who have "dissident ideas, beliefs, and behaviors" should not be allowed to work in the military and that under the constitutional provisions, the decisions and actions of the military cannot be reviewed by the judiciary.

Those who defend the opposite proposition believe:

1. It is perfectly natural for people working in the military to observe their religious duties and be pious. Our nation has prominent military characteristics and the military cannot be isolated from the generally accepted beliefs in society.

2. The members of the military may have diverse opinions and beliefs. As long as they do not violate military discipline, people with different beliefs can serve within the military. Dismissing people from office because of their different beliefs and opinions is a violation of fundamental rights and freedoms. While dis-

---

[39] Members of the military, including the retired high-ranking military officers, were brought to justice in December 2010 for the first time in Turkish history for their infamous Sledgehammer (*Balyoz*) coup plot, which would allegedly struck a heavy blow to the dynamics of democratic process only a decade after the previous postmodern coup in 1997. (ed.)

cipline is a vital element in the military, the protection of fundamental rights and freedoms is much more important.

The problem here is that the debate is not on objective qualifications, but on official ideology and the military's tutelage over civil politics. No public organization or public space should be built upon discrimination among its citizens. If people have the professional skills and competence needed to perform a job then their different opinions, beliefs, and behaviors should not be questioned. A public organization is required to provide services according to its established purpose. If a person has the skills and competence to provide these services, then they should not be prevented from doing so on grounds that they hold different beliefs or opinions. Otherwise this is discrimination, and all forms of discrimination do considerable damage to fundamental rights and freedoms.

We can say that from the early 19th century on, the main function of the Turkish military has been to build a new society, to establish a nation-state, and to ensure the Westernization of the nation—in other words, to modernize it. The modernization of the Ottoman Empire, Iran, and czarist Russia started with the power and influence of their armies. After the establishment of the Turkish Republic, it was the military that supported the modernization of the country. During compulsory military service, young people would not only learn about military science, but they would also become educated in modernization. In many non-Western countries, modernization efforts are backed by the military. We can argue that in many countries, the main function of the military is to act more as a modernizing force than as a defensive mechanism.

A fact about the military officers and those who support the continuation of military tutelage over politics is this: Military officers can no longer foster the modernization of the nation. Instead they create heavy costs for the country due to their anachronistic attitude and methods. Society wants to modernize by civilian and regular methods. The conflict in Turkey stems from the dissidence between "official-military modernization" and "civilian-conservative modernization."

The Military's Influence on Civil Politics[40]

It is no secret that one of the biggest obstacles to Turkey's European Union bid is the military's influence on civil politics. This fact is highlighted in almost every EU annual progress report.

Some groups in Turkey view any shift toward the military in the "military-politics equilibrium" as a "guarantee for protection of the regime" and therefore tend to regard some military activities—such as the expulsion of some officers from the military because of their opinions and lifestyles—as appropriate, even if this means a violation of some fundamental rights. They maintain that those with "dissident ideas, beliefs and behaviors" should not be allowed to work in the military and that the under constitutional provisions (Article 125/2), no military decisions and actions can be reviewed by the judiciary or other institutions. Opponents of this thesis, however, rest their argument primarily on the following:

1. The military is taking advantage of Prophetic traditions; therefore, it is perfectly natural for those working in the military to be able to observe their religious duties and lead a pious life. The Turkish nation has prominent military characteristics and the military cannot be isolated from generally accepted beliefs within the society.

2. Military members may have diverse opinions and beliefs. As long as they act within the limits of military discipline, those with different beliefs can serve within the military. The removal from office of people for their different beliefs and opinions is a violation of fundamental rights and freedoms. While discipline is a vital element in military practice, the protection of fundamental rights and freedoms is much more important.

However persuasive these theses may seem, this should not be ignored: No public organization or public space should be built upon discrimination between citizens. If people have the required professional skills and competence, their different opinions, beliefs, and behaviors should not be considered as criteria to be expelled. A public organiza-

---

[40] First appeared in *Today's Zaman* daily on May 02, 2008

tion is required to provide services according to its established purpose. If a person has the skills and competence to provide these services, then they should not be prevented from doing so on grounds that they had different beliefs or opinions. Otherwise, the result is discrimination—and all forms of discrimination deal considerable damage to fundamental rights and freedoms.

As for the military's Islamic roots, some groups in Turkey have an established belief in this argument. Apart from its profound historical roots, this argument is, however, somewhat defective in practice, given the main policies pursued since the Tanzimat era and the current practice. In the history of Islam, there was a disruption in the Islamic military tradition after Muawiya, i.e., after 660 CE. There is a fundamental difference between the military services before and after Muawiya. The Islamic military organization was not professional until Muawiya's time. What's more, the tradition of using the military as a guarantor of the regime started when the Turks were employed by the Abbasid caliphs as the caliphate's military force.

We can say that in the early 19th century, the Turkish military's main function was to build a new society, to establish a nation-state—in sum, to ensure the nation's Westernization/modernization. The modernization of the Ottoman Empire, Iran, and Czarist Russia began with the power and influence of their armies. After the Turkish Republic's establishment, it was the military that supported the country's modernization. While performing their compulsory military services, the youth would be trained not only in military science, but were also educated in modernization. In many non-Western countries, modernization efforts are backed by the military. We can even argue that in many countries, the military's main function is to act more as a modernizing force than as a defensive mechanism.

By its very nature, the military cannot be expected to be democratic, as discipline, hierarchy, and the chain of command are essential elements of the military art. But not every member of the military can be expected to have the same political opinion, and therefore the only way to protect the military from excluding different political views is to put

an end to the military's potential for coups and purge all military officers who favor coups.

Social Psychology of Military-Civilian Relations[41]

This year's Supreme Military Council (YAŞ) meeting, which convenes
every year in August, was a painful one. The possibility of an "agreement,"
in the words of the prime minister, eventually emerged. Even the news-
worthiness of this "agreement" is sufficient to show that there is a certain abnormality in this regard in Turkey.

In a country where civilian authorities are not able to fully exert their
authority, military authorities who are nothing but "civil servants with
weapons" can flex their muscles against the true representatives of the
people. Still, this year's decision will serve as a roadmap for military-civilian relations in the coming period. Either the military will maintain its
tutelage within the status quo, or it will submit to the civilian authority.

This form of military-civilian relations is not unique to our time.
There is an established tradition about them. If we are to talk about a
true "established practice," we need to have a look at the series of practices that stem from the institutionalization of the military tutelage over
civilian politics.

There are historical, social, and psychological factors in the background that nurture established practices. For most of the time, we
have to resort to tools afforded by social psychology in order to make
sense of today's group, administrative, and political conflicts.

The treatment afforded to Hatice Şenocak, who was badly brutal-
ized by a woman named B. P. for swimming while wearing a haşema—a
loose fitting swimsuit conservative women wear at public beaches and
pools—in İzmir last week, was an expression of the underlying causes
of the recent YAŞ crisis. The assailant B.P., who was apparently the wife
of a military officer, reportedly said, "Let's drown her. You spiders! You
are ashamed to pollute the sea, but you pollute Atatürk's republic. I am
the wife of a military officer. You can't do anything to me..."[42]

---

[41] First appeared in *Today's Zaman* daily on Aug. 10, 2010
[42] *Zaman* daily, Aug. 8, 2010

The traumatized victim, a teacher, filed a complaint with the gendarmerie but was ignored. Doesn't this story remind you of the Ergenekon case or the Sledgehammer (Balyoz) coup plan trial in which commanders who were summoned to court as "suspects" or "defendants" failed to comply with the court order and high-ranking officers could not be arrested despite arrest warrants issued for them? A lawyer who recently spoke to the CNN Türk TV station shouted, "Of course military officers don't care about the law or courts. Atatürk's reforms still apply."

In the final analysis, the aggressive wife of a military officer mentioned above can be said to be equating this country with Atatürk's republic, and claims possession of it. According to the assumptions in the subconscious of this woman, this "country belongs to M. Kemal Atatürk," who founded the republic, and because she is a Kemalist, she has inherited the right to rule and dispose of this country because she is the wife of a military officer, and military officers are the protectors of this country's regime and the republic. This is even mentioned in the law (Article 35 of the Turkish Armed Forces [TSK] Internal Service Code).[43] Türkan Saylan, the late founder of the Support for Modern Life Association (ÇYDD), had previously said, "We are the original ones. Nothing can happen in this country unless we allow it."

According to the assailant, B.P., one of the basic characteristics of Atatürk's republic is revealing one's body, and the teacher who wants to swim while wearing a swimsuit that covers her body according to the requirements of her religion is polluting the sea with her image, and she does not feel ashamed of her behavior. On the other hand, Şenocak covers her body because she feels "a sense of shame" in the presence of other people and God, but the military officer's wife regards this as "shamelessness." There is obviously almost no common value between the headscarved teacher and the attacker, and they are completely at a distance from each other. Some women who do not wear a headscarf and who come from certain groups can be very aggressive. Some claim

---

[43] According to this Internal Service Code of 1935, which has been amended quite recently, the Turkish military had long had a strange and eerie constitutional right to step in and stage a coup in the name of protecting and defending the Turkish homeland and the republic. (ed.)

that one reason for the continuation of the headscarf ban is the existence of wives of military officers who do not wear a headscarf. They urge their husbands to act uncompromisingly with regard to the ban.

It is possible to think that fear plays a role in the sociopolitical tension to a certain extent. The more important thing, however, is that the military as a privileged state group since the Ottoman era claims possession of the country with its regime, land and people. The state's task was to protect "the religion" during the classical period of the Ottoman Empire. After the administrative reforms of the Tanzimat in 1839, the state undertook the mission to modernize the country. It was originally thought that only the military could achieve this. This belief continued to be held during the Committee of Union and Progress (CUP) and the Republican periods. After the end of the 1960s, the society wanted to take over the duty of transforming and modernizing the country. The military responded violently to that request and reasserted its possession of the country. Currently, the military can neither ensure modernization nor try to understand the many social groups struggling for their fundamental rights and freedoms.

Chapter 4

The Steep Slopes of Democracy: Pinnacles and Pitfalls

The Austere Passageway of Democracy[44]

There are several important factors that prevent the full adoption of democracy in our political culture. Since these factors are not taken into regard by political scientists most of the time, people don't realize the important role they play in the political regime.

Above all, the fact that democracy was adopted by us exactly as it had been shaped by the historical experiences of Western societies prevents its cultural internalization in Turkey. At this point, democracy must be forced to face our traditional political culture and historical experience and, most importantly, the religion of Islam, which forms the fundamental cultural code of this country. After Islam was quickly associated with terrorism and fundamentalism, it was claimed that it was in no way compatible with democracy, and soon this was made into a refrain sung by nearly the whole press. This association gave rise to a significant "mental pollution." Any sort of parallel drawn between Islam and politics in general—and democracy in particular—or any sort of comparison made in this context is accused by secular segments of being a reflection of "political Islam" or "fundamentalism." However, democracy cannot take root in any Islamic country unless it faces Islam. It cannot be internalized mentally and thus cannot constitute a referential borderline for political attitudes in a social sense. In fact, many Western political scientists have said democracy has arrived at a point where it

---

44   First appeared in *Today's Zaman* daily on Feb. 15, 2008

is consuming itself and that it is in need of a new injection of rejuvenation from other cultures. Democracy is not a process that has seen completion and the toughest challenge it faces today is the need for it to develop in a way that will include cultural and social pluralism as well as political pluralism.

The second important point is that the claim that the dominant worldview in the Islamic world constitutes a direct obstacle for democracy is never scrutinized at length. Although the problem is not at the level that some often claim, it is true that harsh, so-called Islamic political rhetoric—which does stem partially from the Islamic world—doesn't benefit us much in terms of democracy. It is possible to say that some Islamic countries will create a political system peculiar to themselves and gradually switch to genuine multi-party systems in the middle term. However, in certain countries there is nothing visible that alludes to a democratic culture so it is not possible to make any such hopeful predictions for them. Although it is not taken into regard as much as it should be, there is a high demand for democracy in almost the entire Middle East, and this demand is, of course, being made by the young generation. One of the most important elements that fans opposition to democracy is the fact that no accurate relationship has so far been established between democracy and religious needs and demands. When introduced as an absolutely secular system and as the political regime of the irreligious, democracy may sound to some as an attempt to share God's authority. An important problem perpetually suggests itself here with regard to the Islamic science of Kalam—the Islamic philosophy of seeking theological principles through reasoning and verification. This problem should be discussed by Muslim theologians, intellectuals, and politicians altogether; putting aside basic (humanist) philosophical assumptions, it has not been discussed comprehensively enough whether the democratic system—meaning elections, representation, pluralism, organized opposition, and participation—is really tantamount to trying to share in God's authority.

A third factor is that the process initiated with the administrative reforms of 1839 (popularly known as *Tanzimat*), which immediately meant an absolute severance from the classical Ottoman administration, was followed by the Committee of Union and Progress (CUP) and culminated in Republican culture. This new political process doesn't include a complete democratic culture in any way. This is because the power elites find contradictions between the existing republic and a full-fledged democracy. The main problem is not whether we will go back to the regime of the sultanate—there is simply nobody in Turkey who defends that regime; our problem is a republican regime that has been unable to democratize itself. And what underlies this problem is a concept of positivist despotism fed by the Enlightenment. Positivism has collapsed, but the mindset that emanated from it still persists. The austere passageway of democracy can be crossed through mutual negotiation and dialogue

The 2010 Referendum Campaign: "Not Enough, but Yes"[45]

There are two critical items on the agenda for Turkey: The first is the referendum to be held on Sept. 12, 2010, while the second is the early elections that could potentially be held shortly after the referendum. That's not all. Depending on the outcome of the referendum, there will be municipal elections in 2012 and a presidential election in 2014. If the result of the parliamentary elections in 2011 does not provide stability, then the possibility of early elections will be brought up. In other words, the next three or four years are going to be politically hot for Turkey.

This is why the "partial constitutional amendments" being put up for a referendum are crucial.

Political parties are already taking sides. Both parties with seats in Parliament and no seats in Parliament are going to determine their position according to the "Constitution." This is very normal considering that it has become impossible to continue governing Turkey with the military regime's Constitution, which will be revised again for the 17th time in the Sept. 12 referendum.

The main issue that we have been putting across ever since the Justice and Development Party (AK Party) came to power in 2002 is this: The only way Turkey can get rid of its military-bureaucratic tutelage is with a

---

[45]   First appeared in *Today's Zaman* daily on Aug. 24, 2010

new social contract. Both the domestic and foreign political scene calls for this. In contrast to how it used to be in the past, a substantial portion of society, in particular the religious and conservative groups, is demanding a new constitution. Perhaps for the first time, intellectuals, or at least a portion of them, namely liberal intellectuals from the left or nationalist positions, want a civilian constitution that is free of the tutelage of official ideology. Regardless of the outcome of the Sept. 12 referendum, the demand for a new constitution will be voiced more loudly and clearly.

The successive developments in and the bitter facts of Turkish politics seem to have taught the AK Party many lessons as well. The government has empirically shown that the current laws and regulations allow a party to be "in power" but do not allow it to "wield power." Several center-right parties have come to power in the past but were never capable of wielding power.

They really thought they were governing the country. Whether it was an outcome of absolute political and pragmatic considerations or something else, the AK Party has managed to put a "partial constitutional amendment" to a referendum. It is evident that if the outcome of the referendum is positive, the AK Party will benefit from it.

While this is the situation on the AK Party side, the "front" where opposition parties have united is extremely noteworthy and thought-provoking. The situation on the front we can call the "no/rejection" front is heartrending. It is a disgrace to law, politics, and a more liberal world. The Republican People's Party (CHP), the Nationalist Movement Party (MHP), and the Peace and Democracy Party (BDP) have aligned themselves along the same front. While their pretenses appear to be different, in the end all three:

1. Have formed a "no" front against the partial constitutional amendments;

2. Are trying to prevent even the slightest attempt to foster the expansion of rights in Turkey just for the sake of undermining the AK Party;

3. Are trying to hinder the referendum and are avoiding offering an alternative or a new civilian constitution that is based on negotiations.

Furthermore, the Kurdistan Workers' Party (PKK) and other dark forces are trying to stir social chaos and conflict in the country in order to obstruct the referendum.

That said, attempting to undermine the Sept. 12 referendum just because it is going to give the AK Party extra points is neither ideal politics nor realpolitik. If we bear in mind that the amendments will provide the much hoped for partial improvement to the country's judicial and executive branches, we can see that it is more reasonable, nay essential, to say "yes" in the referendum, even if it will be to the advantage of the ruling party.

In particular, the changes to the composition of the Supreme Board of Judges and Prosecutors (HSYK), which has a profound impact on the judiciary and the Constitutional Court, which has assumed the function of the legislative branch, are a few of the critical steps that will improve the system. What's striking is that in a country governed by a democratic parliamentary regime, the "no front" and political parties that have lined themselves up on that front defend a constitution that was produced by the 1982 military regime and that can clearly no longer respond to the needs of Turkey, and they oppose reform. The slogan for the upcoming referendum is fitting: "Not enough, but yes."

"Nay" to the Century-Old Military Tutelage[46]

In the referendum which took place on Sept. 12, 2010, "58 percent of voters said 'yes' while 42 percent of the voters said 'no'." Turkish society has ended a bloody military coup that took place exactly 30 years ago (on Sept. 12, 1980) with this referendum vote. While 42 percent of the population didn't wish for the status quo to change, the result is paradoxical.

A portion, and not all of the "naysayers"—and these are individuals who reserve their powers thanks to the tutelage that the military has over civilian politics—have partially said "yes" to the Constitution of the Sept. 12, 1980 military coup and thus military coups. And those who voted "yes" have said "no" to the military tutelage and its constitu-

---

[46] First appeared in *Today's Zaman* daily on Sept. 14, 2010

tion. In short, the paradox of this referendum was that those who outwardly said "yes" were saying "no" while those who said "no" were in essence saying "yes."

The referendum campaign was turned into a vote of confidence for the Justice and Development Party (AK Party) and in actuality the theme of the matter at hand was "the coup and the constitution as the by-product of the coup." Prior to the referendum, the AK Party's support in Turkey was around 39 percent. The 58 percent result attained in the referendum will at most give the AK Party 3 percent more support, totaling 42 percent—which is not bad at all. We can say that Prime Minister Recep Tayyip Erdoğan, who practically steered this campaign with a great deal of determination and energy, as well as the AK Party, have benefitted fully from this referendum.

It was the Republican Peoples' Party (CHP), which conducted politics on the grounds of Turkish nationalism; it could neither bring its votes up to the levels that it expected, nor could it stop the dropping level of votes.

How should the situation of the Republican Peoples' Party (CHP) and Kemal Kılıçdaroğlu be evaluated in this referendum? I think it's necessary to separate the two from one another. In my opinion, although the CHP is one of the unsuccessful parties of the referendum, its new leader Kılıçdaroğlu is not "unsuccessful." He was able to raise his party's support to 29 percent, which is an accomplishment in itself. If he is able to demonstrate further initiative in the upcoming parliamentary elections, then the CHP will be able to stop its search for a new leader. However, in order for Kılıçdaroğlu to do this, he must demonstrate that he has complete initiative.

Large cities are giving important signals to the AK Party. The results from İzmir are not surprising. However, the situation in Ankara and Istanbul are not all that promising. In Istanbul and Ankara, no votes were at 45 percent. We can hear the footsteps of the CHP in these two cities. The 2013 municipal elections can be swept up by the CHP even though the National View-AK Party front has been holding down the municipalities here since the 1994 elections.

It is not possible to say that the Peace and Democracy Party's (BDP) boycott campaign didn't work in the East and Southeast. The BDP demonstrated that it has that region under its control, but 35 percent of voters—which included a predominant population of Kurds, Arabs, and Turks—went to ballot boxes and casted a "yes" vote. This is quite informative. Unfortunately, the gap in solving the Kurdish problem is increasing with each passing day; and the opportunities for finding a resolution based on dialogue and common rules are weakening with each passing day. There were some invisible actors in the referendum campaign, some "secret heroes," if you will, who are the people of "voluntary movements," who persevered in spite of all criticisms and attacks: the followers of Fethullah Gülen, who gave powerful support to the referendum all the way from the US. Erdoğan felt the need to cite these "friends across the ocean," thanking these devoted individuals.

Sept. 13 is the beginning of a new era. There was a polarization and division in society as a result of the referendum. A referendum is a democratic procedure and those involved put forth their preferences. The result was that 58 percent said "yes." What is now left for those who voted "no" is to accept this result with maturity and respect. Some members of the judiciary have been giving messages that "the struggle will continue from here on as well," and this is very wrong, dangerous, and extra-judicial.

At this juncture, a lot falls on the shoulders of the political parties, particularly the AK Party. As the prime minister promised in meetings in town squares, while Turkey prepares for the upcoming parliamentary general elections, it must start a period of preparing a new constitution—encompassing all political parties, social and civil groups of different views, and professional organizations and associations. A new constitution must be that of the whole of Turkish society and not just a single party.[47] There is a strong will in Turkish society to this end.

---

[47] The Erdoğan government attempted to draft a new "civic" constitution in 2007 when Erdoğan sought to shift to the presidency and consolidate his position by creating a strong "executive presidency" within the framework of the new civic constitution. However, Erdoğan government's unenthusiastic effort to draft the new civic constitution was abandoned during his third term in office after it became

The Meaning of a Civilian Constitution for Turkey[48]

While getting prepared for the general elections on June 12, 2011, the Turkish people were told that Turkey is also getting ready to draft its first ever comprehensive civilian constitution with the help of various civil society actors. Prime Minister Recep Tayyip Erdoğan announced that the new constitution would be prepared by the public.

The previous constitutions, drafted in 1961 and 1982, had been prepared by the military. Earlier constitutions drafted in 1924, 1921 and 1876 were prepared according to Western constitutions. The military was not involved when the government attempted to draft a new constitution in 2007, but the way the issue was handled was wrong. A total of six experts were going to prepare the country's basic contract. At that time I tried to explain that it was wrong and that it would not help to solve basic problems in Turkey.

Just think about it. Two adults decide to get married but a professor from the neighborhood prepares their marriage contract. Of course business contracts and other contracts have technical formats, but that comes into play after the sides reach an agreement and start discussing legal issues. The conditions of an agreement cannot be imposed on sides, such as couples who plan on getting married or entrepreneurs who want to establish a business partnership. The contracts between them cannot be dictated. In this respect, it is unreasonable for experts to prepare a constitution on behalf of the public, even if before they start writing, the drafters say, "There are many written constitutional texts in the West; let's look at them. Let's see what the Germans and French have done. What do the criteria set by the EU and liberal philosophy foresee? Let's create a text from this mixture and be very careful not to step outside of it."

---

clear that the inclusion of a powerful office of presidency was unfeasible under the prevailing circumstances. Indeed, the government's attempt of drafting this basic contract of the country without a general consensus and only with the participation of a total of six experts of constitutional law from within the AK Party proved that it was only a strategic move to lure voters ahead of the coming elections and not to solve basic problems in Turkey. (ed.)

[48] First appeared in *Today's Zaman* daily on Jan. 21, 2011

It just shows that we haven't learned a single lesson from our 200-year history and that we are quick to repeat basic mistakes.

There is an important reason why we should focus on the procedure and method of drafting a constitution more than its content. One of the most prominent features separating a modern society from a traditional society is its constitution, which is the essence, foundation, and continuing ideology of a modern state. Even if, from the liberal point of view, constitutions protect the individual from the state and, from the socialist point of view—which prioritizes democratic participation—they protect society from the state, in reality modern constitutions protect the state from individuals and society. It is because of this that if members of a society with the will to live together cannot develop a contract based on the principle of offer and acceptance, then a constitutional draft penned by experts will simply make the state the judge of its own court. This judge will always make rulings in favor of itself and the individual and society will lose their rights and freedoms against the state in every case.

Maybe pre-modern societies did not have written constitutional texts and their leaders ruled arbitrarily, but they still enforced customs. For example, sultans and caliphs in the history of Islam were not tyrannical rulers like leaders in contemporary states. There was Islamic law, which was independent from other contracts and invited them to be respectful and obedient. There were traditions, valid legal practices and the Divine Provisions, which were above all else. Together they formed a set of values that was the essence of legal and administrative life. In this respect, while benefiting from the experience of Western countries when preparing a new constitution, we should also turn to our own social history and primary moral codes.

A constitution is not just a legal framework that defines a state's structure. It is also closely related to the structure of a society and, by extension, to the way people want to live. Since a society's organizational model affects a society's lifestyle and its system of values that plays a role in the manifestation of this lifestyle, we can see that the text to prepare a constitution does not consist of merely "quotes from Europe or the EU," or of "a technical document penned by legal experts." This is the point that our liberal legal experts fail to understand. By drafting a constitution you impose a philosophy, a vision, a world view, a mentality of power, and a system of partition. You must involve the whole of society when determining the articles of a constitution.

The Question of Party Closures[49]

Party closure has become a general custom of Turkish politics, with 24 political parties having been closed down so far. Two parties are currently facing closure cases: the ruling Justice and Development Party (AK Party), which received 47 percent (16.5 million votes) of the vote in the July 22, 2007 elections, and the Democratic Society Party (DTP), which received 4 percent (2 million votes) of the vote in the same elections. The choices of 18.5 million voters are now subject to a political ban. In democratically governed countries, political parties are the warranty of the regime. It is impossible to describe a political regime as a multiparty democracy unless it includes more than one competing party. Turkey moved to a multiparty system in the 1950s in response to external pressures and developments; however, circles eager to maintain the single-party mentality have had a difficulty accepting this development.

From a practical perspective, does party closure have any benefit? Undoubtedly, no. It bears no benefit or outcome other than undermining the democratic tradition of the country. The Welfare Party (RP), Turkey's largest party at the time, was closed in 1998; subsequently, the Virtue Party (FP), which ranked third in the April 18, 1999 elections, was banned from politics. The closed-down parties were well supported by society and were not marginal parties. Whether the criminal elements referred to in the closure cases of these parties and used to justify this action actually constituted an offense or crime under the law was very controversial. But what is worrisome and of concern is the style used by the chief prosecutor that permeates the entire text of the indictment prepared in relation to the party closure case. Because style can be considered a sign of substantive content, it is possible to make a

---

[49] First appeared in *Today's Zaman* daily on May 20, 2008

plausible comment on the mindset of those who prepared the indictment on political parties and democracy.

The chief prosecutor described FP members as "bloodthirsty vampires" and "malignant tumors." These expressions are not proper for a legal text, which should be based on substantiated facts, logical explanations, and convincing arguments. These were simple attempts at denigration and insult. A judge, regardless of his political views, religious beliefs, philosophical alignments, ethnic background, and personal attitudes, may not reflect any element of these views or beliefs in his professional capacity simply because he is in a position to make a decision on legal or real personalities. Because he is obligated to ensure the preservation of confidence in the law and the legal system, a judge is required to remain patient, impartial, and calm vis-à-vis a defendant even if the latter is his political or ideological opponent. Even if he believes that the defendant is guilty as charged, the defendant remains a defendant until the final verdict and, as a defendant, he is entitled to some basic rights.

The Prophet Muhammad (pbuh) said, "Beware! When you bring a case to me, one of you may speak eloquently and the other may become unable to explain his part. I make my judgment based on how the case looks." Basing the final judgment on the outer appearance means that the decision is made in reference to concrete, objective and substantive facts. A judge may not make his decision based on his ideology or the potential intentions and thoughts of the defendants. Because crime or offense requires material elements, the evidence should also be clear and substantive. Intended actions, thoughts, and designed plans may not be considered crimes unless they become actions. Because crime is individual, the punishment should also be individual. No one may be held liable for someone else's actions. Punishment may not be collective and based on vengeful feelings and sentiments.

These are the values enshrined in the universal legal culture. When these are not observed and the judiciary is politicized, the legal protections and guarantees over the people who live under this legal or constitutional system are significantly undermined. Law is as essential to people as water and air. When justice, the final outcome and goal of law, disappears or is not served, nothing bears any value because it is justice that keeps the government alive and sustains it. As is frequently stated, "Legality and law are essential for everyone," for fundamental rights to be protected and for justice to be maintained.

Penetrating into the Codes of the Gezi Park Resistance[50]

Every [manipulative] social movement is characterized by the involvement of illegal organizations, marginal groups, or agent provocateurs of states, i.e., "internal and external forces." The intent of these forces to manipulate the masses is not important, but whether they have the capacity to do so is. These forces may enjoy extreme sophistication, experience and skills, but the decisive factor is the sociological, political, and structural texture of each social movement.

Internal and external forces may have been involved in the incidents that started happening in May 2013 in and around Taksim Square in Istanbul. Each of these forces may nurture their unique purposes. This is easy to see here. But if we explain this social movement, which has a high potential of spreading, only by referring to the acts and ways of certain organizations or forces, then we end up deceiving ourselves and closing our eyes to the social facts and underlying dynamics.

No agent provocateur can make a perfectly healthy person shout, "Oh, my stomach is aching!" or "My head is throbbing with pain!" If a person is shouting, then he has a problem that can be abused by internal or external forces. In this regard, we can suggest there are common characteristics of the social explosions in Turkey, Brazil, Indonesia, and other countries.

An examination of the social nature of the protests that started in Taksim Gezi Park before the violence and clashes with the police stepped in reveals that the protesters form three groups. Each group has its unique problems.

   a) The individually unhappy, dissatisfied, and angry ones: They are dominantly young, well-educated, urban technophiles; they communicate via social media. They have expensive tastes and are quite eager to consume modern and postmodern culture.

---

[50] First appeared in *Today's Zaman* daily on Jun. 24, 2013

They believe they don't get their due share from the rapidly growing economy and, therefore, lack the money to buy and partake in modern freedoms and culture. Some of them are rich, but they too have accumulated stress and anger at the government due to other reasons. Attending mass protests comes as a comfort to them, as this allows them to release the monster inside. Just as some people work as distinguished professionals during the week but wear the jerseys of their teams and turning into hooligans on the weekends, this group participates in the Taksim Gezi Park demonstrations to protest a world they don't like.

b) The Çarşı group: This group is symbolized by the famous fan group consisting of the fans of the Beşiktaş soccer team, and it consists mainly of the people from the middle and lower segments of the middle class who have suffered damages from the government's neoliberal policies. These are the small business owners who lost their jobs because big shopping malls opened, the civil servants with low incomes, workers without trade unions or social insurance, victimized subcontractors, people who earn minimum wage, and the unemployed. The members of this group are authentic segments of society, not marginal people. They refuse Marxist forms of protest—like vandalism, anarchy, demolishing public buildings, and clashing with the police—and they just protest an unjust system. Özgür, spokesperson for the Çarşı group, says, "To live is to resist the powerful."

c) Alevis: They have had problems for a long time, but their reasonable and justified demands have never been met. They have been concerned about the Syrian crisis and have been angered by the naming of the third bridge over Bosporus in Istanbul after the Ottoman sultan Yavuz Sultan Selim.

Excluding the small, destructive groups of vandals, these are the sociological and socio-political profiles of the main body of the protesters. Of course, officials must take measures against provocations by internal and external forces. But they should also correctly understand social movements and protests. Sociology has the power to change politics.

The Impact of Social Media
on the Gezi Park Resistance[51]

According to a survey conducted by Istanbul Bilgi University, 39.6 percent of the protesters who actively took part in the Gezi Park demonstrations were between the ages of 19 and 25, and 24 percent of them were between the ages of 26 and 30.

Almost 40 percent had never participated in a mass demonstration before, while 70 percent have no political affiliation. While 56 percent of protesters were in Taksim Square because they opposed the planned demolition of Gezi Park in Taksim, 44 percent said they participated in the Gezi Park demonstrations to protest the police's use of disproportionate force against the protesters. The partisans of a coup are limited to 9 percent, while 79.5 of the protesters are not in favor of any military coup to overthrow the government.

No matter what we may or may not like, there is a new youth profile in front of us. Social media has played an important role in the incidents at Tahrir, Taksim, and Rabaa al-Adawiya squares, and in other countries where mass street demonstration have been held, such as Brazil. From the perspective of political sociology, social groups that oppose the central and vertical political structure of modern nation-states that function via political parties, a constitution, and other institutions, want to change established political practices.

Social media, which is essentially a virtual and horizontal way of communication, is shaping up beneath the surface. Print and broadcast media is by nature hegemonic and privileged. It is hegemonic because the viewers and readers are unilaterally informed by an organized structure. They are delivered a monologue; they cannot answer, object a claim, or join the conversation. It is privileged because media is an expensive investment field. Everybody cannot express their ideas on TV or in newspapers; only a few hundred people such as media bosses, editors-in-chief, editors, columnists, and commentators enjoy this privilege.

---

[51] First appeared in *Today's Zaman* daily on Sept. 02, 2013

Over time, these privileged people formed a sort of clan of solidarity and established close relations with political, economic, and financial powers. Thus, they have become indifferent toward the demands of the people. An incident becomes important for the people only if it was on the agenda of the media, otherwise no one would be informed about the suffering of the masses.

Those who actively use social media tools are saying, "Here I am." They voice their objections, criticisms, and opinions. These people are everybody except politicians, columnists, commentators, academics, and opinion leaders. Their communication is not vertical; it is horizontal and beyond time and space. Social media put an emphasis on horizontal communication.

There are a few questions we need to ask: Is the center of public debate shifting from broadcast and print media, and organized civilian institutions, to social media? Can those organizing via social media establish new political subject-oriented practices? Can social media, which made the public authority backpedal in the Gezi Park incident, force the public authority to adopt a similar stance toward other issues?

There is another issue that we need to contemplate: The fact is, social media has an individual character. People using social media tools are actually acting alone and are not involved in real communication; they close their doors to the real world. But things have changed after social media's role in the Tahrir Square protests. Social media allowed people to enter a new world: The era of chat rooms, celebrity gossip blogs, and online games ended when the central-global powers discovered its real potential and social media turned into a mass political and social power.

Social media has never been the autonomous, private space of individuals. On the contrary, it makes individuals more open to the inspection of hegemonic powers. It is a hidden cave for identity, but when things hidden in this cave surface, they flood everything that stands in their way, just like a tsunami.

Power Politics and Restricting Freedoms[52]

Does a conservative party in power have the right to restrict those freedoms it doesn't agree with?

This question has been increasingly posed owing to the past decade of the Justice and Development Party (AK Party) being in power and even more frequently after the coup d'état that overthrew the Muslim Brotherhood in Egypt. It is best to answer this question in terms of contemporary political theory by looking at what happens in practice. Because anything can seem possible in theory, but most ideas cannot be substantiated through practice.

This fact also refers to international legislation, international covenants, and agreements and, thus, legal situations. The issue is also deeply tied to educational and cultural policies. In contemporary textbooks, the differences between the sexes are overlooked. For example, names are increasingly more unisex such as Fikret, Suat, and Deniz. And there are heroes in television series that do not have reflections of themselves in traditional culture. The traditional understanding of the father-husband as head of the household is less prevalent, and traditional gender relations are changing.

The understanding of "the individual" is being injected into newer generations. These people are the products of their schools, the media, and consumption culture. Young people make a point to highlight their own uniqueness. They define themselves based on the music they like, the clothes they wear, the relationships they develop with the opposite sex, or the movies they see, without politicizing their identities. They prioritize being an "individual." But there are differences between being an "individual," and a "personality." Individuality is associated with modernity, while personality is associated with religion. People who believe they are individuals through education, media, and pop culture do not want the life spaces they have drawn up for themselves to be interrupted. They are at the center of their worlds and if they are happy, the "others" related to them, such as families, spouses, ex-spouses, or children, are also happy. They can move in with a member of the opposite sex easily, and break up with them with the same ease.

---

[52] First appeared in *Today's Zaman* daily on Aug. 12, 2013

These young people have no ideologies; they don't attach importance to political parties. They are not into "organized group activities," and they are not inclined to become a part of a disciplined and structured group. The Internet and social media are their major past time. They are not loyal to liberalism, which is what has formed their political, intellectual, and social presence. They have a tendency for civil disobedience; they develop a language of opposition using humor and jokes. They don't resort to violence. Those who resorted to violence in Taksim Gezi Park protests were, however, organized groups. Contemporary young people are not fans of official ideologies. Their response to Jacobinist [elitist] groups' slogan of, "We are the soldiers of Mustafa Kemal," was a joking reply that made reference to a singer, "We are the soldiers of Mustafa Keser."

These young people who do not question themselves and believe that their parents did not try to understand them and that they deserve much better, do not pay much attention to anything. They go after what pleases them. They also believe that they have the right to have whatever they want. They were mad at the government because they felt they were being ignored by the political administration.

This new generation has a global dimension. Its members are products of the neo-liberal democracy. If governments attempt to restrict their freedoms and interfere with their lifestyles, the global system will speak for them. The system is being designed in accordance with their demands and lifestyles.

When the freedoms and liberties defined by liberal philosophy are taken into account, generations focusing on worldly pleasures will emerge. You will reap what you have sown. We are currently dealing with a postmodern reality that is focused on the exhaustion of freedom over the body.

Heading in the Wrong Direction[53]

A group of people who got lost in the woods are seeking a way out. It is not possible to move due to trees in the way. They advance by cutting down those trees with a chainsaw.

---

[53] First appeared in *Today's Zaman* daily on Jul. 14, 2011

After lengthy deliberations, they have come to an agreement: they hold that there is no other way out, meaning that the only way to get out of the woods is to implement the solution they have thought up. However, they cannot see ten steps away. The direction they picked as a way out is actually taking them to an abyss. At the edge of the abyss is a tree standing and if they cut this tree down, they will fall down along with this last tree. They are not aware of the coming danger. They need someone to warn them of the approaching danger, someone who can see the danger and who has a bird's eye view of these people and the woods.

Culture and social life, which have come to serve as a set of guidelines for life, are similar in this regard. We are surrounded by lovely green trees. In the beginning, many wrongs appeal to us; we do not notice the wrongs or we can tolerate them at the initial stage. The wrongs we have tolerated may turn into big mistakes over time. Mistakes and wrongs are products and outcomes of our decisions, actions, and attitudes. As the Qur'an says, God creates the good, and man is responsible for the bad.

To this end, the statement that failure to see the woods while taking a look at the trees refers to a human flaw and weakness. We cannot possibly see the whole reality with all its dimensions. Like our knowledge, our ability to grasp and our observations are limited. Somebody with greater abilities should serve as a guide for us. They should have a comprehensive view inclusive of depth, integrity, a principled dimension, and a future forecast.

And this is exactly what Plato's cave allegory tries to explain. People whose hands are tied facing the wall are only able to see the shadows of those standing beside them. Interestingly, they think that all of reality is just these shadows because they do not see anything but the reflections of these figures on the wall they are facing. Somebody outside this setting should untie their hands, take them out, and introduce them to the truth. The Prophets have historically assumed this mission.

Sometimes society and political life are comparable to a reverse current in a strait. Water flows in one direction on the surface, and in the other on the bottom. Wise and keen observers can point to an invisible current. It should be noted that man cannot be wise all the time and he does not always respect those with wisdom and prudence.

There are instances where not only the leaders but the societies as well need to be alerted and warned. Society may not make wise and reasonable decisions all the time. Democratic votes, as well as the decisions taken by the majority, cannot always save society. The statement, "The majority of the people would not come to the true path; most of them would not use their mind and most would not be thankful," shows that the decisions of the majority are applicable to only a limited number of issues. If the preferences and choices of the majority—even if implemented through democratic means—were in fact sufficient in providing wise and reasonable decisions, then murderers, looters, and occupiers would not have come to power in some countries. In this case, would it not be safe to argue that democracies should be backed by spiritual sources rather than mere decision-making procedures?

Like individuals, societies may go astray; despite this state of affairs, they may want to remain so. We will then have to be able to speak out like the great Turkish poet Necip Fazıl Kısakürek, who said, "You crowds, stop! This is a dead end!" Is it easy to tell the people they are heading in the wrong direction and that they are seeking a way out in the wrong place? The greatest form of bravery takes place when this spiritual and ethical mission is fulfilled.

The Illusion of Progress:
Two Steps Forward, One Step Back[54]

Unlike the commonly held conviction, the progress that Turkey has made to become a livable country under a democratic regime based on respect for human rights, the rule of law, and a place where everything can be discussed, is not that large.

It sometimes moves two steps forward, one step back, and sometimes two steps back and one step forward. When compared to countries that are making no progress at all or are seeing a worsening of their

---

[54] First appeared in *Today's Zaman* daily on Dec. 12, 2011

human rights record, this may even be considered good. However, when we consider those states that are making swift progress toward a pluralist democracy, the situation is not very promising in Turkey.

For instance, the majority of Eastern European countries that emerged out of the former Soviet regime are better off than Turkey. However, it should also be noted that there is a stable progress; and from a certain historical perspective, we may also say that we are doing better in general terms. The most important aspect of the Turkish experience is that its Islamic groups have never favored violence as a method. This is important in terms of the interpretation of the Sunni political doctrine within the political climate of modern times.

The headscarf ban was only recently lifted at universities, albeit partially; it is still in effect in some places. Some universities continue to impose this ban. Some political parties have been dissolved; the Justice and Development Party (AK Party) survived such a dissolution case in 2008, brought against it because it introduced a constitutional amendment concerning the headscarf ban. Never mind the fact that it received the votes of half of the people. Parties in which Kurdish nationalists have a political platform have always faced this danger of dissolution.

The most recent court cases taking place in Turkey, such as the Sledgehammer case, show that there are still coup attempts. Some circles, after having concluded that they cannot hold power through democratic means or will not come to power via a popular vote, will not hesitate to stage a coup when the conditions are proper. Those who seize the moment and the opportunity want to add to their power by referring to an undefined threat and danger, making the lives of innocent people a living hell. Having an internal threat that is sometimes undefined leads to almost all social groups being repressed; this threat could be "fundamentalism" that allegedly seeks to take society backward, or the partition of the country. The "danger of religious fundamentalism" has been in effect for a century.

Up until 2003, when the AK Party came to power, those who looked at this side of Turkey from an outsider's perspective saw a depressing scene characterized by economic crisis, political turmoil, a lack of passion from the people, depression, and disillusionment, as evidenced in many people. The criticisms raised by the EU towards Turkey could not be attributed to the biases held by the European circles vis-à-vis Turkey alone. The world has achieved some legal and administrative standards; countries that have lagged behind these standards do not want to revise their domestic legal orders. You would say, "I want to maintain pressure over those whom I can pressure," on the one hand, but would also like to be placed in the same category as countries enjoying first-class standards in the field of law on the other. This is not going to happen!

It is not that good things did not take place. Over the last decade, political stability has been achieved; we owe this to the mobilization of the internal dynamics of society. Democracy is not purely a political regime; it needs to be supported by strong social demand. We will not imitate Europe in every field from now on, but we will not go back to the former authoritarian setting. It is a solution to copy and paste some reforms; we will develop our unique perspectives.

Undoubtedly, the stage of respect for human rights, and a rule and government based on the recognition of freedoms and the rule of law was not achieved overnight in Europe. Behind this achievement stand 700 years of struggle and a painful past. Of course, we do not have to wait seven centuries or be exhausted by religious or class wars, as was the case in the West. However, we need to admit that not everything is achievable so easily and in a very short amount of time. The most important thing that we have to consider in the recent upheavals in the Arab world is that political change is not handled by the elites alone and that the main body of the community is involved in the process. Religious groups and communities have been the driving force behind the change in Turkey; without their insistent demands, none of the political parties or elites could have been successful.

The Kemalist Stumbling Block to the EU Membership[55]

Outwardly, Turkey has a desire to be integrated with Europe and to formulate its policies to that end. According to some circles, Turkey becoming a lasting and organic part of Europe actually dates back to 150 years

---

[55] First appeared in *Today's Zaman* daily on Feb. 26, 2008

ago. However, there have been major discrepancies between the European view of Turkey and the things Europe demands from it, and the Turkish view of Europe and the things Turkey demands from it.

We can underline three major issues that unsettle Europe with regard to Turkey's possible full membership to the EU. The first major misgiving is Turkey's progressively growing population; the second is its Muslim identity; and the third is the free movement that Turks would deserve and enjoy using as a right once full membership was realized.

These are structural obstacles that cannot be eliminated within a certain period of time. Whatever sort of policy Turkey might choose to follow in the future, it cannot exchange its Muslim identity for some other. But, according to the assessments of some political circles, it can enforce repressive policies against the Muslim religion, coercing it into withdrawing from the public sphere, thereby eventually reducing it to a merely symbolic existence at the administrative, political, and institutional levels. The fundamental policies that have been followed for a long time and that continue to this day suggest this. Europe can accept a Turkey that has forsaken all its religious demands and that has thus no religious reservations, alternative claims, or objections. It can even use this as an argument: "See, the EU is not a Christian club." Curbing Turkey's population growth and limited free movement of that population, which will have a more "diluted" religious identity, will be tolerated to a certain extent by Europe.

However, while this process is continuing, another issue comes up: the establishment of the standards declared and imposed by Europe as a cluster of ideals, and the protection of these ideals. These standards are human rights, democracy, and the free market economy. This is what puts Turkey in a difficult position, as Europe demands Turkey adopt these three standards and radically revise and amend its laws in accordance with them. There are still groups that are resisting this change.

These groups perceive the implementation of these standards as Turkey's renouncement of a major part of its sovereignty in terms of its political independence. National Turkish policy, the fundamental strategy of which was mapped out by Mustafa Kemal Atatürk, is based on full and unconditional independence. The Kemalist modernization project has another fundamental policy: Westernization, or "keeping up with contemporary civilizations." According to this policy, Turkey was going to be a fully independent country and it was going to exert all its power and means toward Westernization. A not-much-mentioned formula within this policy is "Westernization despite the West and the Turkish people."

An important question suggests itself at this point: Will the EU require Turkey to maintain its current course of "Westernizing despite the people," but renounce the project of "Westernizing despite the West"? While Europe perpetually brings up topics like the Kurdish issue, Article 301, democratization, and minority issues, it turns a blind eye to the repressive system encroaching on religious life, the ban on religious education, and the willingness to shut down any political party that pushes the secular boundaries a little. Despite this reality, some religious segments of society still hold out hope that full membership in the EU would relieve this pressure. In other words, they still haven't started despairing of the EU. Be that as it may, the Western public generally takes a dubious approach to the religious segments of Turkish society.

Since the Kemalist viewpoint perceives the EU membership process as a demand that abrogates, albeit only partially, the notion of full independence and national sovereignty, it rejects it. Looking from this perspective, it is possible to say that it is in fact the Kemalist modernization project that is the fundamental factor preventing Turkey from becoming a full member in the EU.

What the EU Fails to See[56]

The EU progress report, published around this time every year, is a document demonstrating Turkey's performance with respect to its EU membership bid. It gives a basic idea of how much progress has been made.

The decision makers in the EU, the issuers of this report, draw a roadmap. Turkey then determines its course of action in accordance with this roadmap.

---

[56] First appeared in *Today's Zaman* daily on Nov. 11, 2008

A brief review of this year's report shows that it is no different than those published in previous years. The report can be summarized as follows: "2009 should be a year of reforms."

It is obvious that Turkey needs reforms; there is no arguing otherwise. There are a number of problems in major fields, including the making of a new civilian and democratic constitution, civilian-military relations, torture and freedom of expression. Apparently, there has been no concrete progress in these fields. The report also makes references to the flaws and errors of the main opposition Republican People's Party (CHP), as well. Quite rightly, the report stresses the fact that the CHP took 16 bills supporting democratization moves as part of the EU reforms to the Constitutional Court (AYM). The attitude of the court should also be considered. But, frankly speaking it is not just the pro-status quo circles, the bureaucratic center and the CHP, the historical ally of these actors that serves as their speaker in Parliament, that are reluctant about the EU process. The ruling Justice and Development Party (AK Party), too, is hesitant to take steps toward the EU. Many intellectuals, liberals and leftist democrats have openly criticized this reluctance on the part of the government.

There are understandable reasons for this reluctance and slow movement. The governing AK Party, which has apparently changed its approach to the Kurdish issue dramatically, now adopts a political approach close to that of the bureaucratic center and the state. In this respect, there is hidden cooperation and implicit agreement and consensus on the strategies to be followed among the actors opposing Turkey's EU membership both in Turkey and Europe. Asked why Turkey is not given a specific date for full membership while a precise date has been announced for Croatia, EU Commissioner for Enlargement Olli Rehn gave this interesting response: "It is not proper to compare Croatia and Turkey. This date issue is used as a pretext by both Turkey and the EU. Full membership in the EU is possible via political reforms, not pretexts and excuses."

Rehn's statement shows that the EU authorities now know Turkey better. This may look a little strange, but I think that despite their long-standing relations, the EU only knows Turkey a little. The start of negotiation talks provided the opportunity to get to know Turkey. From this perspective, it has been a huge asset and help because Turkey's EU policy has for a long time been shaped by an evasive approach, in which Turkish authorities never want to get serious. Turkey's fundamental state policy is this: EU membership will be insistently demanded but obstacles will be created before realization of this goal by remaining reluctant to introduce further reforms.

The primary reason for the AK Party's eagerness and sincerity to take Turkey to the EU as a full member between 2002 and 2005 was the extensive support for the process by religious people. This support opened the way for the AK Party to come to power and accelerated the EU membership bid.

Today we are not at the same point. The vast majority of religious people are no longer hopeful about the EU. EU circles and the intellectuals supportive of the EU bid in Turkey have failed to adequately respond to the demands of religious people. They have failed to take proper action to ensure the inclusion of their problems in the progress reports. The domestic intellectuals, in their attempts to inform the EU authorities, suggested that there was no serious religious problem and no trouble in regard to religious freedoms in Turkey. While the latest progress report makes references to the problems of all disadvantaged groups, including gays and transsexuals, it does not make a single mention of the problems the religious majority is facing. This is the primary reason for the decline of popular support for the membership bid. Intellectual inquiry and support will not suffice to get full membership; it will also require popular support.

Religion and Politics in Turkey – Part One[57]

What I mean by "Islam in Turkey" is not Islam defined by its theoretical law and general political philosophy, but the political attitudes and preferences of Muslims—or, in other words, the impacts of Islam as a dominant religion over political attitudes and voting behavior. This issue has always attracted the attention of political scientists.

---

[57] First appeared in *Today's Zaman* daily on Mar. 29, 2012

Social and political life in Turkey is two-layered, even though it is not very visible or comprehensible: In the upper layer, which is more visible, there are Turkey's official assumptions—its appearance to the outer world; in the bottom layer, or the real Turkey, we could make reference to the unchanging material, social, and cultural realities of Turkey. When we try to understand Turkish democracy from this perspective, we have to consider the relationship and inevitable link between these two layers of the country. Even though the official discourse of the political regime is based on the strict implementation of secularism, in practice, the official ideology and the policies based on this ideology do not determine the political and social developments and events alone. Most social scientists acknowledge that the invisible determinant in the political life of Turkey during the republican era is the relationship between religion and the state, or Islam and politics.

The involvement of Muslims in political life during our long history is relatively recent. The participation of Muslim people in political life with a mild or strong impact on political decisions or behavior was first observed in the 1950s. In fact, it is not possible to talk about the influence of religion on civilian preferences during the single party era between 1923 and 1950. Where repressive regimes are influential and dominant, social life is repressed and limited. Turkey's transition to a multiparty system in the aftermath of World War II because of conjectural conditions against the will of the elites holding control over the bureaucratic center cleared the way for the political participation of Muslims. In the aftermath of World War II, Turkey had to align with the Western alliance because of Joseph Stalin's threats. In this case, it also had to change its political system that had been based on single party rule.

However, the importance of the domestic factors that complemented this external dynamic cannot be ignored because the people who had suffered through 27 years of repression also sought a way out of their misery. In response to the Democrat Party (DP), which emerged as a reaction to the repressive policies of the single party administration in the May 1950 elections, the CHP, which had relied on state ideology as the founding party, supported the pro-coup military servicemen in the 1960 coup. The political identity of the DP was center-right conservatism. After the coup on May 27, 1960, the CHP adopted a policy of center-left. In the aftermath of this change, leftist groups became dominant in artistic and cultural developments, whereas right-wing groups and their religious/conservative voters and supporters started to determine political life. It was as if there was a division of labor suggesting that the artistic domain is to be controlled by left-wingers and the political sphere by right-wingers.

During the single party era, CHP administrations relied extensively on an education style based on pro-Western ideology. To this end, these administrations banned religious training and people's involvement in religious life. In 1946, the CHP administration did not, for instance, allow the publication of a book on the life of the Prophet Muhammad. During World War II, many mosques were converted into barns and warehouses. In the 1930s, Mustafa Kemal allowed the foundation of a political party in an attempt to take the pulse of the people and their reaction to the new regime. At a political rally of the party in İzmir, a man offered his son to Fethi Okyar, the leader of the party, saying: "This is my son; take him. I would love to sacrifice him like Ishmael if that would save us from repressive rulers."

Religion and Politics in Turkey – Part Two[58]

Muslims, who constitute the majority of the population, are extremely influential in the formation and development of political life in Turkey. In a country where 99 percent of the people are Muslim, this is only normal. Even though religious life, repressed by the state, is weak, it has always influenced politics. For instance, ordinary people who do not observe all of their religious obligations will still align with the right-wing/conservative parties when the Republican People's Party (CHP) makes a move against religion. This has been the case so far.

From this perspective, it is no coincidence that religious groups or Islamic movements and their relation to politics have been extensively discussed within Turkey's democratic political experience. Without under-

---

[58] First appeared in *Today's Zaman* daily on Apr. 02, 2012

standing the religious dynamics in Turkey, it is hard to understand the political dynamics and processes of social change.

The growing discussion about Islam in the world is another factor that makes the link between religion and politics an important issue. However, the discussions in media and academic circles fall into the same mistake: These discussions appear to have assumed that the Muslims in Turkey are homogenous and constitute one group. However, like anywhere else in the world, the Muslims in Turkey are fragmented into a number of groups and communities; this is consistent with the nature of the universe and of social structure.

Overall, it is possible to see that the Muslim groups in Turkey are divided into three parts:

1. Religious communities and Sufi orders: Some scholars refer to the groups in this category as "organized religion" in their sociological research. From this, we can conclude that these groups are institutionalized, and have organized activities in addition to being religious communities. Maybe it is possible to argue that these communities constitute the main body of Muslims because they are the most populous groups.

2. Political groups: This group includes the National Order Party (MNP), founded by Necmettin Erbakan in 1969, and its subsequent extensions; the National Salvation Party (MSP), the Virtue Party (FP), and the Felicity Party (SP), which have created their own support base. In this sense, they differ from other organized religious groups and communities.

3. Independent groups: It is not possible to classify these groups properly. But it has been observed that the vibrancy of intellectual discussions in Turkey depends upon the frequency and quality of the activities by these groups. These intellectual or cultural Islamic groups affect both the social Islamic groups and political Islamic movements.

The political behavior and decisions of these three groups are different from each other. In general, the approach held by the religious communities towards politics is practical and pragmatic. Their main area of interest is to imbue civilian life with a particular moral and social perspective, revive religious life, and hold charitable events, and for these reasons politics is not the center of their attention.

What matters for them is to ensure that the political administration pursues policies that would facilitate their activities. As a type of pressure group, they try to exert external pressure upon politics. In general, with the exception of the CHP, they are ready to support any right-wing, conservative, or even nationalist party. They show their support during certain periods, but especially during elections. Turkey's secular circles and intellectuals welcome the direct or indirect influence by professional and civilian organizations in politics; however, they do not like the attempts by the religious groups and orders to influence politics. They find these attempts inconsistent with the principle of secularism. And they further ask the state to keep these groups under control.

It is almost impossible to refer to a common denominator in the attitudes and behaviors of the independent groups. Their loose organizational style and structure is also apparent in their political attitudes. Independent groups range from radical groups opposed to any type of political participation that relies on democratic mechanisms, to those who support a political party only during elections. However, the fundamental factor that keeps the independent groups away from active political involvement is their ideological stance rather than considerations over interests. The religious communities, on the other hand, view politics from a pragmatic and practical perspective and base their behaviors and actions upon this stance.

Change of Political Names[59]

One of the Turkish political arena's recurring agenda items is why the political parties designated as "left-wing," "leftist," "social democratic," or "liberal" fail to secure comprehensive electoral support to gain control. This question has been nagging Turkey since the country started to implement a multiparty parliamentary democratic regime in the second half of the 20th century.

---

[59] First appeared in *Today's Zaman* daily on Jun. 11, 2012

Political scientists know that Turkey actually lacks a truly left-wing, socialist, or liberal political movement. In the final analysis, Muslim societies never experienced an industrial revolution and they did not experience a class-based society shaped by class conflicts. Leftist, left-wing, socialist, or liberal political movements are nothing but efforts by certain intellectuals to adapt what they translate from Western languages to their Eastern societies.

An ordinary voter, as the subject-matter of democracy—a Muslim—does not describe himself as a leftist, socialist, Marxist, or liberal. He may refer to them as the forms and names of some political movements, but he never internalizes them mentally or spiritually. This means that we are talking about things that do not exist. Yet, we also know that expert political scientists just write off leftist or liberal intellectuals as "bad translators of the West."

We should of course not do an injustice to true representatives and advocates of these political movements who act properly within their respective environments and in line with the background of the historical developments of their own societies. In Turkey and across the Muslim world, there are people who call themselves leftists, socialists, social democrats, or liberals and engage in political activities with these borrowed identities.

In Turkey, the failure of the left-wing or social democratic movement can be explained easily: How can a party whose ideological and political route was decided by the authoritarian CHP leader İsmet İnönü, who declared himself the "National Chief" after Eternal Chief Mustafa Kemal Atatürk died, be left-wing/leftist or social democrat according to the European standards which it claimed to take as its references? The odd thing here is not how a person who designated himself as the "National Chief"—this may be translated into German as "Führer" and into Italian as "duce"—during his 12-year rule (between 1938 and 1950) attempted to shape the party's political course but how a political party that had haunted the country like a nightmare for 27 years—the Republican People's Party (CHP), which had been nurtured on the political heritage of the Committee of Union and Progress (CUP)—attempted to adopt a social democratic identity as if it could stave off its past and true identity.

Moreover, after this party, which was the indisputably dominant party of the single-party dictatorship through 27 long years, secretly lent support to the bloody coup of 1960, it not only maintained, but also fervently embraced its name (the CHP), its original philosophy (the state-founding party), its historical heritage (to Westernize Turkey by coercion), its symbols and canons (the six arrows), but pretended to be a social democratic party.

Since 1850, Islamic movements have been trying to change Turkey in compliance with the principles of legitimacy, participation, the rule of law, freedoms, and rights. Bediüzzaman Said Nursi, Mehmet Akif Ersoy, and other Muslim intellectuals and their followers strongly resisted autocratic regimes and dictatorships. However, because of their Muslim identities, they were always treated by Europe with suspicion. Europeans believed that they could maintain their semi-colonial regimes in the Muslim world only through their mediators or political parties that represent the single-party mentality, so they treated Islam-inspired approaches with doubt. On the other hand, when we look at the anti-religious and oppressive regimes in the region, we can see that just as Europe was unhappy with the Hafez al-Assad and Saddam Hussein regimes, it was also concerned with the fascist single-party government that pretended to be social democratic.

Elites (in Turkey and the Middle East) know that their raison d'être is the continuation of autocratic regimes because their policies do not appeal to the general public. So far they have been successful in controlling political power in one way or another. Now, they change their identities and appearances in order to put the developments in the Middle East back on their original course. Their nature is the same though their name has changed.

Coup Plots and the Disgruntled Voters of the AK Party[60]

We are now into the final week before the June 12, 2011 elections. The general outlook looks like the Justice and Development Party (AK Party) is enjoying 47-49 percent voter support, whereas support for Republi-

---

[60] First appeared in *Today's Zaman* daily on Jun. 06, 2011

can People's Party (CHP) is at 26-28 percent and the Nationalist Movement Party (MHP) is around 11-12 percent. It also looks like 25-28 independent candidates supported by the Peace and Democracy Party (BDP) are likely to be elected as deputies. We can say that this will continue to be the general picture as we enter the elections; however, every single day matters in politics, so these figures may change.

We are facing interesting and yet equally important elections. It is interesting because for the first time since 1957, a political party is expected to win a third consecutive term by increasing its votes. The AK Party won with 34 percent of votes in 2002 and 47 percent in 2007; this time, we are expecting something in the range of 47-49 percent. The Democrat Party (DP) won its third elections in 1957 and enjoyed a great advantage against its political rival, the CHP; however, it was stopped by a military coup staged on May 27, 1960.

There are still some actors around who are eager to stage a coup. Despite ongoing investigations, detentions, and legal cases over the last four years, the illegal structure and organization known as Ergenekon still survives. Maybe the chances of provoking or sponsoring a coup have diminished significantly; however, there are still those with aspirations for this. Some even uphold that the exposed aspects of the clandestine Ergenekon organization are merely the tip of the iceberg, implying that a large part of the infamous organization still exists uncovered.

Even so, it cannot be ignored that people have become more sensitive towards coups and a guardianship regime. In the past, a lack of social awareness vis-à-vis non-political interventions were primary reasons for two bloody coups (May 27, 1960 and Sept. 12, 1980), and two military interventions (March 12, 1970 and Feb. 28, 1997), as well as an attempted intervention (April 27, 2007). The main criterion for the sensitivity and awareness of the people is the reaction by religious people.

For the first time, people have faced the painful reality of the Feb. 28 Intervention with their eyes open. This does not necessarily mean that they were not affected by the bloody coups on May 27 and Sept 12; however, they did not quite understand what happened on May 27. On Sept. 12, the coup was justified by the presence of a chaotic and terror-ridden environment that claimed the lives of thousands of young people. On Feb.

28, there was no justification or reasonable grounds for an intervention; the intervention targeted religious people, which constitute the main body of society. The Feb. 28 intervention raised questions about guardianship by the military over the political system. It also made the legitimacy and credibility of the higher judiciary, the Istanbul-entrenched big capital, and the pro-coup media questionable and controversial.

Whether it is accepted or not, the most important factor that has attracted significant electoral support for the AK Party since 2002 is a strong response by the people to Feb. 28. The April 27 e-memorandum of the military had no chance at all because the people were already aware and sensitive towards coups and interventions. The government, enjoying this awareness, declared that the military was under the command and control of a political authority.

The primary reason why the AK Party will have a landslide victory and win office for a third consecutive time in these June 12 elections are the presence of coup attempts and the possibility of military guardianship over civilian politics. A political party rarely wins office three times in a row.

A careful review of election behaviors will show that a substantial number of people who said they will vote for the AK Party are actually disgruntled. When asked about the benefits of the party's time in government over the last eight-and-a-half years, some respondents say, "What can we do? Is there any other choice?"

Choices other than the AK Party are out there; but the BDP and the MHP are basing their political actions on an extremely nationalistic discourse from opposing camps. The majority of voters in Turkey (85 percent), including Turks and Kurds, are trying to keep themselves distanced from these two parties. So, only one other party remains—the CHP. The masses are also skeptical of this party because of its internal disagreements, its preference to nominate controversial figures who allegedly played a part in coup plans, and its failure to defend the rights and freedoms of the main body of society.

Voters hold some key expectations from the AK Party, the most prominent of which is a new civilian constitution.

Chapter 5

Prelude to the Tragic Account of the AK Party

Wrong Acts Defining the End[61]

We need to look at judgments of religion and other intellectual and information disciplines in order to determine where our acts are positioned in the map of meanings. Mentioning intellectual disciplines in connection with religion does not mean we attach an equal or parallel value to these disciplines. Rather, it is a conceptualization inspired by Ibn Sina (known in the English-speaking world as Avicenna) for facilitating comprehension.

Ibn Sina says that "correct" and "wrong" judgments belong to philosophy while "good" and "evil" judgments belong to "religion." Accordingly, we assess the correctness or wrongness of our deeds with our reason and the goodness or evilness of our deeds with religion. It is "correct" to find a suitable vehicle and follow the right track to reach our destination, while it is wrong to choose an inappropriate vehicle and follow the wrong path that will not lead us to our destination. Our goal and our deeds to attain that goal may be described as good or evil as well.

We can say that human acts of contemplation and learning are the "reasoning" activities which are frequently mentioned in the Holy Qur'an. There are various forms or derivatives of reasoning, seeing, and hearing: Observation, contemplation, reflection, consideration, and deliberation equip us with perspectives about human acts, world affairs, and

61 First appeared in *Today's Zaman* daily on Jul. 21, 2014

existence and help us to have beneficial and instructive information. As noted by the Holy Qur'an, the intellectual processes that will guide people to wisdom and knowledge occur at a place where the eye (seeing), the ear (hearing), and the heart (feeling) meet. When reason relies on these derivatives in the light of divine revelations, it can take us to our goal. At this point, there should be compatibility between the road and the destination. Indeed, if a right path leads to a bad result, then there is a problem.

If, without bothering with the naming, we seek judgments about the correctness or wrongness of our deeds as individuals or as a society in philosophy or, in more acceptable terms, in "systematic intellectual reasoning," we need to look at the practical results of our decisions. Prophet Muhammad (pbuh) said our deeds will be assessed in terms of initial "intention" and practical "results." For Bediüzzaman Said Nursi, every profession or idea may have "good and beneficial elements" and we need to look at the practice and outcome in order to decide to what extent they are good and beneficial. There are four forms of relationships between correct and wrong, and good and evil.

1. Going to the "good" from the "correct path": We get on the Medina plane in order to go to Medina. In this category, our intention is good and our path is correct. This is the ideal form.

2. Going to the "good" from the "wrong path": We get on the Cairo plane in order to go to Mecca. Our intention is good, but our path is wrong. In this case, our good intention is not enough to make us attain our goal. The saying "The road to hell is paved with good intentions" signifies this category.

3. Going to the "evil" from the "correct path": We find the address of a casino by looking at a map. Our intention is evil and our path is correct.

4. Going to the "evil" from the "wrong path": We divert to a wrong path as we go to the casino. Our intention is evil and our path is wrong.

The first option is the ideal one. The second option does not get us to the goal. Indeed, a religiously permissible and legitimate goal can be attained only via religiously permissible and legitimate methods. Illegitimate policies and means will not take you to the religion's primary goals. The third option is a perfect description of modern politics, in which every method or means is considered permissible for political success. The fourth category is both evil and wrong. When the first option is abandoned and the second option is selected, the means defines the end; in other words, the wrong transforms the good. This inevitably leads to the third option. Muslims should base their political activities on the first option.

The Crux of the Problem: A Lack of Ethics and Morality[62]

Using the concept of "modernity" as our basis, we can examine "politics" through the lens of three main historical periods: pre-modern politics as "the art of leadership"; modern politics as "power-centered"; and post-modern politics in the era of "divided society" under a mixed order.

One of the two reasons I have for taking "modernity" as my basis is that, unfortunately, Western modernity continues to shape our mental and physical worlds, as it is the author of contemporary history at this point. The other reason is that in these ambiguous times, with the splintering of reality we see all around us, we are in the midst of a post-modern chaos in which everything is at odds with and in conflict with everything else.

At the same time, we see that while Muslim minds might be offering some much-needed order in the midst of this chaos, they are not fulfilling this duty. Instead, we see that in Egypt, Muslim minds have been put under oppression as part of a dark era; on the Indian subcontinent, a complete rejection of the nation-state in the place of the caliphate, followed by complete submission to the Islamic world; in Iran, pragmatism (in the form of Rafsanjani) and populism (in the form of Ahmadinejad) derailed Islam from what might have been its revolutionary legacy; in Turkey, Islamists have been so overwhelmed by the promises of power that is not really belonging to them, thus blatantly entering

---

[62] First appeared in *Today's Zaman* daily on Dec. 15, 2014

the supervision of the state. Of course, there are exceptions to these examples; I am leaving them aside for now.

In the pre-modern traditional worlds that existed in Islamic, Indian, Chinese, and other non-Western societies, politics was the "art of leadership." In fact, the same was true even in ancient Greece. The word "politics" in Turkish—"siyaset" (from Arabic "siyasa")—is linked to the word "seyis," which means horse groomsman or hostler. A "seyis" has the job of using artful work, skill, love, and intelligence to transform a wild horse into a well-bred and noble steed.

Society is filled with disparities and wild savagery; its leader needs to use such skill and mastery to bind all the differences together, and in doing so, be the orchestra conductor of society.

In modern times, "power relations" in government have shaped the politics. And as modern nation-states have gathered all the divine attributes they can under one roof, what emerges is injustice in the form of totalitarianism, privilege, and ideological tyranny in every arena of life. If power relations are to be taken as the basis, those in power must recognize all real powers in society, including the will of the people of the nation; secondly, classic functions must be used to rein in the state as much as possible; and thirdly, the only real and acceptable target of the leadership must be the creation and spread of "justice."

But now, in post-modern times, the vase of enlightenment, so to speak, has broken; reality has splintered, and all the flaws and sins have been scattered in every direction. Debates over the character and use of power will no doubt continue until the last person is alive on this earth. In post-modern times, there must be agreement reached in society as to what the universal values are, so that those in power can rule with fairness and justice.

The most essential problem facing modern (or post-modern) politics is an utter lack of morals and ethics. When there are no disputes when it comes to morals, then religion is not necessarily separated from politics. This does not mean we have to pass up on either religion or politics. People from various religions can come together on shared ground to find shared principles and solve their problems by identifying and understanding the problems, compromising, and forging social agreements.

AK Party's Non-Islamic Policies[63]

Tension between the Justice and Development Party (AK Party) and the Hizmet Movement; the military coup in Egypt; the survival of President Bashar al-Assad's regime in Syria; and even the election victory of President Hassan Rouhani in Iran have been cited as supportive evidence for the decline of the Islamist project.

The developments in Egypt, Syria, and Iran should be analyzed separately. If developments in Turkey are taken as the demise of Islamism, there are serious flaws in this assumption and conclusion. Above all, let me discuss the proper parameters so that we can analyze the subject matter in the right context.

First, Islamism is the collection of social, political, and cultural movements that emerged in the second half of the 19th century. It states that the universe, creation, and the meaning of life should be perceived and elaborated with reference to Quranic revelation, that a social order based on the Qur'an and the Sunnah should be established, and that unity should be maintained between Muslim elements. No Muslim would object to these three major goals. However, out of impositions based on conjecture, Islamism has emerged as a response to and as a byproduct of modernity. But this does not mean that it is inherently modernist or reformist. A slight portion of it is inclined toward modernism. There are five major basins of Islamism: Turkey, Egypt, Iran, the Indian subcontinent, and Indonesia/Malaysia.

Three main currents and strands—social Islam (which refers to religious communities and modern versions of religious orders and foundations), cultural Islam, and political Islam—are represented under this broad term. Some pay greater attention to social aspects of life whereas others place emphasis upon political priorities. Social Islam remains influential as long as it does not undermine the importance of politics and the inner struggle; the same also applies to cultural Islam as long as it does not erode society and politics, and also to political Islam as long as it does not deny the significance of society and the inner struggle. All these three strands are acknowledged versions of the Islamic ummah.

---

[63] First appeared in *Today's Zaman* daily on Jun. 07, 2014

From this perspective, we need to evaluate whether or not, as a political party, the AK Party is Islamist or a party representing political Islam.

When founded, the AK Party declared that they had adopted a conservative democrat identity rather than an Islamic democrat version. To this end, defining them as Islamist would be unfair to them and to Islamism as well.

They declared that they take religion (Islam) as a point of reference when devising their political philosophy and program. They later noted that they gave up on this because they realized Islamist politics are not realistic or practical.

On various occasions, Prime Minister Erdoğan has stressed that there is no relevance between monetary issues or the economy and religion. He advocated the view that economic life can be irrelevant to religion.

He also recommended that the Muslim Brotherhood, which came to power in Egypt and other Arab nations, prescribe the principle of secularism in their constitution; Arab nations were shocked by this proposal. He upheld that the AK Party was exemplary as it proved that religious people could practice secularism. More recently, Deputy Prime Minister Bülent Arınç said they now enjoy the principle of secularism.

A review of the AK Party's economic policies, family and social affairs policies, cultural policies, foreign policies, urbanization and planning policies, and other preferences have nothing to do with Islam, Islamic thought, or imagination.

Westerners, particularly scholar Olivier Roy, have been arguing for the past 35 years that Islamism is over. If the AK Party is not doing well today, it is not because of Islam or Islamism, which it never took as a reference; it is because of the liberal thinking, nationalism, and moral pragmatism that constitute the backbone of its philosophy and program. These are responsible for its failures.

Is the AK Party an Islamist Party?[64]

Is the ruling Justice and Development Party (AK Party) the main determinant of the fate of Islamism in Turkey? Conservative columns suggest

----

[64] First appeared in *Today's Zaman* daily on Aug. 18, 2014

that the fate of Islamism is dependent upon the AK Party remaining in power.

This suggestion is incorrect. Islamism is inspired by Islam. When the Prophet of Islam (pbuh) passed away, Abu Bakr issued the following historic warning in response to Umar's reaction. "Whoever worships Muhammad should know that Muhammad is dead, but God is eternal." Both Islam and Islamism are alive. Hasan al-Banna died, but the Muslim Brotherhood (MB) is alive—although they are currently experiencing tribulations. Bediüzzaman Said Nursi died, but the Nur movement is still alive.

It is wrong to associate Islamism with a specific party or person. Let us examine this: Is the AK Party an Islamist party? No, because:

a) at the time of its establishment, they announced both for the domestic and international public that they don't use religion as a reference and they are not Islamist;

b) the political identity they adopted (conservative democracy), their programs, the social and economic policies they have followed since 2002, their conceptions of culture and civilization, their religious orientation, the role they accord Islam within public life, and their regional and international policies are not Islamic. For example, despite their flaws or shortcomings, the MB and the Jamaat-e-Islami are Islamist political movements; they declare this publicly and their policies are generally guided by Islam. But the AK Party is neither an Islamist party nor does it represent political Islam. With its conservative democratic identity, it has blended liberalism, social democracy, nationalism, and so on.

An Islamist may criticize the AK Party in connection with principles, but not procedures. These criticisms should not be hostile and they should be guiding. When necessary, due support should be given to the party. When the closure case was launched against the AK Party in 2007, I defended their right to exist. That was because I thought that this might pave the way for a critique of principles. I support any effort to expand the sphere of freedoms and reinforce the rule of law. I will adopt a similar attitude if a threat similar to that of 2007 emerges. Thus, I support

President-elect Recep Tayyip Erdoğan when there is an unlawful, illegitimate attack against him. A leader who is elected to office should be removed from that office through democratic means. Political offenses should be punished through democratic means, while criminal offenses should be penalized by the law.

As an Islamist, I have criticisms about the very essence of the AK Party, and my criticisms differ fundamentally from those of leftists, socialists, nationalists, or liberals. I am not voicing these criticisms in the name of a community or another political movement.

I am solely concerned with Islam and the Muslim world. Islamism is one of the oldest movements in this country. Although it was influenced by the West, it is never pro-Western. It is an ideal or goal that will improve democracy and uphold rule of law in the region. Millions of believers have contributed to this movement. First of all, we must question the politicians (of the ruling party) who declare, "We are not Islamists and we don't take religion as our reference," and we must ask them: "Why were you initially part of this movement then? Didn't the Islamist struggle or heritage pave the way for your coming to power? You amply use this heritage, but you claim to disown it."

Oddly enough, their opponents don't believe in this claim, but bill Islamism for their errors and mistakes. Thus, their achievements are attributed to conservative democracy while their mistakes are assigned to Islamism. Islam and Islamism are held responsible for the problems despite the fact that Islam and Islamism do not make the slightest contribution to the country's domestic or foreign policy.

Taking off the Garb of the "National View" and Islamism[65]

After the demise of Necmettin Erbakan, people started to ask, "What will be the fate of Milli Görüş [National View] now?" The people who ask this question generally want to know about what will happen to the Felicity Party (SP) in particular. They do not ask this question with respect

---

[65] First appeared in *Today's Zaman* daily on Mar. 04, 2011

to the Justice and Development Party (AK Party), which seceded from Milli Görüş some 10 years ago and came to power, because they think that politicians who are affiliated with the AK Party have already put a great distance between themselves and the Milli Görüş movement.

Obviously, both the AK Party and the Voice of the People Party (HAS Party), which has also seceded from Milli Görüş, have developed their own unique political strands. The founding members of the AK Party had made it clear during the establishment stage that they "have removed the garb of Milli Görüş." This is true. It was a break-up. But what is the extent of disagreement between the two? This question is important. If we are to liken parties to human beings, a man is not a garb alone. He has a body and a spirit.

A "garb" signifies actual policies, concepts, approaches and methods employed for political purposes. On the other hand, political strategies can be likened to a body and principal ideals to a spirit. I believe that the ideals that make the AK Party and the HAS Party legitimate and acceptable in the consciences of masses are the very ideals of Milli Görüş. I believe that these ideals can be summarized as follows:

The first is to ensure that the people who take their religion seriously become visible in the political, social, and public spheres and that they are not forced to conceal, suppress, or deny their religious and existential references as they engage legitimately in politics and the political competition for power, and that they can resist those who try to force them to do so. This goal has been achieved to a certain extent. Milli Görüş, or Turkey's Islamism, characteristically chooses to cling on to the democratic plane to further its political goals and try to be democratically elected to office both at the governmental and municipal levels. This places Turkey's Islamism clearly away from violence, terrorism, and radical methods.

The second is to defend the "social center" with all its heterogeneity and pluralism against a small and privileged minority that unfairly controls the social, cultural, commercial, economic, political, and bureaucratic center as well as the bureaucracy and the public budget. In Turkey, it is Milli Görüş and its parties that defend Anatolia, broad masses of poor people, and Istanbul and Thrace with their middle classes against Ankara's bureaucratic center and the traditional hard core of the system.

The third is to ensure a regional integration via Turkey's active role and initiative. In Erbakan's jargon, this is called the Islamic Union and the major step toward it is to establish the D-8. This is an ultimate ideal which can be traced back to today's Islamists, Mustafa Kemal [Atatürk], and Jamal al-Din al-Afghani. Atatürk had said that Muslim nations would one day unite if suitable conditions emerged.

If it is possible to reduce Milli Görüş to these three ideals, then we can assert that Milli Görüş has not ended; rather, Turkey and the Middle East have been pushed by underlying forces to act along this course. We can further say that the ongoing social and political developments in the Middle East derive their power from these ideals—Islamism and Milli Görüş—despite external manipulations. These ideals are shared not only by "the Muslims who struggle on a political plane," but also by "the Muslims who fight a life-and-death struggle on a social and cultural plane." But these two groups may resort to different methods.

Our intellectuals panicked along with the Westerners as they were trying to make sense of incidents in the Middle East, and they raised concerns by asking, "Is it the advent of Islamists?" Thankfully, as usual, Western Islamologists came to their rescue; thus, Oliver Roy, who is known for his flawed observations and biased arguments, stepped in and gave assurances to them with his newly invented concept of "post-Islamism." Looking at the political methods followed by the parties and groups of the Islamist tradition as well as the actual language of the time and fashionable approaches, Roy and his followers in our country declared the end of Islamism and Milli Görüş.

Parties come and go; fashion changes and new garb arrives in the marketplace every day. What matters is whether the body is healthy and pursues its ideals with perseverance.

Erdoğan's 2023 Target Lacks Social Capital and Peace[66]

Prime Minister Recep Tayyip Erdoğan has recently announced his party's election manifesto as the elections slated for June 12, 2011 draw near.

---

[66] First appeared in *Today's Zaman* daily on Apr. 19, 2011

Election surveys indicate that the ruling Justice and Development Party (AK Party) is very likely to secure 47 percent of the national vote while the main opposition Republican People's Party (CHP), the Nationalist Movement Party (MHP) and the pro-Kurdish Peace and Democracy Party (BDP) may get 26, 12, and 6 percent, respectively. This picture allows Erdoğan to act with extreme self-confidence in the face of his rivals. This makes his election manifesto not a simple text for the June 12 elections, but gives us the AK Party's vision for the next 12 years. The following conclusions can be made from this text:

a) The AK Party and Erdoğan intend to stay in power until 2022 (or 2024). Even if the AK Party fails to be elected to office in the 2015 elections, Erdoğan may assume the top state position as prime minister or president. Will Erdoğan continue to assume the top position until 2023 or 2024? We can answer this question with certainty only after the debates over the tenure of Abdullah Gül are over. If Erdoğan thinks that his becoming president might do harm to his party, he might change the party bylaws in order to continue to head his party.

b) The election manifesto is actually hinting at the outlines of the AK Party's 2023 perspective.

c) Erdoğan refers to the next governmental term—which may be his last as prime minister—as the period of "mastery"—that is, the term of huge projects and reforms. Depicting the 2002-2007 period as his "apprenticeship" and the 2007-2011 as his time as "qualified workman," Erdoğan tells us, "We have not managed to implement our actual plans during the last two terms. This was because there were significant challenges we had to overcome and we did not know the system well and were not proficient about its mechanisms. In the post-2011 period, we will implement everything which we previously wished to implement, but couldn't." He also makes an important promise: a new and civilian constitution. A close examination of the deputy candidates nominated by the AK Party reveals that Erdoğan does not want any nuisance or trouble. It is also said that he will place greater emphasis on performing ministries, which have the bulk of the executive workload, as opposed to state ministries.

Erdoğan's speech gives us a concrete idea about his 2023 goals. It is frequently suggested that Erdoğan is planning to make Turkey one of the world's ten largest economies, boost its exports to $500 billion, and make Istanbul one of the world's top ten cities—currently it is the 27th most influential city according to Frank Knight's "global cities" index.

Undoubtedly, these goals are very likely to be accomplished. But there are some problems. I have three reservations about these targets:

1. Although the prime minister referred to such concepts as "advanced democracy, strong community, livable environment, unique cities, and leading country," he basically targets economic growth. This inevitably entails, in addition to improvements in financial markets and macro balances, a mobilization of real productive powers of the society. Also, the existing unequal distribution of income and the ongoing high rates of unemployment and poverty will make it hard to attain these targets. Turkey may attain the target of boosting its exports to $500 billion and becoming one of the world's ten largest economies, but this will not save it from being a country of silently poor and destitute people. Currently, economic development and growth is promoted at the expense of the middle classes and the poor people.

2. Turkey is seriously troubled with issues concerning social peace and social capital. The Kurdish issue is one of them. And sectarian polarization, which is increasingly becoming evident, can be added to this list. The problems concerning freedom of religion and the headscarf issue have yet to be settled. In addition to the above-mentioned poverty, our cultural wealth is weakening and the family structure is decaying and social solidarity is losing its impact. In short, the soft spot of Erdoğan's 2023 target is the lack of social peace and strong social capital. Economic growth alone cannot solve these problems; rather, it will make them worse.

3. The 2023 target lacks a strong intellectual footing. Turkey cannot continue to act as the carrier of philosophical resources and

cultural values of the Enlightenment—which are even criticized in the West—to the Muslim world. It must focus on its own values and should be able to make a healing contribution to the modern world.

We Are on a Wrong Path[67]

Turkey is a country with a growing economy. We are the world's 17th largest economy. The rate of urbanization has reached 75 percent. We are now planning to be among the world's top 10 economies by 2023. Economic growth is accompanied by big problems. "Growth" has turned into a fetish for classical and global capitalism. Growth means more production, more imports and exports, more consumption, and of course, much more use of natural and human resources.

But people are not happy. In our daily lives, we face incredible problems. We spend hours in order to go from one place to another or from our home to our workplace. When it rains, it paralyzes life in the cosmopolitan city of Istanbul. Millions of lira are wasted. Loss of time, labor, and energy come as a package.

In 1994, Istanbul's biggest program was related to transportation, and this has not changed. The municipality and the central administration are trying to find a solution to this problem, but in the meantime they are intensely feeling the pressure to find a solution. However, the measures they take do not do anything but complicate the problem due to reasons beyond their capabilities. The prime minister says that the seven hills of Istanbul are being turned upside down. Yes, it is true.

There are plans for building a third bridge over the Bosporus. The Marmaray rail transport project, which will run under the Bosporus and connect Asia to Europe, will come into service in 2013. Big buses called Metrobuses capable of carrying hundreds of people are shuttling between various points in the city. Construction of the road that will reduce travel time between Istanbul and Izmir to just three-and-a-half hours has recently started. The 420-kilometer road is to be completed in five years.

---

[67] First appeared in *Today's Zaman* daily on Nov. 02, 2010

If your first reaction to this news is, "This will certainly solve the problem to a large extent," then you should know that you are utterly wrong. Rather, the problem will not be solved even partially, but will grow exponentially.

This is one of the big paradoxes which modern society, development, and the ubiquitous use of technology has put us into. We drink saltwater in order to quench our thirst. But the more water we drink, the thirstier we become.

If you are an avid observer of sociological facts, you can see that every new investment designed to ease transportation will complicate the transportation problem further. It is not difficult to support this subjective observation with academic and technical data and studies. Universities and relevant institutions don't, however, conduct such research because the founding principles that form the basis for their execution of ideas don't allow for this. Yet, it is an undisputable fact.

Before the introduction of the Metrobus, Istanbulites needed one-and-a-half to two hours to travel between Avcılar and Zincirlikuyu. With Metrobus, this duration was reduced to half an hour. Of course, it is a big relief. However, supposing that before Metrobus, some 100,000 on average would travel from Avcılar to Zincirlikuyu daily, this figure has now risen to 500,000. That is, the circulation was boosted fivefold. Thus, Metrobus is triggering a new population movement. There are several factors that increase the population of Istanbul. One of them is the bridges over the Bosporus. As a person who studied migration to Istanbul, its demographic structure, and urbanization blueprint, I can safely assert that the third bridge over the Bosporus will add at least 2 million people to Istanbul's population. People from all around Turkey will flock to Istanbul. In short, technology attracts population, and we are investing in new technologies for the emerging needs of the increased population.

Since the Industrial Revolution, the human population has been growing geometrically. The world today hosts 14 times more people than it did 250 years ago, and the world's population is about 7 billion. Fifty percent of the world's population is moving to cities, and every day 200,000 people migrate to cities.

Whoever challenges technological developments will quickly be labeled a "reactionary." But the unavoidable fact is that we are on the wrong path, and we will end up in this vicious cycle. We and all life on the planet are committing suicide little by little.

To ponder this issue is not the task of politicians, experts, or academics. Rather, it is the duty of theologians, philosophers, literary people, and intellectuals. Unfortunately, they do not exert the slightest influence on global capitalism or the politicians who buy votes by selling saltwater to the masses.

Growth without Social Justice[68]

The first set of expectations from the coming June 12 elections, which it is now clear will propel the ruling Justice and Development Party (AK Party) to power for the third time, are for a new and civilian constitution.

The second important expectation is the demand for the straightening out of the real economic situation and the bringing about of social justice. In the vocabularies used by liberal economists, there is "economy" when they are referring to technical processes, but there is no such phrase as "social justice." For this reason, governments that place importance on market policies that are shaped by liberal philosophies measure their successes by the functioning of financial markets, the financial sector, the stock exchange, interest, and other factors like this, but tend to ignore as much as possible the problems in the real economy, when in fact, the true measures of a successful economy are a) improvement in the real economy and b) justice in income levels.

In countries where liberal economic policies are implemented with strict discipline, fair income level distribution is not achieved and a competitive edge is lost against the large, global capital of the real production powers of the world. When we look at the macro balances, we see that between the years 2001-2011, per capita income rose from $3,000 to $10,000; that growth shot up from 5.7 percent to 6.8 percent; that Turkey went from being the world's 26th largest economy to the 17th

---

[68] First appeared in *Today's Zaman* daily on Jun. 09, 2011

largest economy; that exports went from $25 billion to $114 billion; and that the gross national product went from $187 billion to $730 billion.

There is growth in production and growth across the board. All right – but what about income distribution? What is the state of the middle class, which shoulders the true real economy, and the small and mid-size merchants and industrialists? If the positive signs in financial markets are visible on these counts, there is no problem. But if growth in production and general growth are only working to the advantage of a small privileged class of elite, while simultaneously against the favor of the main body of the populace, one needs to stop and consider what is happening. Let's take a look at this tableau: The large companies, for example the Koç Group, reached its goals for 2015 in 2008. Doğan Media Group grew eight-fold. The number of billionaires in Turkey has risen to 33. As for the income for the national budget, 67.5 percent of this comes from the people of the nation. A full 67 percent of the money people pay for fuel goes to tax. Whether or not petrol prices go up or down or stay the same, the unchanging fact is that we use the world's most expensive petrol and consume the most expensive water.

According to field reports coming in from MP candidates out on the road trying to gather support, there are three main complaints heard from voters who say they will be casting their ballots for the AK Party on June 12:

1. Poor people, including the pensioners, face great economic problems. According to data from TÜİK; the hunger level is at TL 899 a month, while the poverty limit is at TL 2,900. Out of 9 million pensioners, how many receive TL 900 a month? Not many, because minimum wages are set at TL 639 lira a month, and unfortunately this encompasses around 50 percent of all workers in Turkey these days. We won't even count the unemployed masses, which are approaching 3 million in number.

2. The subcontracting problem has now taken root in municipalities and other state institutions. There is such a serious problem on this front that it deserves to be handled separately in another article.

3. The fact that large shopping malls are basically finishing off merchants and small shopkeepers. While the number of large shopping malls in Istanbul in 2005 was at 106, nowadays it has risen all the way to 279. The growth in this particular sector is at 20-25 percent. The goal is to raise the number of large shopping malls in Istanbul to 400 by 2013. Nowadays, the large shopping malls are trying to take over Anatolia as well. These malls hold an unfair advantage over smaller merchants.

Another great injustice is the distribution of income wealth. The top 20 percent of the society take in half of all income. The lowest 20 percent of society, the poorest segment of society, share only 5.5 percent of the total income. As for the remaining 60 percent middle classes, which are the ones needing real protection and stimulation of their competitive powers, the general economic policies in place are not in their favor.

Even Kemal Derviş, who was instrumental in preparing the current economic program, noted that its "social dimension is weak." In the run-up to these elections, the CHP has tried to strike blows at the ruling AK Party largely on the matters of retirees, the poor classes, and income disparity. What effect all this will have on the election outcome is something we will soon see. But at the same time, no one has any belief that the CHP will really bring any long-lasting or sincere solutions to these problems. Solutions to the above problem will again be expected from the AK Party during its coming third term. It is a problem that up until today has always been pushed to the side by the government, but it needs to be placed front and center once again. Nearly half of all voters in the country will once again be bestowing on the AK Party the chance to solve this problem, though maybe for the final time. Let us not forget, prosperity without justice does not bring about a restoration of any sort.

Chapter 6

Telltale Signs of the Deadlock

Making a Complete Mess of Relations at Home and Abroad[69]

Turkey is going through a huge crisis. There are domestic and international factors that created this crisis. Unfortunately, the Justice and Development Party (AK Party) administration is failing to manage this crisis properly. We see the following when looking at the picture before us:

The current policy of the US, one of Turkey's allies in NATO and a strategic partner, does not approve of the current AK Party administration. Relations are now quite tense. Relations with the European Union, with which Turkey is engaged in membership talks, are also bad. In fact, the talks are hopeless. Regardless of who is right or wrong, we are experiencing tense relations with neighboring Iraq. There is no relationship at all with Egypt and Syria. We are also seeing unusual relations with Saudi Arabia. Qatar, our closest partner, is pursuing a different policy after a change in its administration. A radical change also took place in Iran, our largest neighboring country. The Hassan Rouhani administration is trying to ensure that sanctions are lifted by developing ties with the US and Europe. And maybe Iran will make moves to start a relationship with Israel.

In a TV debate in Iran, it was argued that the Erdoğan government in Turkey is similar to the former Mahmoud Ahmedinejad administration in that country. In short, Iran wants to put an end to the unregis-

---

[69] First appeared in *Today's Zaman* daily on Dec. 30, 2013

tered and illegal trade and financial transactions it relied on because of the embargo. There are now investigations in Iran into the activities of Babak Zenjani, who has engaged in business relations with Reza Zarrab.[70] Turkey's rapprochement with Russia is an option; however, Russia will not give its blessing to Turkey if there is opposition from the US and the West. We have clearly seen that the two big powers reached an agreement in the Syrian crisis.

Making an alliance with northern Iraqi Kurds and defying many countries in the world means becoming a target of such countries. In short, Turkey, which had been quite successful in the field of foreign policy until 2011, is now experiencing problems with almost every country.

And the domestic political outlook is not good either. Due to the incorrect approach taken towards the Taksim Gezi Park protests, 50 percent of the AK Party's opponents have taken an anti-Erdoğan and anti-AK Party stance. Big business, which has become 10 times richer in the last decade, is now opposed to the government. Leading figures of conservative business holdings are also cooling their relations with the AK Party. It is obvious that there have been issues between the AK Party and the liberals since the 2011 elections. And most recently, the Erdoğan administration is close to ending relations with the Hizmet Movement because of the row over exam preparatory schools. The Dec.

---

[70] The 29-year-old Iranian, Reza Zarrab, sits at the epicenter of the massive government corruption investigations of December 2013, which removed the lid on the extent of Iranian Zenjani's money laundering and sanctions-busting trade within Turkey. Zarrab was detained in Istanbul on December 17, 2013 due to his alleged involvement with the ministers of economy, interior, and EU affairs taking bribes of millions of dollars from Zarrab on various occasions to allow his business to run unimpeded in Turkey. The ministers resigned, but the sons of the two ministers were also accused of receiving bribes from the Iranian businessman. Prime Minister Erdoğan acknowledged publicly that he knew Zarrab only as a philanthropist while it became clear that the National Intelligence Organization (MİT) had warned the prime minister about Zarrab's illegal and illicit activities eight months before the corruption investigation was made public, stating that if they were exposed, it would embarrass the government and would pose a grave national security risk. Erdoğan inadvertently acknowledged the existence of this report, but instead criticized those who leaked the secret document to the press. Zarrab was released on February 28, 2014. (ed.)

17 corruption operation exacerbated their already-fragile relations. If the government resorts to strong measures, such as removing officers from their posts, this will cause serious damage within society, and it will not be forgotten for a long time.

A government experiencing splits with everybody cannot stand tall for too long. Maybe some international powers are depicting the prime minister as a bully. I personally believe that the prime minister and the AK Party government were misled in the Syrian crisis, the Uludere incident, the Taksim Gezi Park protests, and the debate over prep schools.

The obvious reality is this: It is not possible to survive by fighting these domestic and international circles constantly, and this is not a sustainable policy. The growing tension provokes the potential for domestic conflict. If the tension becomes uncontrollable, a more serious crisis will take over the country.

Why Are We at This Point?[71]

We need to understand how we have come this point. Let us remember: When the Justice and Development Party (AK Party) was established, the center-right and center-left parties were failing, and the US was planning to intervene in the region via Afghanistan and Iraq.

The AK Party was founded on the concept of "conciliation." Their reasoning was, "The postmodern coup of Feb. 28, 1997 has shown us that we cannot come to power or stay in power if we stick to the mentality of [former Prime Minister] Necmettin Erbakan. Conciliation is the key to coming to power and staying in power. From now on, we will seek conciliation with (a) global powers, namely the US, the European Union and Israel, (b) the military and civilian bureaucracy, and (c) the big capitalists."

This doctrine was inspired, promising to take the party to power. The party was established, and it started to implement this plan. It first announced allegiance to Kemal Derviş's economic program centered on the International Monetary Fund (IMF) and the EU reform roadmap. Even before he was elected as a deputy, European countries started to

---

[71] First appeared in *Today's Zaman* daily on Jan. 06, 2014

meet Recep Tayyip Erdoğan, one after another. George W. Bush met with him in the White House for two hours (according him a presidential reception although Erdoğan was not even holding the prime minister's office at the time). As former US president Clinton had previously noted, "Turkey will determine the fate of the 21st century."

The US and the West were shifting their focus to the Pacific, where big conflicts and perhaps wars might emerge. The Middle East was a vacuum that couldn't be integrated into the system, and the US couldn't leave it alone. The US had two doctrines: firstly, to establish a system using the military power of conservatives, and secondly, to transform the region using the soft power of democrats (through women's movements, civil society organizations [CSOs], democracy, liberal philosophy, education, TV series, and so on). AK Party-led Turkey was willing to implement these two doctrines. The regimes in the region (autocratic administrations and military dictatorships) were detrimental. Finally, global powers—including the non-Likud Jewish lobbies—had also demanded that Israel's energy sources and pipelines would be secured and that radical Islamist groups would not come to power.

Only Turkey, Iran, and Egypt could impose order on the system based on these parameters. Turkey would emerge as the founder of a "model" for the entire region, but its competition with Iran would be discouraged. This was because Iran would grow stronger from a conflict between Iran and Turkey. Indeed, since Ayatollah Ruhollah Khomeini, Iran had defined the US and Israel as "common enemies" for all Muslims, and this was causing it to grow stronger. Turkey would take Iran to its side over time, tackle the Syrian predicament, and then, in cooperation with Egypt, put the region back on track.

As the lead role was given to Turkey, a comprehensive renewal started in Turkey:

(a) The global capitalists were channeled to Turkey and money started to pour into the country; (b) Turkey was backed by incredible diplomatic and political support in the international scene; (c) Europeans were forced to revitalize the EU membership process; (d) Assistance was provided for the purging of juntas that would periodically stage coups, and the military tutelage regime was "suspended" but not demolished; (e) Serious fiscal and political relations were established with nearby countries, and with the "zero problems with neighbors" policy, joint cabinet meetings were held; and (f) A corridor was opened to Africa.

In 2011, everything was reversed. Turkish foreign policy failed to correctly analyze the social movements in the Middle East. The success that had relied on external support resulted in a deceptive sense of self-confidence and independence. With its "neo-Ottomanism" project, Turkey displayed its intention of dominating the Arab Middle East as it had in the past, competing with Iran, just as the Ottomans had competed with the Safavid Persia, and using the Kurds as its cat's paw in the region. In response, global policy makers took action. Turkey was violating the agreement.

Breaking the Promises That Paved the Way for the AK Party[72]

It is clear that today I stand justified in the critical attitude I have adopted regarding the Justice and Development Party (AK Party) since its establishment.

For a detailed account of my criticisms, you can consult my book titled, *Göçün ve Kentin İktidarı—Milli Görüş'ten Muhafazakar Demokrasi'ye AK Parti* (Power of Migration and the City: the AK Party from "National View" to Conservative Democracy). The book offers my criticisms from an Islamist perspective in three categories.

First, the AK Party wanted to take and use "modern power" as it is, without questioning it. Modern power, by nature, is unequal, unfair and leads to corruption. It is like a curved ruler; with it, even Umar, the second caliph, famous for his just and fair rule, cannot draw a straight (i.e., fair) line. If you use modern power, you will end up with injustice and will deserve the hostility of those who are left outside the system. And if you do this with your "religious identity," which you market as "conservatism" after casting off your "identity of political Islam," the cost of

---

[72] First appeared in *Today's Zaman* daily on Feb. 10, 2014

your failure will fall on Islam in general and Islamism in particular. The main victims of this unfair and corrupt process will be Islamism and the religion of Islam, which will both bear the brunt of that cost.

Second, throughout the 20th century, religious communities and orders or other religious groups traditionally relied on their own resources and kept a distance from public ones. Their main sources of income were donations from the middle class and even from the poor—the skins of sacrificed animals, prescribed purifying alms (*zakat*), the prescribed alms given during the holy month of Ramadan (*fitrah*), and charity (*infaq*). These groups established schools and foundations and supported the Islamic movement; they brought forth increasing piety in society. They were proud that they did not take from public resources.

With the AK Party's rise to power, civilian religious communities, groups, and foundations were introduced to public resources and they started to get their share of funding from commissions. However, a businessman does not donate any sum to a charity if he does not expect returns as high as several times the original sum. Therefore, awarding this businessman with a public contract in return for his donations to a charity leads to the misuse and abuse of public resources. It is wrong to establish imam-hatip schools and build mosques using the funds from irregularly collected commissions. In the course of time, this makes civil Islamic entities addicted to public resources.

As these communities and groups benefit from public resources, they unwittingly lose their "civilian" character and transform into "governmental" organizations loyal to the state. And they are stripped of their dynamism. In this process, the civilian/Islamic entities start to tolerate unfairness; irregular transactions; and even corruption, bribery, and theft. They may even suggest that such irregularities don't have to do with corruption. This is the end of the essential and authentic missions of these religious entities.

Third, the AK Party wasn't established in the face of regional or global policies of Turkey's Western allies, NATO, the European Union, and, in particular, the US. We know that during the establishment of the party and following the 2002 elections, Western countries and global powers lent great support to Recep Tayyip Erdoğan, and even the most influential Jewish lobby in the US gave Erdoğan a "Courage to Care Award."

The AK Party promised in return that it would pursue policies in harmony with the US both in the region and around the world, and that it would bridge the West with the Middle East and Asia. Accordingly, the AK Party promised it would make the region more moderate, prevent radicalism, and assume co-chairmanship of the Greater Middle East Project.

In the past, I wrote many times, "You cannot keep this promise; you have assumed a heavy burden. You will eventually attract the fury of the 'boss.' There is another way. There is another vision that better fits the interests of Turkey and the region. You have volunteered to assume a role in a process whose nature you don't know. Instead, you must restrain your desire to come to power. This policy will spell trouble for you." And that is what happened. Since 2011, Turkey has started to defy its boss, which brought trouble not only for itself but also for Syria and Egypt.

Defying the Boss[73]

It is not possible to justify or explain the current deadlock and impasse in Turkey's foreign policy or the cost generated by the argument that Turkey is fighting a war against global powers and should not submit to their wishes. Some go even further claiming that Necmettin Erbakan also pursued such an independent policy, which was not a mistake in the first place. This rhetoric will work only for those who rely on (the misleading and empty) slogans for public relations purposes. Let me fix some errors in these arguments:

1. This government has never told the actors it is in cooperation with, such as the US, the EU, and NATO, that it would pursue an independent policy in the region. In fact, it was quite the opposite, when this government first came to power it pledged to stabilize the role of Western actors in the region, take the EU to the Turkic republics (in Central Asia) and the greater Muslim world, and establish a new order in the Middle East in line with

---

[73] First appeared in *Today's Zaman* daily on Nov. 17, 2014

American priorities and requests. Archival information and documents would confirm this.

2. Erbakan's project was the ideal plan to create an Islamic union that would have been initiated by the D-8 during the first phase. However, he never made pledges to the West nor relied on their financial, diplomatic, and political support. He was not strong enough and was taken down. There is not the slightest similarity between the foreign policies of Erbakan and the Justice and Development Party (AK Party) government.

3. The AK Party thought it could establish some sort of political and military domination and control in the region by bypassing its strategic allies and the international forces that had extended their support, but this strategy backfired. You should either act like Erbakan and stress that you will act without seeking permission from others or bear the consequences when you break your deal with those who extended support to you in return for your assurances and pledges.

4. The AK Party does not have a vision of pursuing independent foreign policy through intellectual, political, and social resources. The political administration did not pursue a non-Western foreign policy. Instead, it wanted to create a regional emirate for itself. The components of its strategy and power, including capital, emphasis on the construction sector, development and consumption, as well as nationalism, were all of Western origin. Moreover, the development model it relied on was a poor imitation of the outdated Western-style development strategy.

5. Turkey argued that it was a pivotal actor in the region and that nothing would be able to move without its permission. It even further implied that it would reestablish the pre-1911 borders and take back all the lands it had lost. However, it should have considered how global powers, including the US, the EU, Russia, and China, would react to such a statement. These powers are influential in the region. The NATO alliance and the US have powerful facilities and bases on Turkish soil. Atomic bombs have been installed at the İncirlik military base. Turkey is under

the military control of foreign powers as are the Gulf countries, so how could it "re-establish" the Ottoman Empire? Instead it would have been better to create relationships with regional actors to keep the global powers away from the region. However, regional actors distanced themselves from Turkey because of its attempts to maintain an upper hand. Through the current foreign policy, the government disappointed Islamists in Iran, Egypt, and other Arab countries that were sincere advocates of an Islamic union. The Turkish government was mesmerized by the belief that everyone in the region sought Turkey's leadership. However, amid this assumption, a coup took place in Egypt and Syria was torn apart.

Turkey's recent foreign policy has been based on flawed assumptions and unrealistic predictions that will have longstanding repercussions. Above all, the West no longer trusts Turkey as they once did, nor does the Muslim world believe that Turkey's regional vision will work.

Mistakes in Foreign Policy[74]

It is not a surprise that we have been dragged into a process of instability as a result of the deadlock in foreign policy. The US will collect the debt for the economic, military, political, and diplomatic support it extended to Turkey in the early 21st century in order to make it a political actor that would establish order in the region.

At first, the Justice and Development Party (AK Party) government had two options: rejecting this role and offer, or honoring its commitments. I have argued since the beginning that this would cause huge trouble for Turkey. And when, in 2011, Turkey defied the global powers that had sponsored and financed its policies, it should have predicted the counter-moves.

A power and actor that defies the global powers should make a fair assessment of its opportunities and conditions as part of its strategy. You do not have the material, military, and economic power to deal with the global system, and you want to defy it after some achievements that can

---

[74] First appeared in *Today's Zaman* daily on Feb. 17, 2014

be attributed to its support. When the US and its allies promised to make Turkey "the Japan of Western Asia" while shifting their focus to the Pacific region, Turkey should have tried to attract the good after eliminating the evil. The elimination of the evil was the US withdrawal from the Middle East region, and the good of the future was the establishment of a new order through collective action.

Turkey failed to achieve this for the following reasons:

1. The new foreign policy vision was lacking in clarity and sharpness. The implied intention was: We will drive out the global forces when we declare political independence, at some point, and we will rule the entire region by ourselves.

2. Turkey has an unspoken nationalistic and nationalist foreign policy perspective; the vast majority of religious groups and political movements, including the National View movement, radical Islamists, and conservatives, view Turkey's regional leadership as a given and a right in the region. What they mean by the union and unity of Islam is a union under Turkey's leadership. Of course, there are some exceptions, but the exceptions have no or minimal influence on Turkish foreign policy. However, all the countries in the region are also modern nation-states designed on the premises of nationalistic political philosophy; even the smallest Gulf State holds ambitions of regional leadership. The concrete proof of this is the foreign policy of Qatar, a small state the size of Üsküdar, a district in Istanbul. The idea of a region under the leadership of a particular country is observable in all nations and countries in the region, including Iran, Egypt, Saudi Arabia, and Pakistan.

3. Non-Islamic arguments have governed Turkish foreign policy for the last decade. They said, "History and geography give us the responsibility of regional leadership; we have no option but to serve as leader of the region." Let us say that we'll be reviving Ottoman rule. This means that we attribute determinative power to history and geography, but this is contradictory to Islamic tenets and premises. It has no value in practice, because

every country in the region holding leadership ambitions can attribute such a mission to its history and geography as well.

4. Unless the countries in the region, particularly Turkey, Iran, and Egypt, give up their ambitions for regional leadership, they will keep fighting each other on the one hand and will turn the Muslim world into a sphere of invasion and exploitation for global powers on the other. In Islam, leadership is held by the *ummah*; even an ordinary person can play this role, under Islamic precepts.

A Policy That Did Not Work![75]

In the aftermath of World War II, Turkey sought refuge in NATO because of the growing Soviet threat. And so far, it has played a passive role in this organization. Unlike this passive role, Turkey attempted to take part in the US-led invasion of Iraq in 2003. However, the AK Party government's motion authorizing its involvement was returned by the Turkish Parliament on March 1, 2003.[76]

There was a problem in the government's policy: that if a Muslim country was to be invaded by foreign forces, Turkey, a predominantly Muslim country, could not lend military support to the invaders; Saddam would be toppled, but it would be Muslims who were killed. The government based its cooperation with Western powers on the consideration of national interests. However, the national interests could not be in the interest of the global Muslim community. Likewise, Turkey, by relying on its soft power, would secularize and Protestantize the Muslim world. It was risky; there were serious gaps and differences between the Muslim world and the West. Turkey, in the final analysis, should have sided with the Muslim world, not the Western powers. But in a critical

---

[75] First appeared in *Today's Zaman* daily on Jan. 20, 2014

[76] The Erdoğan government mobilized support for the US military action in Iraq, but on March 1, 2003 the majority of the Turkish Parliament voted against the government motion to permit the deployment of the US troops and aircrafts in Turkey, thus granting no access to Iraq through the Turkish border. (ed.)

conflict, if Turkey sided with the Muslim world, it would also experience problems with the system (of the West).

The US and its allies were withdrawing to the Pacific; they asked Turkey to establish order in the region, promising to make it the Japan of West Asia. The Justice and Development Party (AK Party) government gladly took up this offer, and by following this roadmap, it became successful in political, social, and economic matters. The Arab world welcomed Turkey: Islamist Iran adapted to this—it even offered Turkey opportunities to extract oil and natural gas. There were Jewish lobbies in the US supporting this process, but the Likud in Israel did not like this. Some nationalist circles in Iran also expressed their discontent. The Likud, nationalist Iranians, and Gulf emirs were expecting a mistake from Turkey.

Turkey made this long-awaited mistake in 2011. That year, popular uprisings emerged in the Middle East. In addition to other Arab states, Syria also experienced civilian rebellions. All of a sudden, Turkey abandoned its soft power policy and adopted a hawkish stance. Of course, not only Turkey made mistakes, but Iran's stance was also flawed. The hosting of a radar station in Malatya as part of the NATO missile defense plan was the last straw. Iran sided with Syrian President Bashar al-Assad, whereas Turkey supported the Syrian opposition groups.

At the beginning, the Western powers provoked Turkey so that it would adopt a militarist policy; they even considered a military operation. But then they withdrew their support and left Turkey all alone. And when the tragedy in Syria worsened, everybody tried to get away from this and blame others. This was a trap, and Turkey fell right into it.

The reason the West secretly dragged Turkey into the quagmire in Syria is that since 2011, Turkey has been trying to establish its control in the region despite opposition from the West and voicing its dreams of new-Ottomanism. To this end, Turkey would stop Iran, take the Kurds under its protection, and establish domination over the Arabs as it had done in the past.

The Westerners upheld that Turkey did not honor their deal and that it wanted to use their support for its own interests. The Turkish foreign minister said we would "return to the borders before 1911, we will take all the land we lost back; we are a country that establishes order and nothing can move in the region without our consent."

Turkey was defying not only the West but also Russia in the region; it was being argued that Russia could be isolated. This was like defiance against a tank by using a gun. It was the repetition of the policies of [the ambitious political adventurer] Enver Pasha (1881-1922). Not only the global powers that sponsored us, but also the regional powers were bothered by this.

The Root Cause of Flawed Policies[77]

During his recent trip to Japan, Prime Minister Recep Tayyip Erdoğan made some important remarks. He said, "Turkey's goal is not to be a regional or global power. It is simply by virtue of the fact that Turkey carries out the responsibilities that fall to it that it is being placed in an important position in its region and the international community. This is what is happening, and this is what should be happening. Otherwise, one could define it as ambition, and ambition is always dangerous."

These remarks by the prime minister signal a change from the "mistaken, risky, and non-Islamic foreign policies" which have been pursued since 2011. Let me try to explain these three points as follows:

Mistaken: The point that has been reached in terms of its Syria policy is clear for all to see. More than 100,000 dead, millions of refugees, cities in a state of ruin, and fiercer and fiercer sectarian violence. In the meantime, doors throughout the Middle East are closed to us. Of course, Turkey is not the only party to blame for this; Saudi Arabia and Iran bear just as much responsibility. Whether a little or a lot, everyone is responsible for the part they've played. This includes nongovernmental organizations, foundations, media organs, and even certain individuals.

Risky: In the past, Turkey would be deceived by the West and would later form alliances with Gulf monarchies, which were bound to lead to catastrophe, thereby placing the country and the region as a whole at risk. Whether right or wrong, the allegations that Turkey has formed significant relations with the Syrian opposition are placing Turkey under

---

[77] First appeared in *Today's Zaman* daily on Jan. 28, 2014

great risk. Currently, the Syrian government is taking legal action against Turkey on the grounds that Turkey is "assisting radical organizations that are prolonging the war."

We have arrived at a sad point. Hundreds of people left Turkey to fight on the side of innocent Muslims in Syria. Some lost their lives, others—the majority—are still fighting. While there is at least the widespread perception in the West that "Turkey is handling the situation with caution," the Foreign Minister Ahmet Davutoğlu has said, "Compared to ISIL [the Islamic State in Iraq and the Levant], [Bashar al-] Assad is the lesser of two evils," adding that al-Qaeda is a "terrorist organization." With these naïve words, he both insults those who left Turkey to go and fight and, at the same time, incurs the anger of al-Qaeda. But won't they ask: Was it only "now" that you received information about ISIL? Was it only after global actors—the US and Russia—put al-Qaeda and the others up on the target board that they became "terrorist organizations"?

These policies are not Islamic! Had they been, they would not have been "mistaken and risky" and they would not have led to so much cost. No matter what anyone says, Turkey put its Western alliances on the backburner and, in a bid to become the dominant power in Syria and to leap from there to forming a neo-Ottoman order in the region in general, suddenly became the target of not only global powers but regional players as well.

This is certainly ambition; it was a nationalist, imperialist project. It was not realpolitik and, as was expected, it collapsed. That which is nationalist and imperialistic is not ethical. The correct framework of regional policy is this:

1. No state can try to single-handedly dominate a region simply because of national interests; this is not allowed by international powers or by regional countries. When it comes to "national" interests, every country of course has them and, quite naturally, they clash with the interests of other countries. Imperial-type domination can be brought to an end only through the partici- pation and effort of all the countries in the region in which this imperialism exists.

2. No sectarian group (Sunni, Shiite, Salafi-Wahhabi) can dominate one region; all religions and sects are obliged to have a shared vision of where their region is headed. Otherwise, we are set to experience even more terrible sectarian violence and clashes than what Europe had in the distant past.

3. No race or ethnicity has a hold on any particular region. Regional laws can embrace and encompass various tribal groups, basically building a large regional roof for them all. Otherwise, racially fueled clashes will also continue.

The only way out is through a union and alliance between all the various groups of Islam. At the basis of incorrect policy lies the same ambition that the prime minister referred to in Japan. Ambition is potentially poisonous. By changing its foreign policy at its very foundations in this sense, Turkey could well trigger a new wave of excitement in the region. There is still hope.

Take It from the Top Again: Failed Foreign Policy[78]

During his official trip to Japan in January 2014, Recep Tayyip Erdoğan, at the time in his capacity as prime minister, delivered an important speech in which he said, "Turkey has no goal of becoming a regional or global power. Turkey is just doing its job; and by performing its roles, it is situated in its region and in the international community. This is what happens and this is what should happen. Any other sort of action is called ambition, which is always dangerous." These remarks promised a retreat from the "flawed, risky and non-Islamic foreign policy" that had been pursued since 2011.

a) It was flawed: The current state of the Syria policy is obvious. More than 200,000 people have been killed, millions have been displaced, cities have been destroyed and sectarian violence reigns. The doors to the Middle East are closed for Turkey. Iran is the boss in its own sphere of influence. Egypt and Saudi Arabia are creating their own. Of course, Turkey is a big country, but its ties are not good with any Middle Eastern country other than Qatar. Of course, Turkey alone cannot be held

---

[78] First appeared in *Today's Zaman* daily on Nov. 10, 2014

responsible for this. Other countries in the region have also played a role. There are many actors responsible for this, including nongovernmental organizations, associations, media outlets, and individuals.

b) It was risky: At the beginning, Turkey was trapped by the West. After, it made some terrible alliances with the Gulf monarchies, putting the entire region at risk. The coup in Egypt and the Salafist state being created at the northern border of Iraq and Syria under the auspices of the petroleum-rich princes shows that nothing was predicted beforehand. The current state of affairs is very worrisome. Hundreds of people moved to Syria to fight to protect innocent people. Some of them died while others are still there fighting. While there is at least a belief in the West that ISIL was tolerated in Turkey, Turkish politicians have only now declared ISIL a terrorist organization like al-Qaeda. Where had they been until now? A state created along the Iraqi-Syrian border, and the emergence of a federal structure in the areas controlled by the Kurdish Democratic Union Party (PYD), exacerbate the whole situation for Turkey.

c) The Syria policy was not Islamic. If it were, it would not have been so flawed and risky. When, at the second stage, Turkey tried to maintain control in Syria all by itself by ignoring Western allies and attempting to create a neo-Ottomanist order in the region, which global powers and regional actors rejected. This was an ambitious and imperialist project. It was not realpolitik; and as expected, it collapsed. What is national and imperial is not moral. The Islamic framework of the regional policy is as follows:

1. None of the states in the region shall maintain hegemony by focusing on national interests. Global powers and regional actors would not let this happen. Every country has its own national interests and if one is being pushed at the expense of others, this inevitably leads to conflict. Imperialist domination can be eliminated with joint action by the countries in the region.

2. None of the sectarian groups (Sunni, Salafi, Wahhabi, Alevi/Nusayri) shall dominate the region. All religions and sects have to develop a joint approach to regional politics. Otherwise, we

will experience sectarian wars that will be more brutal than those in Europe in the past.

3. No community (racial or ethnic) shall exist all by itself in the region. The regional actors have to build a comprehensive legal system that includes all tribes and communities. Otherwise, ethnic conflicts will continue.

The remedy is the union of Islamic elements. Ambition is the root cause of these flawed policies. Ambition is not Islamic; it is poisonous. It has been almost a year. Foreign policy has remained the same.

Chapter 7

The Saga of the AKP's Fatal Transformation

Turning into a Monstrous Dragon[79]

I t is a challenging task to elucidate the fact that the ruling Justice and Development Party (AK Party) is not an Islamist party and does not pursue Islamic policies, and therefore the blame of its errors and mistakes cannot be attributed to Islam.

Neither the domestic nor the international community is eager to accept this. The reason for this is that the majority of the politicians affiliated with the AK Party have religious identities. This in turn puts people like me, who adopt a critical view of the party, in a difficult situation because criticizing a religious person is seen as betraying the religion itself.

Nevertheless, my guiding principle is that truth towers above everything. An Islamist should speak of and point at errors and mistakes for the sake of truth and refrain from linking the mistakes of a conservative party to Islam itself.

The damage the "religious images" of the members of the AK Party do to the religion is greater than the one done by religious figures of the center-right and nationalist politicians. This is because they hollow out the religion with their basic political preferences and policies, and they sanction the tyrannies and injustices of the ruling party, whose basic philosophical assumptions are not endorsed by Islam but are attributed to Muslims. Even if this is not what they wish for, religion has become

---

[79] First appeared in *Today's Zaman* daily on Aug. 25, 2014

an indistinguishable part of their identity because of their pasts and religious appearances.

What we understand from our past experience is that these religious politicians are protestantizing Islam, making it mundane and materialistic. This in turn will extend the Western domination and hegemony over the Muslim world for many years to come.

There is a political power as defined by the modern nation-state. This power does not belong to us. Religious politicians should first study this modern power with a critical approach based on Islamic jurisprudence and theology. The AK Party's politicians are "religious," but they are unaware of their own political and philosophical references. The following questions are important:

1. To what extent does Turkish society rely on Islamic perspectives to make sense of existence, life, meaning, and the purpose of man and the world, and so on? How many intellectuals have been raised during the time the ruling AK Party has been in office with all of the public resources available to it? How many notable works have been produced during the same time?

2. Can we say that the ruling party's social and economic policies have brought society closer to a liberal, morality-oriented, and justice-based lifestyle? What is the direction of social mobilization? Toward peace and coexistence, or toward profound polarization and conflict?

3. To what extent has the ruling party served the ideal of ensuring regional integration and unity of the Muslim world? Has it brought us closer to this ideal? Or has it moved us away from it? How prestigious is Turkey in the eyes of government officials, intellectuals, opinion leaders and the public in other Muslim countries? Is it declining or increasing?

Political power transformed the ruling party. We have turned into the dragon we intended to kill. Society is disintegrating. The family is in a state of deep concussion. Unfair and inequitable income distribution hurts everyone. Certain people who are protected by the public start to bully other people and they grow vulgar with the income they obtain from the ruling party. They are increasingly insensitive toward the plight of the poor. Society is being lured into mindless and blind consumption. Nationalistic and sectarian sentiments are being provoked. Millions of low-income households are becoming dependent on loans. Our cities are turning into Western forests of skyscrapers. Despite the rhetoric, Turkey is being dragged around by the wind of globalization. It seeks NATO's help for its current dilemma. Finally, religious communities and orders are becoming dependent on public resources, although they are supposed to be independent civil movements that can boost society's moral and ethical values.

Transcendental Conception of State and Power[80]

In traditional societies, a government would rely on a specific person or dynasty for its legitimacy. The king would search for a sacred foundation, but the search was actually about real people. Japan's emperor was referred to as the son of the sun; the Persian ruler Chosroes was believed to have God's blood in his veins; the Roman emperor Julius Caesar or Egypt's pharaoh, who claimed to be a god; and European monarchs' bodies and spirits were consecrated; yet all of them were human beings. Based on such assertions, they could say, "L'État, c'est moi."

The only exception to this rule is Islam's conception of politics, which does not vest rulers with any sanctity. However, the Umayyads incorporated the concept of God's caliphate into their system, taking inspiration from the Byzantines. Following in their footsteps, the Ottomans affixed to the sultans the designation, "God's shadow on Earth," which was an epithet of Justinian. There are a number of fabricated stories about this title. The fact that there is a higher law that is independent of caliphs and sultans saved Islam's historical forms of government from becoming absolutist or monarchic. This, of course, does not mean that rulers always rule their countries in strict compliance with the Islamic law.

There are real people at the heart of absolutist administrations. The modern concept of state has made administration impersonal, giving rise to the idea of the impersonal state. The modern state is actually a secu-

---

[80] First appeared in *Today's Zaman* daily on Apr. 21, 2014

larized version of Christian theology. According to theological assumptions, God was embodied in Jesus and the church is the body of Jesus. The philosophers who sought to take power from the church focused on absolutism, and those who wanted to strip absolutist rulers of power placed emphasis on parliaments. But the impersonal character of the state prevailed. Hegel saw the state as God's will on Earth and history's intrinsic purpose. To him, salvation was possible not through civic affairs that had nothing to do with spiritual transcendence, but through devoting oneself to the transcendent and immanent mission of the state.

As they imported the Western form of state, the proponents of the Tanzimat, constitutional monarchy, and the republic easily translated this form into the ideal of "the eternal preservation of the state" and the sultan's being "the shadow of God on Earth." In their search for power, Islamists have failed to ponder and criticize this modern concept of the state, which is derived from the West and furnished with divine essence, and to which some components were added from our history. They see the state as a savior. Jamal-al-Din al-Afghani almost translated the concept of the modern nation-state into a salvific messiah myth. Just as early Christians fought against the tyrannical Roman Empire for some 300 years but eventually brought Rome to the Christian creed and revived the Vatican as the "religious Rome" in the wake of the fall of the Western Roman Empire, Islamists made the modern nation-state part of Islam's political philosophy. With its historical and philosophical adventure, the modern state challenges God. "Just as God does not accept partners, neither does the modern state." This was exactly what [the Minister of Justice] Bekir Bozdağ, who has a religious background, asserted recently! When necessary, the state shows its power and purges its rivals by killing them, with political justification.

When you accept the state as is, without weighing it against Islam's philosophical and legal heritage, you cannot affix any attribute to the state if you cannot affix it to God. The state needs you for its protection. It submits itself to your embrace readily, but when you believe you have complete control of it, it has already taken complete control of you, nationalizing you and embodying its spirit in you. It is like the ancient Chinese legend: A hero enters a cave to save treasure that belongs to everyone in the village from a dragon. Before him, hundreds of heroes had entered the cave, but none returned. He kills the dragon, and as he touches the treasure, his body begins to change. He turns into a dragon to protect the treasure. The Justice and Development Party (AK Party) is this hero.

Muslims' Monster[81]

I am using the word "monster" in the sense Thomas Hobbes used it: Leviathan, as referred to in Phoenician mythology or the Old Testament.

This monster is a killer crocodile in the Nile River in mythology and the symbol of pagans in the Old Testament. A careful reading may lead us to conclude that the word "taghut" in the Qur'an is similar (yet in a broader context and meaning) to this notion (al-Baqarah 2:256). Hobbes incorporated Leviathan into the literature of politics. Hobbes accurately defined the emergence of the modern nation-state. Conservative politics, liberalism, and socialism-Marxism are derivatives of Leviathan on the European continent.

There have been brutal caliphs, sultans, and shahs who persecuted the people and violated laws in the history of Islam; however, there has never been a state in this world which, as a legal personality, infiltrated in all spheres of life and wanted to shape man to make him comply with its demands. Al-Hajjaj ibn Yusuf of the Umayyads murdered many people, but he has always been remembered as Hajjaj, the murderer.

The only goals in Islam are to preserve high ethical standards and to maintain justice. Even the cruelest rulers in the Islamic world have never thought to rule by ignoring Islamic rules and provisions, which can be taken today as principles of the supremacy of law. They tried to comply with Islamic provisions, violated laws or secured *fatwas*, or legal verdicts on a religious basis, to justify their policies, because the most dangerous thing to do would be to eliminate the concrete provisions of Islam as regulators of social life and to pay greater emphasis upon religious rituals as the foundation of religion.

---

[81] First appeared in *Today's Zaman* daily on Jun. 14, 2014

If they had attempted to redefine the state and power structures by abandoning the cause of saving the state as articulated by the first generation of Islamists, or establishing the state as formulated by the second generation of Islamists, the third generation of Islamists would have made extensive contributions to the political thinking of modern times. They did not do so; they came to power by owning up the state, which is essentially Leviathan. The monster of Muslims comes to life when it places greater emphasis upon the symbols and rituals of religion, whereas it lies on the peremptory policies of modern thinking in the practices of daily life.

Former Islamists, instead of dropping their Islamist claims and proceeding, concluded that they would rely on religious rituals but discard the concrete provisions of the religion. Of course, they justified their preference by a weak religious interpretation that basically stated Islamic provisions are not observed in a secular order because the domestic and external dynamics present obstacles.

However, it was also necessary to become stronger; greater strength was possible only if they came to power. Modern authority offers unilateral power and wealth. In this case, they decided to examine Islamic provisions but observe religious rituals while they were in power. Symbols and rituals preserve a link to religion and offer advantages against secular rivals.

The main factor that created Leviathan in Europe was the secularization of the state or authority vis-à-vis the church and religion, and its emergence as an autonomous entity. Socialism attempted to react to this monster in the name of the oppressed, but it created a greater monster. Liberalism wanted to restrict the power of the state in the name of law, but because its point of reference was rich people, society and the poor were sacrificed to the monster. Islamist political movements could have offered a solution; however, former Islamists who aimed to seize power revived Leviathan in their own rule by gaining autonomy vis-à-vis the provisions of religion.

Fyodor Dostoyevsky once said that everything is justified if there is no God. You would restrict the role of God to religious rituals and symbols and then justify everything. That is what would make a Muslim monster.

Both Religious and Non-Religious[82]

The failure of secularism to perform its classical functions is the result of the collapse of positivism.

Those who believe that man needs a new vision of existence and a new map of meaning outside the structure of the Enlightenment are in search of a solution. However, the majority of the people in both Western and non-Western societies remain in a dogmatic coma. Two types of minds have a hard time accepting that secularism has been transformed into a form of nihilism: First are the supporters of the Enlightenment who believe that rationalism and positivism are still relevant, and second are the conservatives who suspend the worldly provisions of religion and claim ownership over the religious domain. It is possible to see examples of both in Turkey.

Even though it is surprising, the Enlightenment mindset is more suitable than the conservative mindset to acknowledging the unique identity of Islam. They examine the modern and postmodern world which functions outside secularism where they find that their rationalist and positivist foundations are undermined. Many thinkers have come to these conclusions by themselves. A conservative mindset, however, cannot achieve this.

There are two main reasons for this in the case of conservatives in Turkey, a group that now includes former Islamists. First, the conservatives, particularly former Islamists, are insistent on leading a religious life by adhering to rituals.

Second, they seize control over the modern nation-state after abandoning Islamism. According to their self-perception, they have always been religious and supporters of religion. However, they were left with religious symbols and rituals only because they had decided to suspend some provisions of the religion in domestic and international circumstances.

When examined independently, separate from its cause, a religious obligation may perform a function that it was not intended for in the

---

[82] First appeared in *Today's Zaman* daily on Jul. 08, 2014

first place. The wearing of a headscarf was defended because it was seen as the performance of a religious duty, then it was considered a matter of rights and freedoms, and in the end it turned into a symbol of domination. The symbolization of the headscarf led to its redefinition as a means to gain advantages in politics, social status, and daily life. At this stage the headscarf no longer serves as a veil to cover the body [as part of the loose-fitting garment], but a symbol that complements tight pants and a revealing blouse. This does not bother Muslims because the headscarf is now a symbol rather than a religious duty. If you have the symbol on you, then there is no problem. Muslims are not bothered by the dysfunctional religious provisions.

Every "religious" discourse and act, including the headscarf, beards, flamboyant veiling, sacred nights, employment of Islamist language, and many others, have no significance in a religious setting but make the holders of these symbols believe that they own the entire religion. These conservatives become more assured of their religiosity when they oppose attacks on their religion and its rituals. A former Islamist becomes secular when fighting secularists!

Because he owns the language, the symbols, and rituals of the religion, he can rely on the laws of market capitalism for a bitter competition. A conservative politician may employ any method to attain his goals. A pious lawyer may defend a suspect unfairly. A religious trader may take interest money. They may exploit the labor of workers. They may tell lies to win public tenders. They may tell lies about their competitors. They see no problem in earning and spending money in such ways. Irregularity, lies, deception, conspiracy, and everything are justified in their cause.

The question we need to answer is this: How did we make a monster out of the conservatives and former Islamists?

Perception of State[83]

I believe that Muslim intellectuals do not have the correct perspectives on the modern state. They generally confuse the exercise of power by

---

[83] First appeared in *Today's Zaman* daily on Sept. 29, 2014

the Prophet Muhammad and the experience during the reign of the righteous caliphs with the modern state. The following points need to be considered:

1. The power the Prophet Muhammad exercised is not the power envisaged in the classical-traditional or modern state.

2. In terms of the fulfillment of Islamic ideas through politics, the administration of the righteous caliphs should be placed below the politics of the Prophet Muhammad (pbuh) but above the politics and states of the Umayyad, Abbasid, Seljuk, and Ottoman dynasties.

3. The modern state represents detachment from and disconnection with the experiences of the eras of the Prophet Muhammad and the rightly-guided caliphs. If you do not make this distinction, you will attribute the current form of the state to the good and poor qualities of individuals and conclude that those who are like you will exhibit a good performance in state administration, where they will support justice and good governance. In general, the Islamists hold this wrong assumption. You might want to travel along a straight path, but what you have here is not a ruler. If you insist on this ruler, you lose your way, and all of a sudden, you realize that you have made a tyrant, even if this was not your purpose in the first place.

To this end, the relations of Muslim intellectuals, scholars and communities with the state will lead to a further decay or improvement in the modern state. If you look at the current state of affairs from a historical perspective, a few factors affecting state-community relations can be mentioned:

a) Communities had some sort of relationship with the administration, politics, or the state throughout history. Depending on the situation, the administrations pay some attention to different communities in their sphere of authority. This is inevitable; and when the state-society relationship is maintained correctly, the sociological equilibrium is established and based on this.

b) The state-community relationship as the legacy of the Ottoman experience influences the current state of affairs.

c) The influence of the perception of the state that changed during the period between the late Ottoman Reformation era (Tanzimat) and the republican era should be considered; the role of the changing perception of the state on communities during current developments should also be underlined.

d) The communities lost their influence because of these three factors in the late Ottoman period; currently, religious orders and communities identify the pursuit of power and influence within the state as their primary objective and strategy. In this area, intellectual Islamism has never been as eager as social Islam for state power. However, the Naqshibandi order and one branch of the Nur Movement in particular have pursued this strategy incessantly.

e) Another factor which has played a role in state-community relations in the near past is the growing role of religious communities in the public sphere following the Sept. 12, 1980 military coup, when former President Turgut Özal and his aides alleged the involvement of these communities. Özal decided that the military which established the republican regime claims absolute right over politics and society. Indeed, the May 27, 1960, March 12, 1971, and Sept. 12, 1980 coups and military interventions were bloody and antidemocratic responses to the seizure of some power by civilians. So they needed a police bureaucracy that would balance the military and prevent it from exercising its power over the state. This could have been done by the recruitment of individuals holding ethical and moral concerns and responsibilities.

Those who staged the Feb. 28, 1997 coup were aware of this, and for this reason, one of their destructive moves was to weaken the potential of police's ability to stage a counter-coup. Dengir Mir Mehmet Fırat, one of the founders of the Justice and Development Party (AK Party), says that the AK Party has been using this tactic and relied on the Hizmet Movement for this, given that the movement has been producing reliable people for four decades. The reliable figures associated with the Hizmet Movement have protected the AK Party against a possible coup over the last decade. However, what is happening right now is the re-emergence of the old regime and the old state mentality.

Bureaucratic Center Assuming the Identity of the Ruling Party[84]

The most essential problem the newly established Turkish Republic faced in maintaining part of the Ottoman heritage in state governance was that it was torn between the "ideal of ensuring the survival of the state forever" and the emphasis on "raison d'État," or the reason of the State—that is to say, a country's goals and ambitions.

Since the time of Sultan Mehmed II (1428-1481), the ideal of the eternal preservation of the state was represented by the "social center," while the reason of the State was advocated by the "bureaucratic center," and these two centers occasionally clashed with each other.

With a radical breakaway from the heritage of his ancestors—Osman Bey (the founder of the Ottomans) and his son Orhan Bey, both of who relied on a civilian spirit rather than on an institutionalized apparatus—Sultan Mehmed II built the state on four pillars: the Mughal State tradition, the customary law of Genghis Khan, the Arabic right to the sword, and the Byzantine palace politics. The Ottoman palace school of Enderun provided recruits for the bureaucratic center. The sultan was the only security for these recruits, who knew that they were the "servants" of the bureaucratic center. Since they didn't have any historical, religious, or social affinity with or emotional attachment to the public, any misfortune that might befall the sultan would bring their own end as well.

Apparently, astute sultans such as Sultan Mehmed the Conqueror and Sultan Suleyman the Magnificent didn't relinquish the initiative. But we can say that, in general, the initiative was largely wielded by the bureaucratic center. When the initiative was in the hands of the sultan, the state was "generous," but when it was in the hands of the bureaucratic center, the state's emphasis shifted toward the reason of the

---

[84] First appeared in *Today's Zaman* daily on Apr. 07, 2014

State. Thus, coups or revolts were masterminded by the bureaucratic center, not by the sultan or the public. The most tragic example of this was that Sultan Mahmud II took the state banner and urged the public to revolt against the (corrupt) Janissary corps. This is perhaps the only example in history in which a monarch tried to provoke the public to revolt against his own bureaucracy.

The republic took the state from the sultan and handed it over to the bureaucratic center in the form of the cult of personality. While the sultan would say "my servants," the symbolic leader of the bureaucratic center would say, "my nation." While the sultan would say, "This is my edict," the republic's official would say, "This is what we have decided."

The Janissary-led bureaucratic center would reinforce its position and power with periodic interventions. Turkey introduced democracy simultaneously with the West, but the bureaucratic center would maintain it for only 10 years. Interventions have taken place since 1960: in 1960, 1971, 1980, 1997 and 2007. Some of them were open and violent coups, while some others were attempts. This tradition is still in place. Each time, the bureaucratic center acts to reassert the reason of the State with a new disguise and identity. With each intervention, a specific social group is "otherized" or demonized. The thing is that each time, the bureaucratic center adopts the identity of the ruling party or ideology. Thus, when the Republican People's Party (CHP) is in power, it positions itself as leftist/Kemalist, and when a conservative party is in power, it repositions itself as conservative. Their ideology or political identity is just deceptive garb it wears. In the postmodern coup of Feb. 28, 1997, the target was the National View (Milli Görüş), Islamism, and Imam-hatip schools—a type of secondary school with a religious curriculum along with the standard curriculum.

The rise of the Justice and Development Party's (AK Party) to power was not easy. The tutelage regime was forced to withdraw thanks to united efforts from everyone. Everyone, including Fethullah Gülen and the movement he inspired, contributed to this process.

Now, the state's bureaucratic center is once again assuming the identity of the ruling party, using its historic codes, skills, and reflexes, and it is trying to reassert its position within the state apparatus using its customary procedures. The supporters of the AK Party, the National View adherents, Islamists, the religious and pious, and conservative masses belong to the same human ecology as the Nur communities, the Hizmet Movement, and all religious orders. They constitute the main body. If one of them becomes weaker, the others will be influenced from this as well.

New Type of CUP Activism[85]

The Ottoman state reigned over three continents, controlling a vast geography that stretched from the Balkans to Yemen and from Crimea to Central Africa.

The Ottoman dynasty held political power; however, that dynasty-based Ottoman rule was transformed into the rule of the Turks in the republican era. The Justice and Development Party (AK Party) administration believed that it could reclaim domination and influence in the lands the Turks lost in the past for the near and far future.

The point that the leading AK Party figures have been missing is that the "interim period" between the classical Ottoman era and the modern republican era has caused serious alienation and a disconnect in the ways Muslims perceive each other in political culture. In classical states, communities did not have any problem attaching or subscribing themselves to a dynasty—Umayyad, Abbasid, Seljuk, Safavid, or Ottoman. But because a sense of belonging is expressed in the modern nation state by reference to a race or a nation, every nation or community naturally and inevitably assumes sovereignty. Despite the fact that they got along with the Ottoman dynasty in the Ottoman era, the Kurds have experienced great problems with the Republic of Turkey and reference to ethnicity is the main cause of this problem.

The breaking point in the interim period between the Ottoman and republican eras was the Committee of Union and Progress (CUP). Arabs do not even want to recall this period. They hate this period so much that they wrongfully attempt to read the entire Ottoman era through the lens of the CUP; they believe that they were ruled under a colonial regime for four centuries. Associating the Ottoman era with the CUP

---

[85] First appeared in *Today's Zaman* daily on Apr. 30, 2014

mentality is unfair and it is detrimental to the Muslim mentality and perception of the global Muslim community. Our collapsing foreign policy is an example that proves this point.

The problem is somewhere else: from the perspective of a pro-CUP and pro-republican culture, it becomes evident that our general political approach is flawed. This also explains the problems that Turkey has been experiencing in its orientation since the year 2011.

Regardless of our political or religious inclination, we are unable to get rid of the pro-CUP and pro-republican perspective where Iranians, Arabs, and Kurds are considered Muslim brothers but not equal partners. We do not forgive Iran because historically they did not bow to the Ottoman state. There are some figures who are still interpreting developments through the clash between Ottomans and Safavids. The Kurds have been living in a buffer zone between the Anatolian region and the Arabs since Sultan Selim I. They supported the Ottoman state in the fight against the Safavids; but in the end, they are considered subjects who submitted to the Ottoman rule. And from this vantage point, it is obvious that the Arabs have remained under Ottoman rule for four centuries. This leads us to develop a vision that Turkey should become a leader in the region, as if this is its inherent role to play. This is the main source of our mindset that we are a nation chosen by Allah to rule.

Religious groups do not oppose the idea of *ummah*—the global Muslim community; but they ask this question: "Are you referring to the ummah under Turkey's leadership? Why should we seek an alternative leadership under Turks, Persians, or Arabs, given that the ummah itself is considered the leader?" This is contrary to the definition of the ummah. The argument is that Turkey has a strong state tradition. Is that so? Iran and Egypt also have strong experience ruling a state. In the new era, all states are the same. The original version of the present form is the modern nation state as devised in the West. All non-Western states, including Turkey, are copies of this original form. Besides, Prophet Muhammad (pbuh) urges Muslims to obey a ruler even if he is an ordinary man, as long as he adheres to Islamic provisions and precepts. In the early 21st century, we developed a project called New Ottomanism that raised many eyebrows. We declared that we will maintain control in the area where the Ottoman state was dominant before 1911. This is actually a new form of the Committee of Union and Progress (CUP) activism with the title of New Ottomanism.

The Century-Old Nemesis, New Partner[86]

Islamic movements and religious understandings are under huge pressure in different parts of the Middle East and the Islamic world.

On the one hand, modern Salafism, which translated 19th century positivism into a reading of religious texts, is trying to overcome this pressure by addressing (and abusing) the people's sentiments. This generates political and military conflicts and nihilism that destroys hope. On the other, the Khariji groups that promote hatred set aside the legitimate and acknowledged legacy and heritage of Islam and seek to implement the ideas they have derived from their positivist methodology. Even though their political and military leaders have devised some genius strategies, they are making the masses they provoke blasphemous in their actions. Millions of people are negatively affected by the resulting sectarian and ethnic clashes. The Muslim world has been shattered into millions of pieces.

A few years ago, Turkey was a beacon of hope; unfortunately, Turkey is now like the other Middle Eastern countries, as it is evolving to have an authoritarian outlook inside and imperialist nationalism outside. The Justice and Development Party (AK Party), whose support base included the conservative and religious masses, the poor, middle-class groups, and the victimized Kurds, is now acting like the Salafis, unfortunately causing its supporters to question religion by reliance on the same punitive and vengeful method and style.

This stance leads to the emergence of an army of aggressors who recognize no boundaries and rely on a reactionary discourse in the face of the so-called dangers. (Sitting at the epicenter of this army of aggressors,) the "journalists" affiliated with intelligence agencies are provoking this aggression. Unfortunately, people who focus on passion, simplicity, rightful action, and calm are simply ignored. However, this group

---

[86] First appeared in *Today's Zaman* daily on Nov. 03, 2014

that is taking up the fight on the front line is not the actual support base of the AK Party.

Unfortunately, Turkey has returned to its past format. The policies adopted and put in place by the members of the Committee of Union and Progress (CUP) a century ago are now in effect. The reforms introducing the rule of law were rescinded. The powerful figures who were responsible for the coups of May 27 [1960], March 12 [1971], Sept. 12 [1980] and Feb. 28 [1997] are now holding the initiative again. The National Security Council (MGK) is identifying threats again. The Red Book[87] is considered superior to the Constitution. The coup-makers are taking the stage again.

For the first time in our republican history, we had an opportunity to deal with military guardianship in the period from 2007 to 2011; but the critical threshold was not overcome, despite some progress being made. Even in times when coup attempts were exposed, 80 percent of the coup makers were behind closed doors; they were able to remain unidentified. The neo-nationalist juntas were identified, and they were effectively addressed; this gave the impression that guardianship was over. But this was an illusion.

The religious-conservative and pro-Kurdish branches of Ergenekon has taken action to save their neo-nationalist comrades. The AK Party would not have experienced any hardship if it had relied on clean politics and avoided corruption: the rigging of public tenders, illegal money circulating in the market due to the Iranian oil embargo, the neo-Ottomanist dreams, the sources used in the funding of the Syrian civil war, and flawed regional policies ruined everything.

A deeply rooted and well-organized structure is preserving the guardianship system; to preserve this system, this structure relies on all illegal means and methods. The law has been severely breached; the public authorities are committing crimes and making the state institutions dysfunctional. Relations with the Middle East and the Western world are deteriorating. Half of the people hate the other half. The minimal stan-

---

[87] The Red Book is the most secret National Security Policy Document, created and updated once or twice a decade by the Turkish National Security Council (MGK), which is the institutionalization of the Turkish military's influence over politics. (ed.)

dards of a democratic regime are suspended. Freedom of expression is under heavy pressure. Evidence is fabricated by illegal means. What has been happening has nothing to do with Islamism or political Islam.

Interregnum Period (2002–present)[88]

Now that Turkey's intra-regime conflicts are underway—our familiar state is restoring itself with the familiar methods—can Islamism pick up the ball? The answer to this question is more important than ever.

My personal assessment is that after emerging in the second half of the 19th century, Islamism saw two interregnum periods; in the context of Turkey, the first was between 1924 and 1950, and then there was another from 2002 up to the present. The first lasted for about a quarter of a century. If Islamism cannot substantially reform itself, the second one may last longer than the first one. Given the fact that a ruling party can narcotize the brains of the masses, even though it has nothing to do with basic Islamic assumptions and happily enjoys the illusion that it is entitled to rule the country and generously distribute benefits and advantages to its supporters [including especially the religious communities and foundations that lose their essential quality of being civil society organizations (CSOs) and turn into state establishments], the second interregnum period may be extended to 50 years. The restoration I referred to above should focus on the state apparatus and the ruling party.

The first generation of Islamists (1850 to 1924) essentially tried to "save" the Ottoman state that was founded upon Islamic principles. The second generation of Islamists (1950 to 2000) focused on establishing a "new state." The first Islamists—in particular, those that emerged after the second constitutional monarchy—failed to realize that the Committee of Union and Progress (CUP) had triggered the transition of the traditional Ottoman state to a "nation state" and that the state they were trying to save was neither the old Ottoman state nor the modern nation state. The second generation inherited this legacy of the first generation. Believing that the state was genetically engineered, they assumed that they could establish an "Islamic state."

---

[88] First appeared in *Today's Zaman* daily on Jun. 24, 2014

Some time ago I realized that our reference state was not a genetically engineered one and therefore, cannot serve the purpose of promoting Islamic ideals, justice, and living a moral life. Consequently, I dedicated considerable time and effort to the study of the concepts of a modern state and modernization. However, in the post-1950 era, the Muslim Brotherhood (MB) started to lean on political Islam in Egypt. In Iran, former Presidents Ali Akbar Hashemi Rafsanjani and Sayyid Muhammad Khatami dominated the political scene in the wake of the death of Grand Ayatollah Sayyed Ruhollah Mostafavi Moosavi Khomeini. Failing to sufficiently criticize Pakistan's experience with an Islamic republic and not heeding any warning, Turkey's National View (Milli Görüş) went in a direction based on the wrong foundation and using the wrong means.

I must note that the religious communities and groups that refrained from participating in a political movement that used Islamic references did not show the slightest interest. "We have nothing to do with politics," they said, and they did not meddle with the process by which secular parties dominated the public and social decision-making mechanisms. However, they recently realized that this was not the proper method and started to think and act about the state and political power. All hell broke loose when they said, "We are part of the social sphere and we are entitled to have our say in politics." The state, which is the son of a marriage between the Ottoman state and the modern nation state, does not accept "partners."

What the third generation of Islamists was supposed to do was not to "save" or "establish" the state. Rather, they were to "redefine and transform the state and political power" and develop a new philosophy of politics taking into consideration the social opportunities and developments in the global culture. Referring to the failures of the first two generations, Islamists should now come up with a new definition of "state" and "power."

Now, we should try to minimize the damage, and at the same time, ensure that political, social, and intellectual Islamic groups establish a dialogue with other social groups to come together and discuss ways to develop a social contract with reference to rule of law and a redefinition of power.

Chapter 8

Identity, Community, and Politics

Nationalist and Religious Movements[89]

Looking at the chronology of nationalist movements within the Ottoman Empire, we see that the first nationalist movements emerged among the Balkan nations of the Greeks, Bulgarians, and Albanians, seeking to secede from the empire. The second nationalist wave was seen among the Ottoman elites who did not believe the empire could be saved through Ottomanism or Islamism.

The third wave was seen among Arabs. Finally, nationalist movements emerged among Kurds, and in a sense, the Kurdish issue, which still causes difficulties today, corresponds to a form of late nationalism that originally started in the 19th century Ottoman Empire.

We can say that after surviving this last nationalist trauma we have experienced with the Kurdish issue, we may move toward regional integration in line with the spirit of the times.

Abdülhamid II believed that the Ottoman Empire would lose the Middle East in the medium term and be deprived of its influence in the Caucasus. So, he concluded that the major Islamic nations (*anasır-ı Islam*) of the empire should be concentrated in Anatolia, which could then be fortified against destructive external forces. And he took measures to this end. Abdülhamid's strategy had two main targets: first, to delay the collapse of the state as much as possible; and second, to reinforce the empire in material and social aspects during this time. If Abdülhamid II had not been deposed, and if he could have developed a

---

[89] First appeared in *Today's Zaman* on Feb. 19, 2010

healthier dialogue and cooperation with Islamists, the empire might not have collapsed.

The first and most important ideology that developed among Ottoman intellectuals in this chaotic environment was Ottomanism. Ottomanists argued that by uniting diverse elements of the empire or by drawing them closer to each other, the empire could be turned into a crucible or a common land where every diverse unit could live happily.

Another major intellectual and political movement that deserves to be discussed is Islamism. Like Abdülhamid II, the Muslims of the time thought that the Ottoman State would lose the Balkans and a serious problem would arise in the eastern provinces that held sizable Armenian populations. Islamists thought it might be possible to keep the Muslim nations of the Caucasus and the Middle East together by stressing Islam as the binding force. This was the main theme of almost all Islamic scholars, including Bediüzzaman Said Nursi. The theoreticians of Islamism maintained that there are different elements under Islam and it is necessary to promote the unity and integrity of these elements, which could be done with reference to a common identity as Muslims.

The third major movement was Turkism. The major proponents of this movement came not from within the Ottoman Empire, but from the Caucasus and Asia, such as Yusuf Akçora, Velidi Zeki Togan, Ahmet Ağaoğlu, and Sadri Maksudi. As the first movement of modernization was triggered by Kavalalı Mehmet Ali Pasha (the Ottoman Viceroy of Egypt, who was also known as Muhammad Ali Basha), and Egyptian intellectuals, those who gave rise to nationalism based on ethnicity and secularism were the authors who originally came from the Caucasus.

This is an important point because Ottoman intellectuals and political elites were still cool toward nationalist ideologies. They were perfectly justified in being so as there was an empire in their hands and both non-Muslims and Muslims were living together; promoting ethnic nationalism would certainly lead to the separation of diverse religious and ethnic groups.

The proponents of Turkism introduced two major concepts:

1. Advocacy of the Turkish language. Proponents of this movement, particularly Ömer Seyfettin, tended to attach great importance to language. They criticized the traditional literary forms for not

using the language naturally used by the people. They slammed the literary texts of Servet-i Fünun as elaborated beyond being comprehensible and suggested that it was not even a language. They advocated that the language should be the language spoken by the ordinary people, i.e., Turkish.

2. The proponents of Turkish defined "homeland" within the ideological context of the French Revolution. The new homeland was foreign both to Ottomanists and Islamists, who scorned it. Similarly, the concept of "race" was considerably weak until the establishment of the second constitutional monarchy (1908-1923) and the rise to power of the Committee of Union and Progress (CUP) in 1913. This concept gained currency particularly after the establishment of the republic. In this way, new Turkish nationalism, based on the Turkish race, was formulated with emphasis on the Turkish identity.

Our Identities[90]

Any discussion of identities should start with the definition of identity. Identity is the answer to the question, "Who am I?" Everyone asks this question to themselves in this or that way, but this question is not always answered by the person who asks it. Rather, an identity can be given or imposed on him or her from outside. Four distinct categories of identity can be identified:

1. Natural identity. This is the identity a person acquires by birth without any involvement on their part. For instance, a person's skin may be black or white or yellow or red by birth.

2. Acquired identity. This is the identity a person acquires through social processes. For instance, a single person may be married and then have children, thereby becoming first a wife or husband, and then a mother or father, and thus adopt new roles and identities.

3. Volitional identity. This is the identity a person acquires voluntarily or of their own volition. Religion is one of these identities. While people are generally born into a religious environment,

---

[90] First appeared in *Today's Zaman* on Nov. 24, 2014

they can still acquire another religion at a later stage. Acquiring a new worldview or adopting a specific political attitude or being a member of a certain religious community—or democratic association, an illegal organization, or any other group—can be considered in this scope. These are volitional identities.

4. Given or imposed identity. This is the most problematic category both in Turkey and around the world. This is the identity given, attributed to, or imposed on a person or society by external groups or individuals. In modern times, this is generally done by states, and the problems related with this identity were rare in traditional societies before the advent of modernism. In a traditional society, people belonged to a political power, but there was a dynasty that represented that power in the eyes of the people, like the Umayyad Caliphate, the Abbasid Caliphate and the Ottoman dynasties. When the state emerged as an impersonal device and acquired a corporate personality—this is the modern state—it felt the need to give an identity to its citizens.

In this framework, we can divide the nature of identities into two:

a) Identities that rely on physical or material aspects or qualities. These identities are constituted by their natural physical essence. For instance, color, language, gender, race, geography, being eastern or western or northern or southern, being a member of a class or group, or being rich or poor imply physical or material qualities.

b) Identities that rely on spiritual or transcendental qualities or memberships. These identities are acquired through a volitional process because their adoption requires selection or effort on the part of people. Adopting any religion falls into this category.

A large part of these identities are natural identities. People would not feel ashamed of them, and they would not regard them as a source of pride or supremacy over other people. For instance, a person who is born to a Turkish, Arab, or Kurdish family becomes, respectively, a Turk, Arab, or Kurd. But this is not a source of supremacy. We can assert that the practice of using identities as a source of polarization, conflict, or absolute supremacy, and as a support for discrimination, relies on Satan's ideology back at the beginning of creation:

Satan refused to fulfill God's command and did not prostrate to Adam. "Why don't you prostrate?" God asked, and he replied, "You created me of fire, and Adam of clay." Thus, Satan compared the two physical essences. However, the point was not whether Adam was created from soil or whether Satan was created from fire but that God breathed into Adam from His spirit and taught him the names of things and made him His vicegerent (or representative) on earth, thereby glorifying Him.

Satan, however, shifted the context and emphasized material origin or physical qualities. This is the original source of racial or gender discrimination as well as other conflicts.

The Qur'an cites "piety" (*taqwa*) as the sole source of supremacy, and the alienation of Muslims from the essence of Islam—i.e., "piety"—is the source of all conflicts among Muslims.

Return to Religion: Cause or Effect?[91]

The cultural and historical heritage built on Islam's sacred references (the Qur'an and the Practice of Prophet Muhammad, peace and blessings be upon him) is being perpetually exploited by current political standpoints.

But when we look at it from a different perspective, we can say that the heritage in question actually offers great opportunities to overcome the crisis we currently find ourselves in.

As everyone can easily observe, there is a general and broad-scale movement of religious orientation in the Muslim world that needs to be analyzed from several different angles. Developing a proper understanding of the dynamics and targets of this new phenomenon will help in providing explanatory information on how the world will be shaped in the near future. Social scientists, researchers, and experts highly interested in this issue are trying to explain this phenomenon. While this is a very beneficial effort, it is critical for the issue to be properly ana-

---

[91]   First appeared in *Today's Zaman* on Sept. 04, 2009

lyzed, for an inaccurate explanation has the potential to lead the public and especially those who work on this issue to incorrect results.

To link this Islamic phenomenon strictly to geopolitical developments and the deep social and economic injustices in the Muslim world would be misleading.

The biased stance of international politics and the double standards big states apply to other countries does cause the Muslim world to develop a sentiment that "Muslims are being oppressed by the Christian West and their rights and legitimate demands are not being taken seriously." While analyzing this sentiment on a calmer platform is necessary, what are most important are image and perception, and not necessarily reality.

The wide-scale social migration in the Muslim world, the rapid transformation of traditional cities into major metropolises, and the continuous disappointment of millions of people that have migrated from rural areas to big cities, are also important factors that need to be taken into consideration.

Schizophrenics in the cultural world and an extensive search for identity should also be added to these factors. There are segments of the society that have neither become Western nor stayed Eastern because they are stuck between their traditions and authoritarian political regimes that impose modernism on them with official cultural policies.

In this respect and in the context of foreign factors, the Muslim revival movement developed not only as a response to poverty, social injustice, and the unequal international order, but also as a search for identity against mandatory modernization policies.

Although all these factors had an "effective" role, they are not enough to explain the general phenomenon because the return to religion that is becoming concrete in Islam is not only happening in Muslim countries, but also in the Jewish and Christian worlds, and even in the cultural worlds of Buddhism, Brahmanism, and Taoism, though at different levels.

These observations indicate that as humans on this earth we are experiencing a general return to religion. In addition, there are common issues shared by the three Abrahamic religions.

1. The modern point of view (modernity), which is founded on the Enlightenment and the principle of detaching man from God and weakening or marginalizing high ethical virtues, has depleted its own abilities and has reached the end of its lifespan.
2. Man cannot live without God and without the ethical virtues of religion. A completely secular lifestyle is not possible. Mentally denying the transcendent, spiritual, and other dimensions of existence does not separate existence from those dimensions.
3. Regardless of what religion we believe in, we must respond to the call of holy Books and plan a new lifestyle that is appropriate to these callings. Uncontrollable ambitions and desires to win power have made the earth an unlivable place.

These are three main points shared by Judaism, Christianity, and Islam. It is this way because the holy Books of all three religions came from one source. They are revelations from God.

It is at this point that we need to take a look at what Islam recommends and what dynamics it seeks we put into play to be able to live in peace with people from other cultures. And it seems the only way we can do this is by foregoing the habit of looking at everything within the frame of political or geo-strategic interests, and economic self-interest.

Interference with Religion[92]

The discussion of whether religion influences politics or vice versa has been a controversial issue. It is hard to draw a conclusion that can apply to every religion. No generalization is applicable to all major religions.

Both may be true in regards to the teachings of certain religions, their historical backgrounds, and their current state of affairs. For instance, we all know that the Church held hegemonic power and influence over material and worldly authorities in the Middle Ages.

Both Islam and Eastern Christianity remained on relatively good terms with the state; their existence did not lead to serious unease with states. For the Judaic tradition, the period of exile is different from the

---

[92] First appeared in *Today's Zaman* on Nov. 06, 2009

period after the foundation of the Israeli state. There is no need to recall that the actual problem erupted in Europe after the Renaissance and Reformation eras and spread all over the world from there.

Even though different models and styles of relationships with other religions have been tested in the context of history by all three divine faiths and other religions, we may argue that the divine religions have been influenced by different factors in terms of the materialization of their historical goals. Historically, the doctrine of Judaism, the interpretation of Christianity, and the politics of Islam stand out as troublesome areas and factors leading to problems. These three major factors led to the exploitation and abuse of these three religions and the misinterpretation of their fundamental teachings and precepts. This left indelible imprints on the scholastic circles of these religions and caused disruptive impacts.

If we set aside the issue that the doctrine and its interpretation created problems for Christianity and Judaism in some fields and focus now on politics in Islam and its historical background, we would observe that despite the Islamic emphasis on life in this world and a just politic system, the influence of politics has been exaggerated compared to its original focus (on servitude to the Almighty God) and the references to other dimensions in the religion. As such, politics has been made an excessively important element that overwhelmingly occupies minds.

All three divine religions have something to say on life in this world and political order. Of course, the emphasis of Islam on politics is stronger and more visible. Despite this, the influence of politics on religion as an institution regulating the power relations has unfortunately been negative, exploitative, and restrictive. This is a relationship shaped by consecutive political requests and interventions. Political authorities and administrations sought to base their legitimacy on religion, viewing religion as a tool to achieve their political goals. It is redundant to search for the legitimacy of a ruler who views himself as the representative of God in this world in the eyes of the people. The same sultan or ruler would seek to make religion subordinate to the state as an institution, while he would also make impossible requests from religion if he deems necessary.

To make a reference to the current age, it should be noted that this historical relationship has politicized religion. As the state and the political administration relying on the central power of the state made requests from religion in regards to their sphere of administration and policies, religion became more politicized in the state of tension that emerged.

The historical practice is not free of certain tensions even though it did not lead to excessive discomforts over time. It could be argued that our history is the history of the division of power between the administration and the civilian sphere.

Individuals and social groups have tried to make sure that a greater influence is reserved for them, whereas the state sought to consolidate and reinforce its sphere of authority. The process by which the individual and society were included in a sphere of authority of the modern state accelerated with Westernization which led to the emergence of the initial repression of religion and, of course, the politicization of religion.

Religious Communities and Politics[93]

There are some recent changes that require a re-analysis of the relationship between religious communities and politics.

1. During the transition from modernity to postmodernism, there is a sociological change from a monolithic society towards a plurality of communities. This does not mean that society will collapse and be divided; instead, it can be represented by an umbrella. In this change, the actor is society, not the state.

2. Parallel with the growing economic activity needed for further growth and unrestrained urbanization, the middle classes constitute the backbone of politics. The presence of a middle class makes a participatory and pluralistic democracy necessary. However, pressure and interest groups or popular leaders may corrupt democracy through demagogy and perception operations they have built with media support. If pluralistic and participatory democracy is not achieved, internal clashes are inevitable.

---

[93] First appeared in *Today's Zaman* on Sept. 8, 2014

3. This state of affairs requires a reevaluation of democratic theory. Pragmatic social Islam, which takes inspiration from European Union membership and values or liberal theory, cannot perform this reevaluation. Only ideological Islamists can. And Islamists are unable to perform this function unless they free their minds from daily politics and party affiliations.

4. With the new socioeconomic situation and global material developments, we have to realize the following: a) horizontal dialogue and negotiation are required; this dialogue and negotiation has to take place between religious, sectarian, and secular groups and communities; b) vertical negotiation has to take place between these groups and the state. This process should seek to ensure that the state will become an impersonal apparatus and that these groups become influential in the decision-making mechanisms. In this way, the state is transformed and the society of religious communities gets involved in political processes. Otherwise, the given form of democracy acquires a totalitarian and authoritarian identity, referring only to the majority and national will. Politics should take place so that society, as the real actor, is prioritized, and politics should be performed on the basis of ethical considerations. The basic form of this approach is the Islamic teaching that there should always be a leader picked whenever there are at least three people traveling. The leader is primus inter pare; he has no sanctity or superiority. He is only responsible for observing the rules applicable to all three travelers, including himself.

Politics is sociology. Western sociology is based on classes, whereas ours is based on religion and identities. Religious communities ensure the survival of religions, sects, and different identities; if there is no community, there is no religion either, because an individual cannot preserve his religion vis-à-vis an amorphous society and the absolute power of the state. For this reason, the rulers holding the strings of politics have to take the input and consent of social groups. The state takes the law as its reference; but the law is not all about the laws of Parliament, which performs under the authority of a single person. There should be some legal framework that Parliament is unable to change by making laws. If politics ensures the participation of communities in politics, the communities will no longer have to organize themselves within the state. The state has to remain equally distant from all communities; it has to recognize them by their standings and statements. And the state should not favor a certain community or communities.

Of course, a community should not be allowed to seize excessive control within the state bureaucracy. The state should be able to employ a member of any community based on his or her merits. It has to secularize education, and every community should be allowed to offer educational services. Raising a religious generation is not the job of the state; it is the job of religious communities. Communities should check the power of political actors, but their main function is not to force the government to make decisions based on its responsibilities; their main function should be to support society in ethical and social terms.

The "Community" Reality in the Postmodern World[94]

Ferdinand Tönnies, the 19th century German sociologist, argued that there is a necessary progression from the community (Gemeinschaft) to the society (Gesellschaft). In the post-modern world, however, society is disintegrating, leading to the re-emergence of the community. In this new period, democracy cannot turn a blind eye to the reality of communities. I can list my arguments in support of this thesis as follows:

First, individual-centered social life is the very essence of human life. I must note that here I use the word "individual" to mean "a human being with a personality," but not in liberal philosophy's concept of "individual." Personality belongs to Islam, while liberal philosophy's individual belongs to the Enlightenment. A person with personality worships God, while liberal philosophy's individual challenges Him.

Second, individual raindrops are unique and countless; when they come together, they constitute rain, which is perceived in Islam as a manifestation of God's mercy on man, nature, and the universe. Social life is

---

[94] First appeared in *Today's Zaman* on Sept. 15, 2014

a human fact, and for it to become mercy, individuals should be organized in the form of a "community." For, "God's hand is upon the community."

Third, the communities that are formed by individuals and families constitute society. If society is a dome, then communities are semi- or quarter-domes.

Fourth, the totality of societies in diverse geographies constitutes the "ummah," the universal unity. There are two senses in which I use the word, "ummah":

1. The universal fellowship of Islam introduced by the Prophet of Islam (pbuh). The "ummah" is a global organization at the highest moral and spiritual level; it is a form of belonging that is completely different from clans, tribes, nations, ethnicities, people, communities, and the entirely modern synthetic inventions of "nation." The ummah is above all.

2. Political union, which also includes non-Muslims as members. Religious groups that avoid certain kinds of conflict may make an agreement to coexist.

Fifth, the society that does not take this human organization into consideration belongs to modernity. It is fine-tuned to become a nation and it is conditioned to be under the state's control. Islamic political thought is required to reform society to conform to the four articles above, thereby saving it from the refined totalitarianism of tyrannical power.

Sixth, regardless of whether it is refined by Islam or not society is a sociological structure. Learning, culture, economics, politics, and regional and international policies are mediated by this sociological milieu. In other words, society is the garden of culture, economics, and politics, but contrary to what Durkheim proposed, it is not society that sows seeds in this garden, but rather individual or collective voluntary choices and the acts of individuals with personalities.

I refer to three forms of "community": (1) the religious orders that maintain historical traditions connected to salient Sufi figures, (2) the religious communities and groups that emerged largely as a result of migration to cities in the 20th century, and (3) secular civil society organizations (NGOs) and democratic organizations, associations, foundations, and societies.

Groups in the third category distinguish themselves from religious communities in that they don't have historical or religious references and they are autonomous, non-governmental, and voluntary organizations. Thus, they argue that religious orders and other religious communities and groups cannot be considered "civil society" organizations.

However, the historical backgrounds of religious orders and groups differentiate them from others—actually putting them in a more advantageous position compared to others—but undermine their ability to be truly autonomous, like voluntary and non-governmental organizations.

The non-governmental nature of secular communities is dubious as well. But it should be noted that what undermines the religious communities' non-governmental nature is how they perceive the state and how they opt to establish relationships with the government. If they can manage to make this relationship more democratic and civilian, religious communities may pave the way for new political and democratic forms in the Muslim world.

Communities and the State[95]

What happens when religious and other communities or associations start to obtain funds from the state via local administrations and the central government, even though they are supposed to operate entirely within the civil sphere?

After winning several municipalities in the 1990s, Welfare Party (RP) officials concluded that contractors or employers can be asked to donate 10 percent of the contract's value to religious communities or foundations upon being awarded public contracts. On coming to office, the ruling Justice and Development Party (AK Party) maintained this practice. Personally, I have raised the following objections to this practice.

First, upon making a 10-percent donation, a contractor will be inclined to earn several times that donation. He will either lower his costs by using low-quality materials or sell his goods or services at a higher price, eventually making the state pay for the losses he suffered by making that donation. The state contains communities with diverse

---

[95] First appeared in *Today's Zaman* on May 12, 2014

religious and philosophical convictions and political views. It is wrong to favor certain communities to the detriment of others, directly or indirectly, and is a violation of their rights.

Second, Islamic communities are by nature "civil," and they thrive on donations from benevolent people, including prescribed purifying alms called *zakat*, charity called *sadaqa*, and other kinds of benefaction. This constitutes their spiritual bounty and social dynamism. Religious movements derive their energy from activities that seek to attain God's pleasure. If religious communities, orders or associations start to thrive on "public resources," albeit indirectly, this will put an end to their dynamism and make them dependent and subordinate to the state. In this process, they lose their quality as civil society organizations (CSOs) and turn into civil public organizations (CPOs).

Third, the state is willing to ensure the limited subordination of religious communities to the state. Thus, these social entities will lose their quality of being "nongovernmental, autonomous and voluntary" organizations and turn into quasi-nongovernmental entities which are, like company trade unions, autonomous in appearance only.

Fourth, the process of winning public contracts necessarily entails irregularity. This is because it is virtually impossible to finish any public contract if the procedures are performed in the way prescribed. The legislation concerning public contracts is so artificial that it forces even the most honest businessman to perform irregularities, albeit at a minimum level, as otherwise he will be unable to complete the contract in time. The state does this intentionally, as then the case files of those businessmen who commit crime by indulging in such irregularities can be stored to be used when needed. The majority of corruption cases in the public sector involve such irregularities. Therefore, when you say, "There is nothing wrong in sidelining foolishly drafted legislation," you indulge in corruption, become entrapped, and the documents are stored in your case file to be used when needed in the future.

Twenty years have passed since many religious communities, associations, foundations, and organizations were subordinated to the state, losing their purity and dynamism and indulging in irregularities. Eventually, religious communities, associations, and foundations have become stripped of their social dynamism and have become unable to make intellectual decisions. They have grown more and more, to the point that they have become metaphorically obese. They have become numb and anesthetized by political power. Yet, Islam's cause is not about money, aid, or donations from the state. It is the cause of upholding morality and justice.

Scornful Stance against Communities: "After Me, the Flood"[96]

When tension between Fethullah Gülen's Hizmet Movement and the ruling Justice and Development Party (AK Party) was high, Deputy Prime Minister Bülent Arınç, in referring to religious communities, said, "We guarantee everything. You exist as long as we exist. You cease to exist when we cease to exist."

In addition to its connection to the actual agenda, these remarks have aspects relating to political sociology as well as recent and ancient experiences in the Muslim world. The question is: Does society determine politics or vice versa? It must be noted that both cases are possible and one can find examples of both cases in history. Excluding the weak monarchies, politics can play a dominant role in determining sociology during times of strong rulers. Monarchies weren't effective at this level as there are ruling elites which play an effective role in the decision-making processes and these elites generally consist of the military, bureaucratic, economic, and religious groups. We know that in ancient Egypt, elite social groups referred to as the "malaa" (chieftains, notables) and "mutraf" (the elites whose affluence of bounty and welfare of life have made them haughty and neglectful, and have caused them to exceed all limits) played a dominant role in the country along with the pharaoh, who saw himself as the "Lord" of Egypt.

The main innovation introduced by Islam to politics is that it declared that God's will does not manifest itself in so-called "sacred" rulers—be it a caliph, sultan, king, shah, president, prime minister, chief, and so on—or in the state as an impersonal artifact; it reduced the government to a simple trade. Thus, "swearing allegiance" (*biat*) is a form of

---

[96] First appeared in *Today's Zaman* on May 26, 2014

trade. A government owes its legitimacy to the nature of provisions which are taken as a reference in the administration, and not to people.

This implies that politics and administration should be developed on sociological grounds. In other words, rulers or politicians cannot determine social life; rather sociology determines politicians. In the final analysis, politics, like economics, can be defined as a social event. Indeed, political sociology studies politics within the context of changing social events. If politics or rulers can determine sociology, then people will adopt the religion of the king.

The movement the AK Party came from initially started as the Necmettin Erbakan-led National Order Party (MNP), in 1969. Thus, it is not even half-a-century old. On the other hand, religious communities and orders—whose existence this movement claims to depend on—are centuries old. Nakşi, Kadiri, Haznevi, Mevlevi, and other orders are extremely old; the Nur movement is almost a century old. These communities and orders survived pressures from rulers, the single-party regime, and implicit or explicit military interventions and tutelage.

Does "social or cultural Islam" owe its existence to the National View (Milli Görüş) or political Islam—which the AK Party has denied any connection to—or vice versa? In my opinion, we can say that these versions of Islam mutually supported each other, and in the early 21st century, they brought the AK Party to power by abandoning their fundamental assumptions.

With the AK Party coming to power, the majority of the adherents of cultural or social Islam were attracted to public positions and resources, and were bound to the state through politics. These religious communities which feed on public resources do not want this government to go, as they can no longer return to their old days of voluntary, civil, and autonomous work. However, those who are able to review their relations with the state, ruling party, and public authorities [thus saving their independently civil nature] may suffer certain losses in this process, but they will be able to stand on their feet again with the very strength in their independence. Yet this very process implies that there are serious problems with our sociology which should determine politics.

Chapter 9

Seeing the Bigger Picture beyond the AKP-Hizmet Row

Reincarnation of the Tutelary Regime's Ancient Reflex[97]

Those who believe that the ongoing crisis in Turkey is a clash between the AK Party government and the Hizmet Movement are focusing only upon one part of the big picture.

If you take a look at the big picture, you will see that we are currently facing a fairly worrisome situation that goes beyond a government-Hizmet row.

Things are slowly being clarified. The key term to describe the ongoing process is "plot." The remark by the prime minister's chief advisor Yalçın Akdoğan, who argued that "a plot has been staged against the military," reveals that what we are observing is actually the tip of a huge iceberg; I am making this argument because this remark led to discussions on holding retrials in the Ergenekon and Balyoz cases; the retrial may include more than 40,000 cases. It should also be noted that many suspects in these cases have already been released. The Ergenekon suspects, for instance, were released shortly after Akdoğan's remark was made, despite the fact that they had been charged with attempting to stage a military coup.

Turkey is a country that was ruled under a tutelage regime when the Committee of Union and Progress (CUP) maintained control of the state. There are domestic and international dimensions to this tutelage.

---

[97] First appeared in *Today's Zaman* on Apr. 14, 2014

In the early 21st century, the Justice and Development Party (AK Party) came to power thanks to the proper international conjecture and alliance and consensus between almost all religious communities. The AK Party is therefore a coalition and an umbrella party that is able to represent different tendencies and groups under the same roof. Turkey has made swift progress, showing a striking performance in the economy and integration with the world.

However, things started to change in 2011; I dedicated some of my previous articles to the external factors of this decline. Of course, external factors are not sufficient to explain it; domestic factors are also important to consider, as they might be determinative. Akdoğan's "plot" remark was a sign that the state was reviving its ancient reflex. I do not think that AK Party figures understand this; they are just following the current debate on the Hizmet-government row; they are simply asked to evaluate the process from this perspective alone.

The state is something that does not trust anybody else and that assumes inherent power. Depending on the conditions of the time, it relies on a different ideology or group to protect itself. But in essence, it exists for itself; those who assume the role of protecting it believe that they seized control of it, but then realize that they are just guardians. The state does not reconcile with anybody; it may take action against a communist, a worker, a Kurd, a Turk, a leftist, a rightist, or an Islamist. The only thing that can control the state is law. Those who are eager to assume a role of protecting the state avoid legal assurances. The state has its own mechanisms, methods and tactics which may be used when necessary. Interestingly, even nationalists who promote the idea of the supremacy of the state and subscribe to state ideology have been severely victimized by state practices in the past. The state may use nationalists against leftists, Sunnis against Alevis, or secularists against religious people, to protect itself. And now, it is pitting religious people against each other.

The core center takes the vital decisions in this country; the center controls the bureaucratic structure, directly or indirectly. They would introduce communism if they considered it the best option; and maybe they will even consider Islamic law as a mode of government in Turkey.

Would you have thought that people who defined themselves as Islamist would defend an interest-based banking system?

The state itself is a community; it exists to sustain its rule and to protect its privileges. You may eliminate a community or movement; those who destroy it replace the former community; but eventually, they will also be destroyed.

Failed Policy![98]

The Justice and Development Party (AK Party) has not adopted Islam as a reference or source of identity in its policies.

Therefore, neither Islam nor Islamism is responsible for its policies. However, it is not possible to argue that at least two variations of Islamist stances are not responsible: those who have made great efforts to come to power and have taken advantage of it at the first opportunity and those who conclude that the secular order can be utilized until Islamist actors gain greater strength.

We can list the reasons for the current state of affairs in Turkey under the rule of the AK Party as follows:

1. They made impossible promises to the US and Israel when they came to power in 2002. Their grave mistake was that they made bold commitments at the beginning; they could have done this mission, but without claiming to represent the Ottoman legacy through leadership of the region. Their ideology, however, did not allow them to do this.

2. After the 2011 elections, they broke their pact with social, intellectual, and political circles; they thought that the AK Party was all about their support base rather than a coalition and that this support base made the AK Party the ruler of the country. They parted ways with democrats and liberals.

3. The common desire of groups supporting the AK Party was a new civilian constitution. The Sept. 12, 2010 referendum, the election of Abdullah Gül as president and the 2011 elections

---

[98] First appeared in *Today's Zaman* on Jun. 16, 2014

confirmed this. However, leading AK Party figures suspended the work of making a new constitution, implying that the current constitution would work for them. Without a new constitution, chronic problems have remained unresolved.

4. No significant improvements have been experienced in social or economic policies. Income inequality is becoming more severe; retired people are having difficult times; the homes of poor people are taken from them as part of urban transformation plans; social cohesion is disrupted. Marriage is no longer popular; a conservative group of consumers has emerged; they have attracted the resentment of the public. There are rumors about corruption, and charges are not effectively investigated.

5. As the AK Party thought that they had become a center-right party, they developed a doctrine by which they decided to generate a ["religious"] community that would stand against the Hizmet Movement, their most constructive partner over the last decade. Initially, the AK Party government decided to shut down the exam preparatory schools; this government attempt was met with a reaction;[99] the AK Party also cooperated with those who want to [put in place the policies of the Committee of Union and Progress and] re-establish the laic order in response to the corruption and bribery operations of Dec. 2013. [While forming this partnership against the Hizmet Movement] they rely on a rhetoric that suggests that the corruption operations wanted to overthrow the government. This is, however, a broad, far-reaching, and influential operation that has been initiated

---

[99] The AK Party government pushed a bill through Parliament earlier in year 2014 to have these privately run prep schools shut down by 2015. The Hizmet Movement runs one-third of the more than 3,500 prep schools that have been in operation for decades as educational institutions which supplement the failing public schools to help students enroll in top-notch colleges and universities. This move to forcefully close these popular prep schools has sparked outrage among millions of parents. After the prep schools, the Erdoğan administration has also begun to clamp down on private schools; an army of inspectors has been sent out to harass students, parents, and school administrators at Hizmet schools as part of his administration's assault on educational institutions.

against all religious groups and communities, including the Hizmet Movement; it is also against religiosity, which was promoted during the AK Party's term in office. They started with [the strongest faith-based movement of] the Hizmet; others are in line.

The AK Party has made huge mistakes; they have taken Turkey to a fairly dangerous point. Every society experiences problems and crises, but proper politics is the art of resolving these problems skillfully.

All Religious Communities Are under Threat[100]

The ruling Justice and Development Party (AK Party) continues to see the graft and bribery investigations of Dec. 17 and 25, 2013 as a plot against its power.

These operations might have targeted the government in some respects, but so far no concrete evidence has been produced about the deliberate, systematic, and willful inclusion of the Hizmet Movement in this plot. It is true that the Hizmet Movement's media group has been lending support to the graft and bribery investigation. In my opinion, their editorial policy might be a bit attenuated. But this editorial policy is not because the media group is a part of the efforts to overthrow the government, but because the government has made moves to shut down prep schools and there is dreadful uncertainty about where the government's operation to destroy the Hizmet Movement will stop. It may be right or wrong, but the Hizmet Movement believes that the government is trying to annihilate it with a grudge.

Certain prominent figures lend credence to this perception. For instance, Hayati Yazıcı, who was a prominent member of the previous Cabinet, said he didn't believe there was a "parallel structure" within the state apparatus and that evidence had to be produced to prove it. Former Interior Minister İdris Naim Şahin, who had worked with Recep Tayyip Erdoğan for 20 years starting with the municipal elections of 1994—and who closely knows the state—does not believe there is any "parallel structure" within the state. As he resigned from his party, he said that the government is under the control of an oligarchic network.

---

[100] First appeared in *Today's Zaman* on Dec. 01, 2014

Ertuğrul Yalçınbayır, one of the founders of the AK Party, called on Erdoğan to ensure that the members of such a network, if any, are found and tried.

There is no doubt that some bureaucrats sympathize with the Hizmet Movement, but this applies to all groups and religious communities. Administrators, particularly governors, general directors, other public authorities, and even ministers are affiliated with some religious community or order. This is quite normal. What is not normal is civil servants abiding by the instructions of the leaders of their religious communities or orders, using their offices for unlawful purposes or taking part in conspiracies against the government. What should be done? If there is any conspiracy against the government, this should be investigated and prosecuted within the confines of the legal system. However, the government has been reshuffling about 10,000 civil servants without any proof or legal action. The government is implementing a collective and vengeful punishment on a specific community.

As for the investigations of Dec. 17 and 25, there may or may not be a deliberate plan behind them, but this should be investigated by the court. The suspects cannot be exonerated from the charges even if there is conspiracy behind those charges, and the ongoing efforts to refrain from engaging the judicial process will surely undermine the prestige of AK Party circles—regardless of whether they deserve it or not. However, the corruption, the government's "parallel structure" rhetoric (in an effort to cover up the corruption investigations), the incidents regarding the semitrailers (carrying the government's aid to the armed radical groups in Syria in order to topple the Assad regime), and the like, are being used effectively by some internal and external forces. Thus, seeds of hostility have been sown within the government, the Hizmet Movement, and other religious communities, and no one accepts the corruption charges.

Turkey and the Middle East are going through radical changes. There is a global and regional operation targeting religious groups. The aim is to purge all religious groups from public institutions. This purge is being conducted with coups or by abusing existing legislation. Over time, it has become clear that this operation is not restricted to the Hizmet Movement, but targets all religious groups and communities. The ancient forces within the state have seized the initiative once again. At the end of the process, everyone will lose.

The State Restores Itself![101]

The state restores itself periodically. The military interventions of Apr. 27, 1960, Mar. 12, 1971, and Sept. 12, 1980, as well as the post-modern coup of Feb. 28, 1997, are examples of such a restoration.

Many believed that the Feb. 28 post-modern coup was the last of these operations, but they were wrong. In Turkey, restoration of the state implies a reduction of democracy. This is because this restoration is performed not by the public, but by the state itself. Our state has reflexes to protect itself against the public. The state always sees a threat against itself. In the 1970s, this threat came from anarchists and communists. The coup of Sept. 12, 1980 purged them in a bloody manner. In the 1990s, the National Vision (Milli Görüş) supporters and religious people penetrated the state. They were trodden down by the post-modern coup of Feb. 28, 1997.

With the disintegration of the Soviet Union, communists were no longer a threat to the state. Kurdish nationalists and separatists seem to be relatively at ease as they are part of and party to the settlement process since 2009. The coup of Feb. 28, 1997 saw *irtica* (reactionaryism)[102] as its primary threat, but the state lacked the possibility of restoring itself with other groups and it chose to submit itself to the conservative religious groups who were hungry for power and had domesticated themselves. In the early 21st century, the global powers' plans for the region overlapped with the religious groups' quest for power. They kicked off a new period by making an agreement, explicitly or implicitly.

---

[101] First appeared in *Today's Zaman* on May 05, 2014

[102] *İrtica* (or reactionaryism) literally means returning to the dark, olden times. It has long been used as a smear word lobbed at religious "reactionaries," thus trying to take a stranglehold of all religious people and groups and depriving them of all legitimacy.

In 2002, the state was sandwiched between external reform pressures and internal social dynamics for change and had no place to go. It delivered itself to the Justice and Development Party (AK Party), which had declared its divorce from political Islamism. The ruling AK Party emerged as a coalition of all religious groups. Currently, however, both global powers and the central core inside Turkey concluded that the religious groups have gone beyond the limits and scope set for them and that the state organs have started to exhibit a religious character. The new threat was coded as the Hizmet Movement, which encourages Turkey's democratization.

The external and internal powers see three threat categories: (a) the Hizmet Movement, (b) the AK Party, and (c) other religious congregations, groups, and organizations. Although the state is focused on the Hizmet Movement, it targets not only this movement but also all religious communities.

To summarize, the state restores itself. It uses the previous victim as its tool before discarding it, later after having used it for its purposes. The victims of the Sept. 12 coup were the leftists, and the state used them as a tool in the postmodern coup of Feb. 28, 1997. The Workers' Party (İP), the leading actor of this coup, had rallied in Istanbul with placards reading, "Let the laws of Atatürk's revolutions be implemented [against religious groups]" in January 1997, but they were later imprisoned. They were released from prison only recently. The victims of Feb. 28 were Islamists and religious people. Some of them abandoned the "Islamism" ideology to adopt a conservative identity and they purged the actors and juntas of the Feb. 28 coup. In this way, the state was restored.

Someone is making the groups—which are believed to add an extra, unwanted religious character to the state affairs—clash with each other. Those who are scared of the specter of a "parallel state" are advised to ally with the coup-perpetrators who are assumed to have become domesticated.

Obviously, there is a delicate engineering effort going on. If this plan works, first the Hizmet Movement, then the AK Party, and finally all religious communities will be purged. There is only one way to rectify the state: To make it abide by the rule of law, not to take over the state.

The Meaning of This Crisis[103]

In the wake of the Dec. 17 and 25 bribery and corruption operations, the faction led by President Recep Tayyip Erdoğan has directed two main unfounded accusations at the Hizmet Movement: a) that the Hizmet Movement has become involved in a plot constructed by foreign powers—notably, the US and Israel—with the aim of overthrowing the elected government of Turkey, and b) that the Hizmet Movement has gone all the way into people's bedrooms with its wiretaps.

Though an entire year has passed since these original accusations were made, there is still no sign of any concrete proof to back these claims, thus failing to convince anyone. Renata Sommer, a European parliamentarian and member of the Christian Democratic Union, asserts, in her capacity as a member of the EU-Turkey Joint Parliamentary Committee, that allegations of a coup attempt against the Ankara government are ridiculous. As Sommer also notes, there are simply no documents to back these claims.

In addition, the police officers arrested in connection with the wiretaps have not even been asked a single question in relation to espionage. As far as these "illegal wiretaps," the suspects have underscored two arguments: "The wiretaps are completely legal, and our chiefs and the top-level officers all knew all about them!"

The vast majority of Justice and Development Party (AK Party) members, however, do not believe these allegations, and yet traces of the Hizmet Movement have ironically been sought under every stone, while both the government corruption and the transition of the southeastern Anatolian region into a federation are being covered up. At the same time, the operation against the Hizmet Movement is being used as a strategic move to hijack public awareness from both of the issues ahead of the coming general elections.

There are of course sympathizers of the forty-year-old Hizmet Movement. When the AK Party came to power in 2002, it took advantage of help from the Hizmet Movement, both to help close the gaps in the AK Party in terms of personnel as well as to ward off expected coup

---

[103] First appeared in *Today's Zaman* on Jan. 05, 2015

attempts. In the meantime, quite a few coup attempts were revealed. Even if there were occasional legal violations [during this process]— and these of course cannot be ignored—to say that there were truly no coup attempts, to say that there were no military takeovers, to say that there weren't thousands that simply went missing, to say that the country wasn't been shaken by assassinations, to say that there weren't junta-type organizations that had taken root in the Turkish military, all of this would make even a child laugh.

The stark reality is that this country has seen coups, has had its Parliament disbanded, has seen its Constitution shelved and has seen hundreds of thousands suffer gravely. Some measures were taken against the tutelage regime. But if precautions had been taken against this tutelage regime to the full extent, Turkey might have turned out to be a state of law.

Two important developments occurred that derailed this democratic process: One was Ankara's 2011 attempt to try to gain power and authority in the Middle East by overthrowing the regime in Syria via a "neo-Ottoman ideology," and the other was the revelations of the government corruption and bribery.

From the very start of all of this I have believed that these operations were NATO-centered. There are certainly those who know this in the government, that the Hizmet Movement is being used as an instrument. In the meantime, this message is being given [by the government] to those carrying out these operations: "If you are going to harm us, we will create absolute chaos. We will burn down the country and then turn it over to you. And just look, that's what we're doing!"

On the other hand, the AK Party, which has been isolated, has tried to find its savior in cooperation with the clandestine Ergenekon group as well as by leaning on Abdullah Öcalan. The support from these two factions has been provided granted "Erdoğan finishes off the Hizmet Movement."

Thus it is that, unfortunately, the AK Party has formed an alliance with Ergenekon supporters and the Kurdistan Workers' Party (PKK), who want to take revenge on the Hizmet Movement. The AK Party has actually been taken hostage. If the Hizmet Movement is targeted by a blow, one can be certain that next in line will be the AK Party and the other religious communities.

Moral Degeneration and Corruption[104]

Turkey has been experiencing shockwaves from the debate over the graft and bribery investigation and coup charges.

Every incident leaves some residue in us. This residue may be negative or positive depending on our position regarding the incident at hand. This country has seen numerous fights, wars, struggles for power, and conflicts. The current tension will come to an end eventually. The sponge will release the water it has absorbed. We should focus on the residue left behind in the sponge. If we fail to clean up the harmful deposits, the sponge will ossify.

The tension between the ruling Justice and Development Party (AK Party) and the Hizmet Movement has exposed a certain weakness within the country: moral collapse. It is certain that there have been corrupt practices and acts of bribery (prevalent in the AK Party government)— as substantiated by safe-deposit boxes, millions of dollars and euros in cash, expensive watches, ministers forced to resign, and audio recordings posted on the Internet, among other things.

There are some people who claim that all of this corruption evidence is fake, forged, and unfounded. The number of these people is not high. There are also others who concentrate only upon the timing of the investigation, asking, "OK, but why now?" You could only gape in astonishment when you see still many others who fall in the category that ironically say, "Everyone steals, but these guys do work!"

The people in the last two groups attest to the presence of corrupt practices and acts of bribery. Actually, corruption is acknowledged by an overwhelming majority, excluding a small group. The people in this majority tend to raise objections to the investigation, questioning its timing and rationale.

---

[104] First appeared in *Today's Zaman* on Dec. 08, 2014

The fact that these objections are raised by "religious and conservative" groups is proof of profound decadence within society. Imagine a Muslim who says, "OK, I accept that there is corruption, but why is it being investigated now? So I gather there is ill-intention behind this investigation."

All corrupt practices will eventually be questioned. When should prosecutors take action? Should they act when corrupt executives allow them to proceed with the investigation? The scandalous bit: Those who raise objections to the graft investigation refrain from questioning the deeds of corrupt politicians. Normally, a Muslim is supposed to exhibit the following attitude in all circumstances: All allegations of corruption must be investigated immediately.

"Everyone steals. Is there anyone who does not steal?" This objection constitutes the most scandalous form of disgrace. It amounts to saying, "We, too, may steal." If voters continue to support the ruling party despite the allegations of corruption—the investigation into which has been obstructed—does this mean that corruption is legitimate? Even if 99 percent of society voted for the corrupt government, this does not make corruption legitimate.

Elections and democratic processes do not exonerate politicians who are charged with corruption. Democratic support for corrupt politicians is portent only of the moral weakness of a society. "Even if the audio recordings are true, no one believes them," the AK Party MP and lawmaker Burhan Kuzu said, with apparent reliance on this weakness. Even if there is a "political conspiracy" involved, does this legitimize the crime?

Once I was at a barbershop in İskenderpaşa, Istanbul. A man with no connection to the Islamic community entered. "This time, I will vote for Necmettin Erbakan's Welfare Party [RP]," he said angrily. "Is it really you saying this? The RP is not your type," the barber teased him. "This Republican People's Party [CHP] does not work, but it steals. The Motherland Party [ANAVATAN] works, but it steals. The RP is the party of honest people. They will work and won't steal," the man snapped back.

One of the RP's five political promises was "to ensure moral integrity and cleanse the public sector of corruption." We are now in the year 2014. Ironically, all the conservative people can say about the corrupt practices of the current administration is, "Even if the corruption charges were true, voters wouldn't believe them." Or they say, "Is there any party that does not steal? The current one steals, but works in return."

Now, religious people who are supposed to be honest and reliable have become dirty. When religious people become dirty, this damages the prestige of religion as well. If religious people can tolerate corrupt practices with such justifications, this is a sign of the greatest disaster that can befall society. Apparently, there is permanent damage to the foundational roots of our society.

The Shocking Waste of Concerted Efforts[105]

The Battle of Jamal, where two Muslim figures who were very close to Prophet Muhammad (pbuh)—Ali, the Prophet's son-in-law and Aisha, the Prophet's wife—faced off, is one of the few topics that depresses my soul.

Historians provide different figures, but it is certain that at least 5,000 people died in this meaningless battle. One cannot know which side to praise or blame.

On one side was Ali, who was the son of the Prophet's uncle and the first youth to become a Muslim, as well as the Prophet's son-in-law and a distinguished Companion of the Prophet. He came to be known as the Lion of God. On the other side was Aisha, who was the Prophet's dear wife, well-versed in Islamic jurisprudence. Was the confrontation between these two prominent figures really worth it? It is known that both of the Companions suffered deep internal trauma after the incident. But what was done was done. I might be wrong, but it occurs to me that if the Jamal tragedy (656 CE) hadn't occurred, the Battle of Siffin (657 CE) would not have occurred either, and Mu'awiya ibn Abi Sufyan and Banu Umayyad would not have turned the caliphate into a sultanate so easily. Moreover, Hussain, the beloved grandson of the Prophet, would not have been martyred (661 CE), and this tragedy wouldn't have left such a deep scar, which couldn't be healed for ages.

---

[105] First appeared in *Today's Zaman* on Feb. 24, 2014

The Muslim world is fragmented. Sectarian and ethnic clashes are everywhere. Perhaps secularists, leftists, socialists, liberals, and nationalists are rejoicing over the apparent failure of religious prescriptions and over the justification and validation of their nonreligious (or secular) perspective. Still, they are part of this world, where clashes and wars abound. If the fire cannot be contained, it may engulf the entire neighborhood. And Turkey is not safe from this risk of fire. Turkey's return to the Middle East after a hiatus of 100 years gave rise to great enthusiasm and hopes. The revolts that erupted in Tunisia, Egypt, and many Middle Eastern countries came as a shock to Turkey. Syria was a turning point. Everything was reversed.

The critical problems that must be resolved at once in the region are polarization and conflict. Sectarian groups, nations that privilege specific ethnic identities, states that idolize their national interests, and religious communities and groups that cannot withstand the dissent and bickering taking place, all become polarized. We are in a state of chaos in which we will eventually find ourselves longing for the salvation of the Greater Middle East Project. An intellectual/political framework has already been drawn up, and we, as Sunnis, Shiites, Alevis, Kurds, Turks, Arabs, Persians, secularists, women's rights activists, civil society organizations (CSOs) and religious communities and orders, are unable to extinguish this fire.

We are living under the West's guardianship. Our roadmap is being drawn by the big guns of the past and the global powers of today. For the first time in history, during the first decade of the 21st century, external pressures and internal demands have forced the Turkish state to change, although it originally promised not to distance itself from the West's guardianship. During the last 10 years, there were good developments that gave Turkey a significant push. We know that political, social, and cultural Muslim identities are behind this significant achievement. The energy that has accumulated in these three identities has put the country into motion. None out of the ruling Justice and Development Party (AK Party), or religious communities, intellectual groups, and Muslim intellectuals could have done this alone. All labored together and contributed to the success. The achievements between 2002 and 2013 were the product of 90 years of patience and labor.

Parties, religious communities and intellectuals should not act against their raison d'être. The raisons d'être of the ruling party, the communities, and the intellectuals are justice, service, and wisdom, respectively. The current tension in Turkey has the potential to harm the general public. We need to find a new synergy in which everyone will exist in peace and live according to mutual consensus. Jamal is followed by Siffin and Karbala.

Collective Punishment[106]

The ruling Justice and Development Party (AK Party) is preparing for a comprehensive crackdown.

If he can secure sufficient electoral support at the local polls slated for March 30, 2014, Prime Minister Recep Tayyip Erdoğan will not only purge members of the Hizmet Movement from the bureaucracy, but will also try to halt its activities in the media, finance, education, and other sectors. AK Party Istanbul deputy Burhan Kuzu announced he has submitted to the prime minister a list of 2,000 people who will be detained.

Those who suggest that members of the Hizmet Movement must be purged from public institutions justify their position by saying members of the movement receive their orders from their leader and not from their superiors. However, I should note that the problem is not about the failure of the members of the Hizmet Movement to obey orders from their superiors in the public service, but about the unfounded claim that the prosecutors and police chiefs who conducted the graft and bribery investigation are members of the Hizmet Movement—a claim which has yet to be proven. Still, I will try to critically discuss relations between the Hizmet Movement (and other faith-inspired movements and communities) and the bureaucracy.

First, any public servant who is a member of a faith-inspired movement or community is required to obey orders from their superior. If a public servant attempts to use the public resources and authorities avail-

---

[106] First appeared in *Today's Zaman* on Mar. 17, 2014

able to them to promote the interests of their own religious community or movement, then this creates problems.

Second, a community with a certain political ideology may engage in political activity or try to influence political processes within a well-defined sphere. But if it tries to manipulate the bureaucracy for political gains, this indicates a problematic approach as this means "unfair competition" against other communities or groups, and abuse of powers and resources of the executive branch of the state, which is accountable to the public for its actions.

You may find the first argument "problematic" and the second "rightful." Indeed, those who voice these objections tend to portray the Turkish Republic as a state free from any ideologies or value judgments, which is clearly not the case. Given its historical roots, centuries-old experience, and modern version, the state sees itself as a religious community per se. In the Ottoman Empire, the dynasty was the possessor of the country or the estate, and it was a small community of familial and blood relations. When the Turkish Republic was established, this dynasty was purged and replaced with a community of founding fathers. In this tradition, a specific community or group in the bureaucracy tends to see itself as the community or potential possessor—owner, even—of the state. The presence of a community within the state is even perceived as security.

Given the political tradition from which it came—Milli Görüş (National View), its founding members, the fashion in which senior politicians communicate with each other, and its responses to the outside world—the AK Party gives the impression of being a "community" in the final analysis. Indeed, Erdoğan referred to President Abdullah Gül as his "brother" when he nominated him for the presidency. "Our ties go beyond a brotherly relationship," they are quick to note when referring to a potential competition in the future. These reactions do not fall into the category of "individual" relations, which are considered normal in liberal democracies.

Furthermore, it must be noted that when certain public servants are being purged on charges of being members of a specific community, we see them being replaced with members of other communities. This problem will continue to haunt us unless we make our state one that is built on justice.

Here is a more important problem: Suppose a bureaucrat who is a member of a specific community or movement fails to comply with the orders of their superiors. In this case, the political authority is of course entitled to remove that bureaucrat from office under administrative law. But to use the failure of some bureaucrats to comply with orders as a pretext for purging thousands of bureaucrats in all public institutions and penalizing many trade firms and organizations would be to collectively punish individual offenses.

Social Opposition[107]

The social explosions and upheavals in Egypt, Brazil, and Indonesia have come to a point where they need to be analyzed from the perspective of political sociology: In cases where the political opposition organized in accordance with the law fails to stand against elected governments, a new type of opposition emerges. Of course, political parties are inalienable parts of a democratic parliamentary regime. However, the social explosions over the last few years point to another option, a new type of opposition that goes beyond organized political parties; I believe that this could be properly called social opposition.

This new style of opposition, which I refer to as social opposition, has four major characteristics.

1. This type of opposition does not resort to negative politics, which justifies violence and terrorism. The armed opposition waged by the Kurdistan Workers' Party (PKK), a leading example of negative political opposition, has cost more than 40,000 lives.

2. Social opposition does not belong in the same category as legal political parties. In other words, social opposition does not emerge in the form of a political party or a political party identity. For this reason, remarks or suggestions by members of the ruling AK Party inviting the representatives of this type of oppo-

---

[107] First appeared in *Today's Zaman* on Mar. 10, 2014

sition to form a political party are not meaningful, because social opposition does not form political parties.

3. Social opposition is issue-oriented; it has micro and concrete reactions, rather than long-term, political goals.

4. Social opposition does not seek to come to power; its main goal is to issue warnings to the political opposition so that it does not make any mistakes. When the voice of social opposition is heard and its demands fulfilled, its members abandon their opposition and return to their original and natural functions.

This shows that social opposition, in terms of its emergence, is of social character rather than political. If it occasionally raises political demands, it is because of a crisis in representative democracy. In addition to crises of representation, democracy's failure to recognize socio-cultural plurality and diversity makes this sort of opposition inevitable. It should also be noted that political administrations that control legislative and executive bodies between elections sometimes make laws that run contrary to the demands and expectations of their supporters. In such cases, the political administration, assuming that it represents the will and well-being of the people, defies society, which is the real power behind the regime.

If we review the recent developments in Turkey over the last few months [following the break of the unprecedented government corruption scandal] from the lens of this conceptual framework, we will see that social opposition is more influential than political opposition parties and groups. By relying on the Sunni tradition, religious people, for the first time in our near past, are reacting to the Justice and Development Party (AK Party) government, to which they had extended overwhelming support, over its approaches to the prep school issue and the corruption probe. Their reaction is issue-oriented and concrete. But unlike secular forms of opposition, this sort of opposition is being staged by the figures and actors of "social Islam." This is a first in the political history of this nation: Social Islam staging an issue-based opposition. It is also interesting to underline another characteristic of this instance of social opposition: A person, Fethullah Gülen, who adheres to the tradition of civilian scholarship inspired by Abu Hanifa and relies on the precepts and rules of the mainstream Sunni tradition as well as the main references of Islam, the Qur'an and the Sunnah, is orchestrating this reaction and opposition.

Outdated Anachronism: The Perplexity of the AK Party[108]

One way to understand the ongoing tension between the ruling Justice and Development Party (AK Party) and the Hizmet Movement (aka the Gülen Community) is to look at the past.

Our historical heritage seems to continue to haunt us. In the Ottoman Empire, the state was at the center of political and administrative life, and the Ottoman territories were the estate of the sultan and the sultan's dynasty. The sultan did not accept partners when it came to his estate. In order to prevent potential attempts to seize this estate, the military and civil bureaucrats were specifically selected from converts. The mothers of the princes were usually non-Muslim women. Thanks to the fact that the civic sphere was safeguarded by Islamic law (*sharia*), this system functioned without disturbing the subjects for many centuries. Of course, sultans had occasional rivals. There were no clashes among peasants, workers, and other social classes, but local lords (*beys*) revolted against the Ottoman state from time to time.

The Ottoman state adopted the following methods for confronting these lords: They would first be given major posts within the state apparatus. Some lords were even allowed to become viziers. This method generally worked because the lord and his followers abandoned their challenge against the state. If it was impossible to stop the lord by granting him a state position, then the Ottoman state would support "rival lords" (in today's discourse, rival religious communities) against the lord who had revolted. If the competition ended up with a victory by those lords who were financed by the sultan, this meant that the sultan's estate, i.e., the country, was secured. If a formidable lord emerged and defied the rival lords backed by the sultan, then the sultan's last resort was to behead the lord and confiscate his estate, which was risky. But property was also confiscated if it belonged to those who committed crimes,

---

[108] First appeared in *Today's Zaman* on Mar. 11, 2014

revolted against the state, were implicated in corruption, or wronged their subjects.

This method is understandable only through the lens of history. The use of this method in the nation states of modern times or in the new political cultures of the postmodern era is anachronistic, and it perplexes ruling elites about what time they are living in.

The nation state has to delegate part of its sovereignty to (a) local identities and units (e.g., the current state of the Kurdish issue and the reforms regarding this process); (b) global powers (economic policies are regulated according to the requirements of the global economy and metropolitan cities are shaped according to global capital); (c) regional integration (e.g., the roadmap of administrative and legal reforms is shaped within the European Union membership process); and (d) "civil society."

The state can no longer control the estate in its entirety. As a matter of fact, society and politics cannot be perceived as an "estate." Thus, civil forces and communities want to be influential over decision-making mechanisms related to political processes and public polices, not over the state. This is a necessity but, unfortunately, the state of the Turkish Republic has inherited the Ottoman Empire's estate policy and sees itself as the sole owner and possessor of the estate or the country. And it sees any emerging partners as its rivals and adopts a communal identity.

Upon coming to power after establishing a coalition of groups and communities, the AK Party was supposed to introduce a social and legal framework. However, starting in 2011, AK Party sought to get rid of all of its partners and possess power as a single force.

Although it is unacceptable and improper for religious communities and orders to act as an embodiment of the "executive" branch, they are extremely right in wanting to influence the decision-making mechanisms and processes, because this is essential for fair and consent-based functioning of the system. If this cannot be correctly understood by the Turkish state, this anachronism will trigger social conflicts, and the masters of the state apparatus will pave the way for injustice.

Tyrannical State Philosophy[109]

The purpose of legitimate politics is to govern within a legitimate framework and administer justice.

A brief look at our distant and recent political history can teach us why rightist/conservative political movements tend to eventually lose electoral backing and fall from power. The political ideology that we supported since the 1970s suggested it would create a style of politics, based on sound Islamic values, that would refrain from indulging in corruption and bribery, lend additional protection to the poor and weak, establish social peace in the broadest sense, and, if it came to power, implement a fair administration without discrimination against diverse religions, sects, professions, philosophical convictions, or segments of society. This was what distinguished the Islamist political movement from the rightist/conservative ideologies. The expectation was that this movement would enable Turkey to reconcile with its past, close the gap between Turkey and other Muslim societies and push the social center into power, thereby dispelling the curse that has been haunting us for the last 200 years. Politicians and administrators with conspicuous Muslim identities would not step into the traps of the past, but would take into consideration the general course of the world and Turkey's emerging political culture.

The outcome has been, however, tragic and dreadful. Despite its strong Muslim identity, the ruling Justice and Development Party (AK Party) is regressing more aggressively than the rightist/conservative political movements and trying to revive the shameful practices of the past.

Please have a look at the following quotes:

"Neither God nor the state accepts partners" (Justice Minister Bekir Bozdağ).

"Some of the reflexes our state has developed are quite spine-chilling...This is just a reminder," an adviser to the prime minister said, referring to certain extrajudicial methods the state used in the past to finish

---

[109] First appeared in *Today's Zaman* on May 19, 2014

off its enemies. Another adviser (Yalçın Akdoğan ironically) defines legal measures against the coup attempts—which helped to push back military tutelage to a certain extent—as "a conspiracy against the national army."

"We will drive you out of this country and clean you out of the state apparatus by force and never heed your cries," AK Party Erzurum deputy Muhyettin Aksak threatened a spokesperson who made a public statement in the name of 70 civil society organizations. But Foreign Minister Ahmet Davutoğlu's remarks were the most bloodcurdling of all: "We have state traditions. This was also the case in the Ottoman Empire. Many people were sacrificed for the state. Likewise, we cannot accept a structure that might harm the state. We won't allow anyone to seize control of the state."

These remarks indicate how a Muslim mentality can readily accommodate a tyrannical state philosophy. In the Ottoman Empire, the country (state) belonged to the dynasty, and any prince from this dynasty was entitled to claim ownership of the country. If anyone was believed to be challenging the dynasty, he would be beheaded immediately. Let me ask: Does the state belong to a dynasty, according to the Islamic perspective? To whom does the state belong today? Does a political party that was elected to office on a temporary basis see itself as a dynasty, so that it mentions royal fratricide in the context of protecting the state? From whom does a ruling party that is in office now and might fall from power in a few years protect the state, which is the common property of all? How is a state protected? With these (current) illegal and extrajudicial methods? Should we also be talking about attempts to repeal the Constitution, dissolve Parliament, start an armed insurrection, or assassinate someone?

It is tragic to observe that our old tradition, which allowed politically justified killing to be employed to maintain power, has risen from the grave in conservative minds. The concepts of justice, freedom, and fairness have been replaced by security and customary law. Islamic principles and governing provisions have been forgotten. The Mughal state tradition, the customary law of Genghis Khan, Byzantine palace politics, and the Arabic right to the sword have become fashionable in politics. This wasn't the point we originally aimed to get to.

The Beginning of 2015[110]

Turkey is entering 2015 by moving toward an authoritarian regime. On a Middle Eastern scale, authoritarian regimes are autocratic. In a monarchy, a monarch holds all the power in his hand, and the right to rule is passed from father to son. This does not happen in autocracies, but all power is held by one man or organ.

Those who now want to create an autocratic regime in Turkey first argue that a coup was staged against their rule so they can repress this so-called coup (that actually does not exist) to remove all obstacles in creating an authoritarian and autocratic regime. When a regime becomes authoritarian and autocratic, it not only intimidates its opponents and rivals, but it also controls all sorts of dissidence and opposition, abolishes freedom of speech and avoids accountability. Unfortunately, Turkey is moving in this direction. Therefore, those who now remain indifferent to the operations carried out against a certain group [i.e. the Hizmet] will become targets of similar operations themselves in the future.

Polarization is a major characteristic of autocratic and authoritarian regimes. And sadly, Turkey is suffering gravely from this problem now; there are huge tensions between different social groups because of alienation and polarization. We have a heterogeneous society and areas for potential clashes. Up until now, potential conflicts were avoided thanks to the calmness of the parties, mutual compromises and the democratic nature of the political system. However, two important developments may break the fault lines and stimulate clashing: reliance on polarization and a language of conflict in political activities; and ethnic and sectarian clashes in Iraq and Syria turning into civil wars.

Turkey's human geography is not independent from these two neighboring countries, where clashes have become severe. What happens in Iraq and Syria may also happen in our country as well—it could start and never be stopped.

The settlement process on the Kurdish issue has come to a critical juncture. We have no idea about the content of the agreements and negotiations between Kurdistan Workers' Party (PKK) leader Abdullah

---

[110] First appeared in Today's Zaman on Jan. 12, 2015

Öcalan and the state. Of course, the fundamental rights of the Kurds should be recognized immediately without any prejudice. But if both autonomy for the eastern and southeastern parts of Turkey and a new status for the region are being broached, this raises some major issues because it goes well beyond the powers of the government and the PKK in the process.

If a new (geo-political) status is to be introduced, the views of the non-Kurds in the region—as well as the religious, secular, liberal and nationalist Kurds who do not subscribe to PKK ideology and policies—should be considered. Perhaps it would not be possible to preserve a unitary state model in the rest of the country if a certain part of the country gained autonomy. Maybe a federation could be introduced in the future, but this cannot be done without the consent of the social groups I have cited above.

It has been a year since the corruption and graft operations of Dec. 17 and 25, 2013. There are incessant attempts to cover up and seal the whole investigation, but a substantial proportion of the population firmly believes that corruption took place. In fact, government members confirm this. Failures to investigate the allegations also raise suspicions. Increasing authoritarianism may delay the prosecution of corruption, but this will never exonerate those who were involved in corruption and bribery. On the contrary, as society and the media are silenced, there will be more suspicions. Any government failing to be transparent and accountable will have to deal with these deep suspicions all the time.

Chapter 10

National–Transnational
Problems and Prospects

State Elites' Perception of the Middle East[111]

Despite some reservations and possible criticisms, it is fair to argue that Turkey's ongoing policies, vis-à-vis the Arab world, are stable and consistent with the message being delivered in recent years.[112] Of course, stability and consistency do not always mean they are ultimately proper.

The Islamic world has suffered increasingly from western colonialism or indirect exploitation, (in the aftermath of the Ottomans' withdrawal from the Middle East) following the years of the foundation of the republican regime in Turkey. This being the general picture, when we focus on the history of the bilateral relations between Turkey and the Arab states, we can see that it was based on two key policies. First, Turkey paid the

---

[111] First appeared in *Today's Zaman* on May 16, 2011

[112] There was a fundamental paradigm shift in this stable and consistent Turkish foreign policy in 2011—the year this article was written. When the demonstrations began in Syria like the ones in Tunisia and Egypt during the Arab Spring, the Erdoğan government made a complete strategy change in Turkey's foreign policy. For example, Erdoğan abandoned his policy of engagement with the Syrian President Assad. The government rushed to politically engineer Syria by supporting the opponent armed groups there, instead of persuading Assad, who was indeed listening to Turkey at the time and carrying out reforms by taking Turkey as a model—to introduce more reforms over a long period of time. Turkey could have kept engaging with the region using its soft, democratizing power and could thus have had a say in bringing about order in the region. But Turkey failed due to the AK Party's strange reversal of policy in the region starting in the year 2011.

utmost care to not become involved in regional disputes; second, it took action on matters that concerned the Middle East only after the Arabs had done something. In fact, even these two major considerations were not honored all the time. For instance, Turkey took action before the Arabs in the UN session where Israel's independence was voted on. With respect to the Algerian war of independence, Turkish politicians adopted a premature stance that put them in a delicate position because of which they had to apologize. Yet it is fair to argue that the two policies were preserved. During the Gulf crisis, then President Turgut Özal sought to change this concept by replacing it with active intervention, but he failed.

However, it has become evident that Turkey is unable to stick to these two major principles because of the huge transformations affecting the Middle East region, including the Iranian Islamic revolution, the removal of Cold War tensions, and regional conflicts and social upheavals. Turkey's disappointment with its EU membership bid seems to have played a defining role in this change as well.

There is one concrete fact that no one can ignore: Regardless of its political, economic, and military relations with the West, Turkey is a country in the Mideast region. Inevitably, it is affected and influenced by any major development in the region. A wave of wind blowing there may create the effect of a hurricane in Turkey.

The military intervention in Cyprus in 1974 and the outbreak of armed attacks by the Kurdistan Workers' Party (PKK) in 1984 may be cited as two major reasons for Turkey to review its conventional Arab policy. Syria's failure to include the Kurds in the political and socioeconomic system contributes to the PKK's fight against Turkey as it becomes able to recruit a greater number of militants. It could be argued that up until recent political and social popular reactions, Turkey has parted ways with the Arab world as evidenced by its deliberate actions to ignore regional realities and priorities. Due to this state of ignorance, Turkey has been unable to communicate with other regional actors. This has been what the pro-Western Kemalist elite have actually wanted all along. However, it appears that this was not a proper preference. This disconnect with the outside world has caused a neurotic trauma; this applies to states as well. The political balance and social dynamics of the Middle East are going through an enormous transformation, changing the status the international order has chosen for the region into a different concept. At this point, it looks like Egypt and Iran will stand upfront, becoming major actors able to have a determinative role in the region's future.

It should be noted that if it seeks to become a strong, influential, and respected state in the region, Turkey needs to consider the potential Iranian sphere of influence in the Middle East region and to maintain ties with the Arab world. This means that in order to achieve this goal, Turkey should improve its economic and political relations, and carefully review and reconsider Western-style solutions and recommendations before aligning with them. Of course, the mental background of this is completely psychological, and a radical paradigm shift is needed to change this psychology. Above all, the Turkish elite have to reconsider their perception of the region and the Arab people.

Paradigm Shift: Motherly Role in the Middle East[113]

On Apr. 12-13, 2010, a Turkish president visited Oman for the first time in 13 years. I accompanied President Abdullah Gül on his visit. This trip to Oman was organized as part of the relationship developed with Arab countries in general and Gulf countries in particular. According to the president, the Arab Middle East has ascribed three important missions to Turkey in recent years.

First, Turkey is a big country and politically effective. If it uses its power properly, more precisely if it uses it fairly and in favor of regional countries, it could have a positive impact on solving many conflicts and problems. Everyone in the Arab world, from political leaders and intellectuals to the general public and academics, closely follows Turkey. Their expectations from Turkey increase by the day.

Second, Turkey plays a critical role in the security dimension. Dialogue between Gulf countries has been continuing as part of "strategic cooperation agreements." Regional countries believe Turkey's new regional policy is integral to ensuring security and continuing stability.

---

[113] First appeared in *Today's Zaman* on Apr. 16, 2010

Third, Turkey has significant economic potential. It is a country whose gross national product (GNP) is increasing even though it does not have natural resources. Arab countries rich in natural resources such as oil and natural gas find it valuable to observe the performance Turkey is putting out basically through the power of labor.

In order for the new foreign policy Turkey has launched to be beneficial to everyone, diligence is required in some areas. The West and those who look at the developments from the perspective of the West's economic, military, and political interests seek to predicate Turkey's entry into the region on two targets: breaking Iran's influence and achieving what America could not achieve with crude/military power through "soft power opportunities and means" instead. A portion of regional actors that are in a historical and sectarian competition with each other may be pleased with this kind of a mission. But if Turkey enters the region with this purpose, it will jeopardize its legitimacy. When we look at the views and expectations of the Muslim public, we see that their expectations are different.

Despite the propaganda that has been spread, the region's fears do not involve Iran. Even though the official tone is wary over Iran's insistence on carrying out an energy program, the public and intellectuals who can assess incidents independent of international forces argue that presenting "Iran as a threat" does not reflect the truth. In this context, perceiving Turkey as a sort of "competitor to Iran or a wave breaker to its development" and interpreting Turkey's new foreign policy with this perspective is leading to the awakening of deep suspicions. It would be a big disaster for Turkey to be perceived as "a country entering the region on behalf of the West."

An Omani businessman with whom I spoke said, "Turkey needs to turn towards the region. It needs to gather us around itself like a mother." I thought it was interesting that this person used the "mother" metaphor instead of a "father" metaphor. To be able to understand the process the region is in, it's important to understand the social and psychological backdrop. Countries in the region and the Muslim world in general are being insulted by the West, their lands are being occupied, innocent civilians are being killed, historic works are being plundered, natural resources are being stolen and, as if that is not enough, Islam and Muslims are being presented as factors to be feared and that threaten global stability and peace. The use of model mosques by British troops when practicing their firearm skills, the use of civilian targets as entertainment by American troops, and the civilian causalities caused by NATO forces in Afghanistan clearly show how Islam and Muslims have become an object of hatred in the subconscious of people in the West. At this point, the Muslim world is looking for a guard for itself.

It is evident that we are entering a new period. This period is unique because it includes a process of cooperation and coexistence.

Internal and External Weakness[114]

Even though we do not strongly focus on it, the Middle East is Turkey's reality. The Middle East is a problem that we have to deal with. We did not inherit from Islamic history the political regimes that survived in the region, the economic structures, the borders which do not reflect reality and lead to disputes all the time, the administrative structures which restrict fundamental rights and freedoms, or the myriad other issues.

It is also not possible to argue that these issues have Islamic legitimacy. It is possible to view this assessment as an escape from confronting problems. Blaming an external actor for the problems that affect you will only give you relief for a short time. Of course, the Muslim world has its inherent problems. In the previous century, Bediüzzaman Said Nursi stressed that there are three major problems in the Muslim world: ignorance, poverty, and lack of unity.

What I need to underline is that, by nature, the ongoing problems in this region cannot be attributed to Islam. Quite the contrary, Islam does not tolerate repression, exploitation, extravagance, poverty, and national egoism. It is a religious obligation under Islam to address and resolve these problems. We are dealing with these problems, but we are unable to resolve them. The West is the root cause of these problems and it is also responsible for delegating them to us in the previous century. The British and the French in particular left many sources for disputes in

---

[114] First appeared in *Today's Zaman* on Jan. 13, 2014

the lands they withdrew from. They left many potential disasters and disagreements, which could and would lead to problems, between Turkey and Syria, Iran and Syria, Iran and Iraq and Kuwait and Saudi Arabia. We should remember that the Iran-Iraq War, which left behind 1 million casualties, was provoked by a simple dispute over islands. The colonialists not only left behind problems that could cause bigger problems, but they also left their own political regime and administrative structure. A military dictatorship was created in one country whereas a monarchy was strengthened in another. Authoritarian republican regimes were also preferred in some others. However, almost all these countries were ruled by one single regime and administrative style in the past.

The Middle East appears to be a region where there are constant conflicts and social turmoil. But these problems do not stem from the inherent structure of the region. The destruction caused during the colonial period weakened the whole system in the new era of Westernization. The policies of modernization further weakened the social and cultural fabric of the region. The systematic and deliberate destruction of the social and cultural fabric and of the structure of society by rulers is a tragedy that the Muslims experienced in modern times. In the current stage, these social structures and regimes have "expired" and are no longer able to offer a remedy to the ongoing problems.

The Middle East has come to a point where it hurts not only itself but the entire global order. In the 1970s, some Americans classified the states in the Middle East into two categories: remote outposts, like Turkey, Egypt, and Pakistan, and gas stations, like Kuwait, Bahrain, and the Gulf states. Now, these states are not functional. The regimes trying to remain operative under the tutelage of the West are no longer productive. New dictatorships will not work. The answer is the invocation of regional dynamics to deal with these problems. We experimentally know that change imposed externally does not resolve problems; they become part of the problem.

Global powers impose projects that are strange to the region so that the region does not change itself through its own methods. This is one of the reasons for ongoing conflicts. Even so, Muslims have to seek a solution to their problems. External attacks find a home in "internal weaknesses."

A Model in Terms of the Problem Solving Method[115]

Whether the result of a change is internal dynamics or the role of foreign factors, the balance in the Middle East has changed. I am among those who have believed from the very beginning that the social uprisings in the region exploded as a result of an internal, bottom-up thrust and a rupture that occurred in the depths of society. Foreign powers are trying to manipulate the situation according to their strategic interests.

There is an inexplicable chain of events going on. Let's say Western powers quietly lurking in the background started and controlled the events in Tunisia, Egypt, and Libya. The West does not want Islamic groups incompatible with the Western way and that seek to dominate social, administrative, and economic policies outlined by Islam to assume power. As a result, the West is imposing the "limited democracy Turkish model."

A democracy that is under the tutelage of the West (Is there any democracy that isn't under the tutelage of the West?) will be able to ignore the demands of the public regarding the use of natural and human resources, accept every wish of the West, and allow Israel to continue its arrogant and destructive attitude. The West, and in particular the US, also does not want Iran and Shiites to exercise initiative in the region. These are apparent and well-known facts. But then there are some gaps in the details. For example, what is the reason for the Shiites' demonstrations in Saudi Arabia? Is the US provoking them as well?

While these questions still linger in the minds of the people, Saudi Arabia sent troops to Bahrain, where Shiites refuse to leave the streets, to control critical locations (e.g., energy facilities, oil wells, banks, and public buildings). Now what if Iran decided to raise its voice or what if serious bloodshed occurred in Bahrain? How would America, which supported the civilian-led resistance and pro-democracy movements in

---

[115] First appeared in *Today's Zaman* on Mar. 18, 2011

North Africa and openly warned Libyan leader Muammar Gaddafi to leave, saying he lost his legitimacy to rule, be able to justify its stance in the Gulf?

These matters deserve to be contemplated. But more important is the deep-running internal disputes in the region. We need to look at these problems. Either the US and Europe, which are trying to control the region one way or another, are not well aware of the internal problems—if that is the case, then the West has become too unobservant—or they are aware but are trying to cover up problems using different methods to desensitize the regional public and maintain the unjust order.

It is impossible to establish stability in the region without solving major perpetual problems. The current situation in the region is unsustainable. No matter how vociferously autocratic regimes resist or global interest networks write up scenarios, the people in the region want to change. This is the most basic fact. Religion, the religion-state relationship, minorities, the elimination of suppressive regimes, the economy, unemployment, poverty, the loss of resources, the unfair distribution of wealth, ethnic problems, sectarian divides, and an identity crisis are all problems. These problems, depending on their severity, cause social unrest in certain countries in the region. For example, the sectarian factor becomes a bigger issue in countries such as Iraq, Bahrain, Syria, and Saudi Arabia. In Iraq, ethnicity is another important issue. In Egypt, the main issues include economic problems, the elimination of a repressive regime, and the demands of non-Muslims. When we look carefully at countries where social unrest has occurred and is likely to occur, these six problems, depending on their intensity, stand out the most.

Turkey's main problems can be gathered around these six items as well. While there may be a difference in the degree and severity of these problems in Turkey, the same problems that are waiting to be solved in the Middle East are waiting to be solved in Turkey as well. Of course, Turkey has some advantages, but that alone is not enough to make us a "model country" for the region. Our ability to become a model country depends on the conceptual framework we use to perceive our problems, the way we define ourselves, and the way in which we solve our problems. When considered from this perspective, it is only natural for there to be problems. Problems will exist in any place there are humans. The main issue is whether we can solve our problems and whether we have found a way or method to solve our problems.

A Challenging Solution for Syria[116]

The clashes in Syria are growing in intensity and scope, causing large-scale casualties. If the bloodshed cannot be stopped at once, Syria may be dragged into a more comprehensive civil war, in which Syria may be divided along sectarian lines and the clashes may spread to the entire region.

A full year has passed since the start of the protests, and tragically, the regional countries have failed to display the right initiative, willpower, and insight. Iran and Turkey have emerged as the top two countries who have failed the test with respect to the Syrian crisis. Leaving aside the national reflexes along with the rhetoric of public diplomacy strategies and propaganda, both countries have proved that they are actually no different from each other. They put the blame on each other but they appear to be equally guilty. Every sane person knew that the crisis in Syria could be solved before it grew out of proportion if Turkey and Iran had reached an agreement. If Iran and Turkey had exerted peaceful pressure on Bashar al-Assad and the opposition, the crisis would have been averted with an interim solution and general elections would have been held on a date acceptable to both sides, while the way to drafting a new constitution could have been paved.

Tehran repeated the great error it made back in 1982, refraining from developing dialogue with the Syrian opposition. It turned a blind eye to the Baath regime's ruthless killing of Muslims. This again clouded the prestige of the Islamic revolution. In 1982, we learned what the following assertion meant: "Big revolutions occur in the Third World countries, but foreign and finance ministers do not change." The Finance Ministry changed slightly, but the blind Realpolitik attitude of the Foreign Ministry did not.

Since the start, Ankara has pursued a misguided policy with regard to the Syrian crisis. Although it was supposed to offer a model for the

---

[116] First appeared in *Today's Zaman* on Feb. 27, 2012

region by "managing the political change based on calm power, soft power, trade, visa exemptions, dialogue, and social change," it helped to deepen the crisis under the influence of the United States and the Gulf countries. It failed to prevent the Syrian opposition's militarization, and civilian protests soon evolved into armed clashes. Today, Turkey takes special pride in noting that the country's relations with the US are at the highest level.

We now face a picture that is much more tragic compared to one year ago. The regional countries are now divided into two fronts according to the global strategies of the big guns: On one hand are the countries that have secured the relative backing of Russia and China, i.e., Iran, Iraq, Syria, Lebanon, and the Arab streets that fulminate with rage against the US and Israel, and on the other hand are the US, the UK, France, Turkey, Israel, Saudi Arabia, Jordan, and the Gulf countries. Egypt does not show its colors and chooses to be on standby, trying to solve its own problems.

This polarization is horrible and dismal. As we were heading toward a regional integration, we suddenly found ourselves in camps hostile to each other. Lebanese Strategic Studies Manager Muhammad Nureddin says that if Turkey conducts a military operation against Syria, it has to risk a collective war against Iran, Iraq, Syria, and Lebanon at the same time.

Concerning the invasion of Iraq and the shelling of Libya, I have argued that the regional countries should create an Islamic peacekeeping force that would meddle with the crisis regions. Of course, before any intervention, diplomatic initiatives should be exhausted fully. Indeed, peace is essential and peace is always more beneficial. If Turkey and Iran had reached an agreement, there would not have been so much bloodshed in Syria. Actually, visiting Iran in early January, Ahmet Davutoğlu said, "Iran may play a role in the solution of the Syrian issue. We believe that Iran's conveying of necessary suggestions to the Syrian administration would be a great contribution to the process."

As two leading regional countries, Turkey and Iran have failed to effect such cooperation. They could not overcome their narrow national interests, their engagements with the external world, and sectarian fanaticism. Now, the Western countries will assume the savior role and rain Syria with thousands of bombs. As was the case in Libya, thousands of people will die and the country's infrastructure will be destroyed. Or they will force Turkey to conduct this disgraceful intervention. *"O human being! Whatever good happens to you, it is from God; and whatever evil befalls you, it is from yourself"* (Surah an-Nisa 4:79). If we deserve evil, it will befall us. It doesn't matter if it is Turkey, Iran, the Arab League, or the Organization of Islamic Cooperation (OIC); unfortunately, all of them are nothing but useless specters.

The 'ISIL' Pretext[117]

The US-led coalition has been conducting military operations against the Islamic State of Iraq and the Levant (ISIL) in Iraq and Syria. This coalition has two distinct components: the US and its close ally the UK as well as France and Italy at the core, and Saudi Arabia, Jordan, and the United Arab Emirates (UAE) as their regional allies on the periphery. The peripheral allies should be seen as the coalition members that have auxiliary duties such as financing, logistical support, public diplomacy, and public relations, though they also take part in military attacks. But it is the US that is calling the shots.

It should be noted that the US is shelling certain targets, but we don't know about the outcome.

Of course, civilians are killed as well.

Turkey's position is a most delicate one. Now that the hostages have been rescued, the Turkish government has been forced to adopt a clear stance on the operation; however, the US is unable to truly rely on Turkey as its ally. US Secretary of State John Kerry implied that as the hostages are safe Turkey must stop talking and start to act. Rear Adm. John Kirby, spokesman for the Pentagon, was more outspoken, saying Turkey is, will be, and should be, more involved just by way of its location. They expect Turkey to participate in the coalition actively.

The operation against ISIL is questionable in the eyes of region, reputable organizations, social movements, and religious communities. Yusuf al-Qaradawi, head of the International Union of Muslim Scholars,

---

[117] First appeared in *Today's Zaman* on Oct. 13, 2014

announced that he does not approve of the military operations by the US-led coalition against ISIL even if he does not endorse ISIL's ideas and methods. Moreover, spokespeople for Muslim Brotherhood organizations in Egypt and Syria stated they are against any military operation in the region under the pretext of fighting ISIL. Egyptian Muslim Brotherhood spokespeople say that intervention in the Muslim territory is an effort to divide the Middle East once again and will lead to disorder. While they acknowledge that ISIL is a criminal organization that has deviated from Islam, Syrian Muslim Brotherhood spokespeople believe the intervention is a fight against Islam under the pretext of counter-terrorism. They rightly want the US, the West, and related parties not to meddle with this business and to define what terrorism is so that innocent people can be kept out of harm's way. They add that they do not agree with the international intervention in Syrian territories because Syrian people have the power to liberate themselves and overcome radicalism and terror.

We are facing a critical situation. It would be grossly naive to assume that the operation targets just ISIL. Rear Adm. Kirby admits this is not only a military operation but a comprehensive regional, political, and economic approach with military components. US authorities note the fight against ISIL may take years.

The US and the West scare or blackmail certain countries or promise small benefits to others so that regional countries support their occupation of Syria after Afghanistan and Iraq, and the redesigning of the region. Back in March 2003, Turkey faced the critical parliamentary decision of whether to authorize the use of force in Iraq. The ruling party was anxious to get this authorization, but Parliament did not support it because of harsh reactions from the general public.

No one endorses ISIL's activities, but the problem is not ISIL alone. The Muslim world is disintegrating along sectarian, ethnic, and class lines within the context of the "creative chaos" doctrine. The regional countries cannot come together to find solutions to their common problems, but instead they expect the US and Western intervention to solve them. The solution is not military intervention by foreign powers but the well-functioning internal dynamics in the regional countries.

Turkey and Palestine[118]

We are re-living another Israeli classic. As usual, Israeli operations are disproportionate and go beyond limits.

It should be noted that Israel is currently experiencing the most comfortable and advantageous period of its short history. Israel has the advantage due the fact that Iran, Syria, and Hezbollah have suffered great losses. Former Iraqi president Saddam Hussein and Libyan leader Muammar Gaddafi were helping the Palestinian cause but were destroyed. By establishing a new Christian state established in its south with the help of Israel, Sudan was taken under siege. In Egypt, pro-Israeli soldiers staged a coup.

When Turkey came to the stage in 2003, it was a source of great hope. Many reasoned as follows: as a member of the Western alliance, Turkey could establish a dialogue with Israel. As a non-Arab Muslim country, Turkey was also important to Israel. In the past, Iran used to play this role, but it became an enemy after the Islamic revolution. Today, Kurdistan plays this role. When it was preparing to strike Iran, Israel performed training flights in Konya. As "two democratic countries" in the region, Israel and Turkey were going to introduce democracy to the region.

However, Turkey was lured by money from oil kings to reinforce the Sunni world against Shiism and challenge Iran in the region. Turkey began to support armed groups against Syrian President Bashar al-Assad, who closely followed Turkey in his efforts at making reforms. Thereby, Turkey played a crucial role in triggering the ongoing chaos in Syria. Until 2011, Israel needed Turkey in its relations with Syria; this is no longer the case. Due to the Syrian crisis, Hezbollah is no longer a threat to Israel, although it gave Israel a heavy defeat in 2006. If Turkey had intelligently maintained its diplomatic ties with Israel while Iran, Syria, and Hezbollah continued to reject Israel and lend a great deal of support to Hamas, Israel would still enjoy the status of being a regional country and the Palestinians would have found some relief.

---

[118] First appeared in *Today's Zaman* on Aug. 4, 2014

Turkey made a big gamble and lost. Assad was not overthrown, despite Turkey's help to armed groups. Hamas leader Khaled Meshaal left Damascus, relying on the empty bravado of Qatar and Turkey though Syria had been supporting him for years. Iran and Syria had been giving ample military, material, and logistical support to Hamas, including unmanned aerial vehicles. Now, Hamas was left alone and forced to make peace with Fatah. Saying Fatah means accepting the road map of the US and Tel Aviv.

What can Turkey do for Palestine? Nothing! What can it do for Israel? Nothing! Everything is obvious:

1. Despite the apparent tension, Turkey has maintained its commercial relations with Israel at the highest level. Due to the fact that Turkish exports have to use Israel ports—exclusively, except for a few Lebanese ports—Israel earns enormous sums of money.

2. Oil from the Kurdish region in northern Iraq goes first to Turkey and then is exported to Israel by tanker. This way, Israel not only is supplied with oil for domestic consumption, but can also export oil to third countries. There is a hidden network between Kurdistan, Turkey, and Israel. Turkey and Israel are trying to help Kurdistan secede from Iraq.

3. Israel no longer needs Konya for training flights; it can make deals with Greece and Azerbaijan. In short, Turkey is hurling empty good-for-nothing heroic rhetoric at Israel. It is all geared toward manipulating domestic politics. Turkey is making a lot of noise about Israel's aggression, but behind the scenes, trade ties continue to function smoothly. This is the exact copy of the hypocritical policies that Egypt and the Gulf monarchies have been pursuing for years. And in the meantime, the poor Palestinians are wronged. Everyone is exploiting the suffering of the Palestinians.

The Orientalist Language in Gaza Reports[119]

Different instruments are used to ensure that the ongoing Israeli attacks and atrocities against civilians—particularly against children—will not

---

[119] First appeared in *Today's Zaman* on Jan. 16, 2009

lead to moral outrage and that Israel will be tolerated until the predetermined goals have been fulfilled by the Israeli army.

As we witness the collapse of moral values in this scene of murders, media groups are playing a pivotal role. Those familiar with the Western media already know that CNN avoids broadcasting massacres of civilians. The American public is only allowed to watch rockets fired by Hamas. Also, depictions and video feeds accompanying news reports include Palestinian civilian buildings hit by Israeli troops. The British Broadcasting Corporation, known for its impartiality and neutrality, avoids reporting on the events with video footage. The BBC's justification for this is that Israel does not allow reporters into Gaza, where the operation is ongoing.

Orientalism still affects the mindset of Western peoples and institutions because Western media do not consider footage taken by Al Jazeera acceptable because it has not been filtered. According to the BBC, clear footage and live broadcasts do not suffice in depicting what is going on in Gaza; reports not confirmed by Western institutions are not trustable.

What is even more striking is that depictions drawn by those who Orientalize themselves in Turkey rely on such a repugnant discourse in an attempt to justify the ongoing Israeli atrocities. The argument stressed frequently since the beginning of the assault is, "Yes, Israel attacked, but Hamas provoked this." The second argument is that Israeli state terror based on systematic and organized terrorist attacks is equal to Hamas, which in fact relies on its right to self-defense against an aggressor and is trying to save the Occupied Palestinian Territories.

A segment of the Turkish media with little or no concern about Islamic values preferred to belittle the massacres through the language it relies on and even tried to justify these atrocities. The most obvious example of this involved reports detailing an incident in which Hamas leader Nizar Rayan was killed along with his entire family. Referring to the incident, the *Hürriyet* daily on Jan. 2, 2009 headlined with "Family-sized bomb for Hamas leader."

This is language insulting to human dignity. Reading through the article, one can see that extra stress was placed on the fact that he was killed along with his four wives. As if this weren't enough, the daily used an irrelevant photo accompanied by an explanation reading, "Israel hit Rayan and his four wives." In other words, according to *Hürriyet*, what should be emphasized was the Orientalist image of an Arab with four wives instead of the killing of innocent women and children. For the report, the murder of children aged between 7 and 10 was of secondary importance. Whereas the news wires for the story on that day were filed along with pictures of the bodies of the women and children killed, for the *Hürriyet* daily the bodies of these women were nothing other than the four wives of a Hamas leader. The daily did not hesitate to use this opportunity to deliver "modernist" messages with regard to polygamy. The message transmitted to the readers was this: "Yes, Israel kills civilians, but these are primitive Arabs stuck in the Medieval Ages. There is no need for outrage."

This is the same *Hürriyet* daily that published a headline back in 1967 reading, "Dogs are tearing at Arab bodies in the desert." That article described Rayan as a promoter of suicide attacks against Israel and a mentor of suicide bombers. *Hürriyet* did not have any problem with dressing up their reporting of this massacre with Orientalist codes and messages despite the danger of losing impartiality and neutrality.

Trade with Israel[120]

It is said that there has been a "serious crisis" between Turkey and Israel since the 2010 Israeli attack on a Gaza-bound aid flotilla that left nine Turks dead, but in reality, there is no problem with the commercial and economic ties between the two countries.

The foreign trade volume between the two countries rose from $4.022 billion in 2011 to $4.858 billion in 2013. "Turkey is one of the 10 most important economic partners of Israel," says Ekrem Demirtaş, the head of the executive board of the İzmir Chamber of Commerce (İTO). Until recently, there were 11 flights a day between the two countries. Among Organization for Economic Cooperation and Development (OECD) countries, Turkey ranks fifth in terms of Israel's exports and

---

[120] First appeared in *Today's Zaman* on Aug. 11, 2014

sixth in terms of its imports. The commodities sold by Israel are food, machinery, and advanced technology products. Israel buys plastics, rubber, textiles, concrete, ceramics, glass, machinery, and automotive products from Turkey.

Commenting on Israel's recent attacks against Gaza, Deputy Prime Minister Bülent Arınç underlined that the bilateral trade ties with Israel continue uninterrupted and it is impossible to halt commercial transactions. An analysis of the statistics provided by the Turkish Statistics Institute (TurkStat) reveals that Turkey sells military equipment to Israel. Since 2010, Turkey exported weapons and ammunition worth about $11 million.

The recent Syrian crisis particularly played into hands of Israel. As a result of the crisis, giant ferries depart from the İskenderun port and anchor at the port of Haifa in Israel. These giant ferries carry Turkish semi-trailer trucks which can then travel to Arab countries.

In a letter the Mechanical and Chemical Industry Corporation (MKEK) sent to the Chamber of Shipping on Sept. 3, 2013, a tender was to be opened for the shipment of one 20-foot (6-meter) and one 40-foot (12 meter) container full of 31,508 120-millimeter tank shells. However, the official announcement in the wake of the Mavi Marmara attack was that Turkey had postponed arms procurement deals with Israel. "We are no longer buying weapons from Israel," the Undersecretary for the Defense Industry declared in April 2011. However, Brig. Gen. Shemaya Avieli, the head of the Foreign Defense Assistance and Defense Export Organization (SIBAT), had said that "defense exports to Turkey were never halted, and are weighed according to the interests of the State of Israel. The relationship that existed in recent years hasn't continued, but if you look at the numbers—defense exports to Turkey were not zero. There are new demands from Turkey and we are examining them."

There is more. It is no secret that the oil coming from Iraqi Kurdistan to Turkey via pipelines is indirectly sold to Israel via tankers. The Prime Ministry's statement does not deny the indirect sales. Moreover, the Shalom newspaper, the representative of the Turkish Jewish community, reported that according to a news story that appeared in the *Yedioth Ahoronot* newspaper, Prime Minister Recep Tayyip Erdoğan's son, Burak Erdoğan, maintained his trade ties with Israel. The newspaper wrote that Burak Erdoğan's 95-meter cargo ship "Safran1" shuttled between Israel's Ashdod port and Turkey many times. Moreover, his other ships traveled to Israeli and Egyptian ports many times, even after this news story appeared.

Should the Turkish government implement a boycott? A general boycott is problematic. Many Western countries in particular, including the US, are enforcing boycotts which are mostly cruel to Muslim countries. For example, Iran and Iraq suffered greatly from such boycotts in the past. Hundreds of thousands of children have died due to lack of food or medicine in Iraq. Gaza is already a de facto concentration camp.

Islamic scholars do not endorse a general boycott. Even in a case of war, a general boycott is not permissible if there is the risk of any damage to civilians. For Abu Hanifa, the founder of the Hanafi school of Islamic jurisprudence, it is forbidden to sell materials which can be used to produce weapons to those who are at war. The Qur'an prohibits the punishment of people by keeping them hungry (al-Baqarah 2:126). In this case, Turkey should stop selling arms and ammunition and oil to Israel as a minimum.

Expanding Foreign Policy[121]

"Those who try to implement certain projects in the Middle East while excluding Turkey will not be successful," Prime Minister Recep Tayyip Erdoğan said three years ago. "This also goes for our strategic partner, the US."

In order to support his case, Erdoğan provided Iraq as an example: "There were attempts to keep Turkey to one side. Were you able to solve it? You could not and will not solve it. If we had acted as a mediator, it would have been resolved in a short time, but they did not concede to it. Why? Because they are not sincere. Terrorism has claimed the lives of 30,000 people in our country and we will not step back."[122]

---

[121] First appeared in *Today's Zaman* on Jun. 15, 2010
[122] *Zaman*, Oct. 26, 2007

What should we make of these remarks? The prime minister tried to squeeze two themes into the same statement: First, if an arrangement is made in the Middle East, it cannot be done without Turkey's involvement; and second, Turkey is determined to put an end to the atmosphere of violence that emerged in connection with the Kurdish issue in which more than 30,000 people died. These two issues and the connection between each other deserve to be discussed. Indeed, those who claim that there is more than a simple coincidence between the bloody attack against the Mavi Marmara ship, which was carrying humanitarian aid to Gaza, and the murder of six soldiers in İskenderun, both of which occurred on the morning of May 31, 2010, cannot be scorned for being overly conspiratorial.

The question that must be answered is: What really bothers Turkey? Is it "terrorism that claimed the lives of over 30,000 people" or "attempts to redesign Iraq without Turkey's involvement"? How can Israel, which constantly protects itself in the region, dare to launch such a reckless attack, killing nine Turks?

To find the answers to these questions, we need to go back in time. Abdullah Gül attended a meeting in Washington in early 2007 in his capacity as Turkish foreign minister and delivered a speech titled "Turkish Policy at a Crossroads" and in which he said, "We ruled the region for several centuries. We have natural ties with the region. We also recognize today's realities. Iraq belongs to the Iraqis. When we gave Mosul to Iraq in 1926, we gave it to a single Iraq. We want to see a single Iraq before us."[123]

The venue and title of this speech were important, as was the prime minister's speech. Both speeches underlined a "profound uneasiness" and at the same time stressed a common theme.

One thing is quite clear: In the early 21st century, the George W. Bush-led US—under the influence of neocons—dared enter the region as an occupying country without seeking the consent of Turkey and other countries in the region. To borrow a Turkish saying, it acted like an elephant in a glassware shop. It makes arbitrary arrangements in the

---

[123] *Yeni Şafak*, Feb. 9, 2007

region, dividing Iraq into several parts, giving autonomy to some parts, with the eventual goal of making them independent. It conducts all its plans and programs only in consideration of its predictions and its and Israel's interests; it does not deviate even slightly from this main strategy. It does not even hesitate to antagonize its old allies and friends of half a century to this end. Disgraceful murders continue to take place in Afghanistan, and NATO soldiers continue to kill Muslim civilians. The US reminds Turkey that it cannot undertake any initiative in Iraq without its consent or knowledge. For instance, on the day Gül made the above-mentioned speech, US Assistant Secretary of State Daniel Fried clearly said, "If Turkey is planning to conduct a cross-border operation, it should consider its consequences and responsibilities." We would not be exaggerating if we were to take Fried's remarks as "a kind of threat."

The problem at hand may appear to be the Kurdistan Workers' Party (PKK) and terrorism—this is certainly a problem—but this does not preclude the fact that there might be other unpronounced underlying facts.

The Kurdish Initiative[124]

It can be said that two factors play a role in the Kurdish initiative launched by the government.

First is the message US President Barack Obama gave during his address to the Turkish Parliament on April 6, 2009. In his speech, Obama stressed the need for handling the Kurdish issue, improving relations with Armenia, and the issue of reopening the Halki Seminary.

It seems that the US is attaching special importance to the Kurdish issue. The fact that the US is pulling out from Iraq, the potential problems that the regional Kurdish government in northern Iraq might face, and the possible role that Turkey may play as a strategic ally of the US are adding more urgency to the Kurdish issue. New developments have increased Turkey's role. At this point, it is vital to the US that no damage is done to northern Iraq. The US does not want the Kurds to develop feelings of being betrayed once again, and it is trying to make sure that a federation as its own political model is successfully implemented in

---

[124] First appeared in *Today's Zaman* on Aug. 25, 2009

Iraq. Concerning this point, the US believes Turkey may play a critical role. Turkey may protect the regional Kurdish government in northern Iraq and increase its political influence on Arabs so as to counterbalance the regional patronage of the Shiite population and Iran. While sorting out its business in the region, the US is shifting its focus to the Afghan and Pakistani zone.

The other factor is having realized that things will change in this process, Kurdistan Workers' Party (PKK) leader Abdullah Öcalan has declared that he would announce a roadmap for settlement and that he has been in touch with various columnists, authors, leading figures, and nongovernmental organization via his lawyers within this framework. In a preemptive move, the state has launched an initiative and conducted various talks with similar figures. The method Öcalan is following in drawing up his roadmap is the same as the method the government is currently employing. It is as if the government and Öcalan are competing with each other to discredit one another's road map.

Now everyone wonders what sort of improvements the initiative will introduce in the settlement of the issue. It seems that the initiative will progress within the framework laid down by Chief of General Staff Gen. İlker Başbuğ on April 14, 2009. Başbuğ is stressing the concepts of nation-state, the unitary structure of the state, and individual freedoms, still under the influence of the official paradigm. However, we need a more comprehensive solution that goes beyond the established liberal or nationalist perspectives. This issue entails that we resort to another set of values, i.e., that of Islamic values. The intellectual and political basis that will help us settle this issue consists of the main Islamic resources and our historical experience. The state, the government, the PKK, and the pro-Kurdish Democratic Society Party (DTP) are miles away from these resources.

There are also difficulties other than those imposed by the paradigm: Even if, as the prime minister said, some partial improvements are made, we need a basic set of constitutional amendments. Currently, the ruling Justice and Development Party (AK Party) can make neither constitutional amendments nor a new constitution. The seats it commands in Parliament are not sufficient. Moreover, in the past, the Constitutional

Court held that it committed an offense against secularism by amending Articles 10 and 42 of the Constitution and penalized it in this respect. We can expect no support from the Republican People's Party (CHP) and the Nationalist Movement Party (MHP) concerning the constitutional amendments. The support from the DTP will not be sufficient, and even if it suffices, the Constitutional Court will still cancel those amendments. However, we should not ignore a small possibility: if this is a state project backed by the military, then the CHP might be forced to lend support, and in that case, even if the amendments are reviewed by the Constitutional Court, they will not be canceled. Whether this will be the case, we will see in the near future.

Even though a basic set of constitutional amendments cannot be made, some symbolic steps might be taken. These steps include reverting to local names, bringing the majority of the people in the Makhmour camp in northern Iraq back to Turkey, the establishment of a Kurdology institute at Artuklu University in Mardin, the transformation of the Diyarbakır prison—which is among the top five biggest torture houses in the world—into an educational complex, and possibly introducing Kurdish as an elective language course in schools. As a matter of fact, the prime minister says they do not intend to engage in difficult tasks such as amending the Constitution.

Domestic and Extraneous Factors of the Kurdish Initiative[125]

While the "Kurdish initiative" introduced by the Justice and Development Party (AK Party) government is moving forward, it is bringing with it great debates. Opposition parties are stirring up dust as they disapprove of two basic points. The first is that the national and ethnic identity of the Turkish Republic will change with this initiative, and the other is that the Kurdish initiative is being imposed on Turkey by the US.

It must be noted though that in today's world, great powers no longer impose an idea or project onto others by using force or direct inter-

---

[125] First appeared in *Today's Zaman* on Sept. 28, 2009

vention; instead, they employ a more sophisticated, polite, and diplomatic tone. In fact, most of the time they won't even say anything clearly, but influence events and leave you no other choice but to act in a way that is compatible with their interests.

On the other hand, it seems the opposition parties have not fully comprehended the globalization phenomenon. Globalization means the uninterrupted operation of interdependent processes and the continued functioning of decision-making mechanisms in line with these processes. Certainly, while these interdependent processes function, the power between countries and states are not equal. States influence diplomacy and politics, depending on how they utilize their resources for their economic and military potential. But another reality is that former US President George W. Bush's "I decide on my own; you are either with me or against me" doctrine no longer applies like it used to. Although US troops are still occupying Afghanistan and Iraq, today's American government feels the need to persuade the administrations in Afghanistan and Iraq. If the US were to take the liberty of doing whatever it wanted, it may ultimately reach its goals, but the cost would, in the long run, take a toll not only on the countries it controlled but on itself as well. It is this tactic that is one of the main reasons why global hostility toward the US hasn't decreased to a desirable level.

Another point overlooked by opposition parties in Turkey is that in the processes in which globalization requires everyone to engage in interactive relationships, the "my own domestic policy" doctrine barely applies anymore.

In this respect, the Bush era was a deviation. It was like a parenthesis in a process that was otherwise very difficult to stop. But during the international meetings held in Turkey, Bush's predecessor, President Bill Clinton, looked directly at Russian President Boris Yeltsin and said, "Countries no longer have independent domestic issues. Human rights violations are both a foreign policy and an international issue." And he was right.

Justly or unjustly, when big powers decide to intervene in a country's domestic affairs, they make use of "human rights violations, genocide attempts, and policies that harm a certain ethnic or religious group" as an excuse, and it doesn't matter how much the country at hand says that this is their own problem.

With the influence of the media, the international community and dynamic nongovernmental organizations, scholars and opinion leaders that have the power to mobilize society can put pressure on countries that make rights violations. When we look at the government-supported Kurdish initiative project from this perspective, what is the image before us? Without a doubt the most important factor in starting this project was the strong demand by the public to find a solution. As a result of the armed upheaval started by the Kurdistan Workers' Party (PKK) on Aug. 15, 1984, around 40,000 people have been killed, 17,566 unsolved murders have occurred and hundreds of billions of dollars of resources have been used. The economic and human geography of Turkey's eastern and southeastern region has been devastated.

Aside from the group of people that benefit from the "war and terror sector," the majority of people have a strong will to put an end to this problem. This strong will cannot be ignored.

Meanwhile, in consideration of the situation in Iraq, the serious problems the Kurdistan Regional Government (KRG) in northern Iraq is facing, and the new situation on the Afghanistan-Pakistan front, the US wants Turkey to assume an active role in the region and to solve the Kurdish problem within this framework. Now what's important is that Turkey doesn't try to solve the problem just because America wants it to, but because it needs to and that it doesn't make the mistake of accepting America's solution plan as is. It seems likely that the government is going to have a difficult time developing a third method that goes beyond these two choices, and it is for this reason that it is being subjected to harsh criticisms.

How to Turn Turkey's Kurdish Problem into an International One[126]

The first thing that comes to the mind of people in Turkey when they hear the phrase "Kurdish issue" is that it usually refers to "one dimension of

---

[126] First appeared in *Today's Zaman* on Aug. 18, 2009

the problem that the Kurds living in Turkey face." There are, however, various dimensions of the issue. The most important dimension of the problem is cultural. Kurds were a partner in nation-states that were established in the first quarter of the 20th century. But during the making of national identities, they were deprived of opportunities to freely express their own.

To a certain extent this stemmed from the nature of the newly founded nation-states, which had no connection or resemblance to the traditional state forms and models. The modern nation-state was a political concept, and the historical claims and fundamental assertions that formed the basis for this concept envisioned only one identity, prohibiting all other identities from expressing themselves in the public sphere.

People from other ethnicities were expected to express themselves within the set official identity. In Turkey the official identity was set as the Turkish identity. Similarly, in Iraq the Arab identity, and in Iran the Persian identity became the standard. Naturally this process led to the emergence of various tensions.

The problem was not just political or legal, but economic as well. Ethnic groups that did not fit the description of the official identity were deemed to be a potential threat and the region in which they lived was not economically protected. Development programs that were launched in the first quarter of the 20th century did not view this region as a suitable place for investment and employment. Those who reckon there was a conscious preference not to invest in the region are actually not exaggerating the situation. The main justification for the lack of investment in border regions has been the occasional attack by hostile neighbors. However, this justification has very little credibility, at least for the eastern and southeastern regions of Turkey. From the very beginning, 90 percent of investments have always been directed to the western regions.

Historically, the wealth of the region is linked to the existing close trade relations with Syria (Aleppo-Damascus), Iraq (Mosul-Baghdad, Arbil-Kirkuk), and Iran (Tabriz), which didn't come across any customs barriers when trading with each other. Tight controls, heavy taxes, and known and unknown prohibitions that came with the drawing of national boundaries at the beginning of the 20th century not only impoverished the region, but also opened up a gap between the region and other regions and caused disproportionate and sudden migrations that had heavy social costs.

The other dimension of the problem is political. When people want to address their problems through legitimate ways, they encounter politics. Another name for addressing demands through legitimate and open ways is called "positive politics." The method that is applied when legitimate roads are blocked is called "negative politics." This is one of the most important factors that ultimately lead to the emergence of violence and terror. When people can't communicate their demands through politics, this doesn't necessarily mean there is no problem. When demands are mentioned for the first time, the problems are immediately pushed outside the realm of politics, and an issue that would have otherwise not been a problem becomes a serious problem, impacting the future of the nation.

The terror and violence that began in 1984 has kept the regional people between two fires. Harsh assimilation policies were implemented, especially during the Sept. 12, 1980 coup, such as changing village and district names and prohibiting families from naming their children any name they wanted. These practices aggravated the Kurdish problem, and the problem evolved into its present stage.

Certainly, this weakness within Turkey quickly drew the attention of foreign countries. As a result of flawed definitions and policies, a suitable setting for manipulation emerged. The Kurdish problem was turned into an international problem and foreign states systematically became secretly or openly involved in it.

However, what should have happened first was that Turkey should have shown an effective intention to solve the problem inside the country. But such an environment, which was available for many years, eventually disappeared, and many opportunities were lost.

When we look at developments on the regional scale today, we still see that the ground on which to build peace is being eroded, and it is almost as if we are moving away from finding a real solution. Aside from conceptual frameworks extracted from the West, we are in need of new intellectual analyses. One solution that applies to one society may not apply to another. Today is a new day, and we need new concepts and new styles of approach.

The current government has made a declaration of its political will to solve the problem despite the existence of discouraging factors.

The Nest of the PKK and Manipulating Regional Politics[127]

The emerging elites of Iraqi Kurdistan who closely monitor developments in the world and in their immediate region say that "an Iraqi Kurdistan cannot exist without Turkey."

The new administration in northern Iraq clearly states that it can overcome the pressing problems of economic, social, and culture development only with the help of Turkey. They further disclose that they are ready to share with Turkey the benefits from the oil resources that are allocated to Iraqi Kurdistan within the new status of Iraq. While the final status of Kirkuk is still to be decided, if Kirkuk is included within Kurdistan as an autonomous region according to the solution that sounds melodious to the ears of Kurds, this means 40 percent of Iraqi oil resources.

All these are raw ideas, needing further polishing. But none of them can easily be jettisoned. The leading countries have already opened representative offices in Arbil, and the Turkish government is too late to take such a step. The only instance of Turkey acting preemptively ahead of other countries is the [Gülen-inspired] schools opened by Turkish entrepreneurs since 1994. This year, Turkish entrepreneurs opened the third largest university, second only to the US and British universities. The Kurdish administration, led by Massoud Barzani, is considerably satisfied with this as they already tend to do business with the Turks. Barzani says that even their education minister is of the opinion that they are ready to transfer the entire education business of Iraqi Kurdistan to Turkey. They just want to see high quality education carried out in compliance with international standards.

---

[127] First appeared in *Today's Zaman* on Nov. 04, 2008

This is the good part of the story. When it comes to the issue of the outlawed Kurdistan Workers' Party (PKK), things change. The official view of Iraqi Kurdistan is that "the PKK is an internal problem of Turkey and unrelated to us in any way. The areas where PKK militants are located are not under our control. These are empty areas without human settlement." Sero Kadir, the Kurdistan information general manager, with whom I spoke last week, said, concerning Turkish air strikes: "Those areas are vacant. As long as civilians are not harmed, Turkey may conduct as many operations as it desires against the PKK."

When he was asked whether the Kurdistan administration should do something to drive the PKK out of the region, he gave a thought-provoking response: "Let us emphasize one point. In the past the PKK settled in the Kandil region of northern Iraq with permission and with the knowledge of Turkey, Syria, and Iran. If these three countries reach an agreement among themselves, not a single PKK militant can remain in Kandil."

This was a considerably interesting disclosure. I always thought the PKK was never an element completely out of control. Thanks to the PKK, some clandestine groups can still maintain their guardianship over the system and can meddle with politics and manipulate regional policies. What interests me is that about 40,000 people died and animosity increased between Muslim Turks and Muslim Kurds—and billions of dollars were wasted.

The fact that there are 6,000 PKK militants—1,500 inside Turkey and 4,500 in the mountains—is discussed even in Cabinet meetings. It is common knowledge that one-third of these militants are of Syrian origin. The Kurds in Syria are in a worse situation than those in Turkey; they even lack national ID cards. Why doesn't Turkey make an attempt to discuss this issue with Damascus in line with the dominant role it played in launching negotiations between Syria and Israel? Isn't it a bit strange?

The Abdullah Öcalan Factor[128]

Turkey's Kurdish issue is squeezed between those who call the Kurdistan Workers' Party (PKK) leader Abdullah Öcalan "the killer of children"

---

[128] First appeared in *Today's Zaman* on Dec. 22, 2009

or "chief terrorist Apo" and those who prefer to call him "the distinguished Abdullah Öcalan." Both groups use these denominations based on their specific justifications.

But, there is a plain truth irrespective of whether you call him a chief terrorist or distinguished: Öcalan's influence over the PKK continues, newly established Kurdish parties tend to take into consideration his possible reactions, and a significant segment of the Kurdish population, or at least of the supporters of the Peace and Democracy Party (BDP), is sympathetic toward him.

As we meditate upon the Kurdish issue and ways of settling it in the least destructive manner, we must pay close attention to the Öcalan factor. Here, what we should do, regardless of our political views or ideologies, is to follow the sociological method, namely of distinguishing between "what is" and "what should be." In our opinion, Öcalan may be a killer of infants who rightfully deserves the title of chief terrorist, but if about 40,000 PKK militants have been killed up to date and if the PKK can still exist as an armed and active organization and if Öcalan is the only person influential on this organization, then we will have to choose between killing another 40,000 PKK militants—and at the same time losing more soldiers—or taking into consideration the Öcalan factor.

If a leader of a terrorist organization that is serving his prison term for life can change the course of events with a single nod, it is not wise to ignore this and it is more advisable to think about the contributions he might make to the settlement of the issue at hand. It is my conviction that some units of the state already take into consideration this factor. Indeed, Öcalan has confirmed that some state officials intend to meet with him with respect to some "intelligence matters." Yet, the process does not make any progress and armed clashes go on and the children of this country continue to die. The important thing is that the intellectuals who sincerely contemplate on the solution to the Kurdish issue should think about this factor in a cool-headed manner.

One may wonder: Where does Öcalan's power come from? How can he be so influential? Why do Kurdish politicians and intellectuals fail to hold sufficient sway over the Kurdish movement? These questions really deserve deep thought.

In the first place, we need to emphasize that the Kurdish movement is very different from other separatist movements around the world, particularly in the UK and Spain. In these countries, it was the "political" organizations that made the first appearance with certain demands for autonomy or separation. When they failed to get their demands accepted through politics, they either started their armed struggled or maintained the political and armed struggle simultaneously. In both cases, the armed wing of these movements was strictly controlled by the political wing and the militants who resorted to terror and violence were always guided by the course of action followed by civilian politicians. In other words, in these secessionist movements, political parties or political figures who act in the legitimate sphere would sit atop the pyramid while armed organizations were dependent on them. For this reason, even if the UK or Spain conducted secret talks or negotiations with the armed wings of these movements—indeed, they never severed contact with them—they openly addressed their civilian or political wings.

However, this is not the case with the Kurdish movement. The armed struggle first started in 1984. The PKK's first move was to purge all other Kurdish movements and allow only those parties that would act within the limits it set. You may not like it, but this is the truth.

Obviously, the state or opinion leaders, or the leaders of political parties, cannot be expected to talk to Öcalan openly. This is the case from the perspective of political reality. Yet, we also have to stop the bloodshed. Within this framework, the BDP was established in place of the now-defunct Democratic Society Party (DTP). This is another reality. The things that can be discussed with the BDP do not include the laying down of arms, sending armed PKK militants outside the country, and stopping the clashes. The BDP is concerned with the political aspects of the issue. Although he demands that he must be addressed at all times, Öcalan also concedes that "he should not be consulted about everything" or that the "BDP may be consulted." This must surely be taken into consideration.

The Kurdish Phenomenon in Northern Iraq[129]

In a mid-January 2010 visit, some 60 journalists from Turkey and Iraqi Kurdistan met under an initiative by the Medialog Platform, affiliated with the Hizmet Movement's Journalists and Writers Foundation (GYV), to discuss the media perceptions of Kurds and Kurdistan.

The participants also criticized themselves in this context. The main theme of our self-criticism consisted of the following:

We are having difficulty accepting the regional Kurdish government in Iraq. We mumble and stumble in our speech when we are supposed to talk about this regional, international and constitutional political reality. The Turkish general public has concerns and some visible justifications in addition to some aspects related to the subconscious in our indifference to this reality.

We argue that there is a federal state in the making in the north of Iraq and it is backed by the US and Israel. We have certain problems with Israel, but our military and political relations are maintained at the highest level. Our "strategic partnership" with the US has evolved into a "model partnership." The US is disrupting the structures in the Muslim world—including in Afghanistan and Yemen—creating chaos and imbalance. Still, our officials assert that we enjoy harmony with the US concerning foreign policy issues. In other words, we can establish all sorts of relations with the US and Israel, but won't allow others to do so. We are having a hard time confessing that this is only a superficial justification that does not sound at all convincing.

Rather, we have underlying concerns. We say that if a federal Kurdish state is established in northern Iraq, it will be a South Kurdistan, and it will automatically be associated with a North Kurdistan. In time, South and North may decide to unite, and this means the fragmentation of Turkey. While it cannot be said that this is nothing but paranoia or an unfounded concern, Massoud Barzani acknowledges the following: "It is true that Kurds are dispersed in four different countries. They have problems, too. Each Kurdish group will settle their problems with their respective countries. The problems of Kurds are the internal issues of

---

[129] First appeared in *Today's Zaman* on Jan. 22, 2010

their respective countries." Barzani may be using such discourse "for the time being." But will we be justified if we assume that he has dark ulterior motives for the distant future, and if we thus oppose every step Kurds take? We have no choice but to accept what he says as sincere and act accordingly until he or others change their discourse.

The Kurdistan Workers' Party (PKK) is located in the Kandil Mountains in northern Iraq, and this represents a major problem. Currently, the Kurdish regional government offers cooperation with Turkey to deal with the PKK. But before that, if we manage to make some progress toward the ultimate settlement of the Kurdish issue internally, the northern Iraq dimension of the issue will be mitigated to a great extent. In sum, we have to sweep our home before dealing with the external dimension.

Most of us are unaware of the role our subconscious plays with respect to accepting the Kurdish reality. We can recall that some of our politicians and intellectuals would make references to "tribal leaders wearing the *poshu* headdress and [the loose-fitting pants of] *shalwar*" until very recently. We have nearly severed our ties with the traditional state since 1856. Still, we tend to assume ourselves to be a "great nation with a strong culture of statecraft," and we regard the societies of the Middle East as "tribes or clans." However, there is no difference in essence between our modern nation-state and the nation-state that the Kurds are trying to establish today. Both are imitations of certain models in Europe, where the original copy of this model has been preserved in Paris since the French Revolution. Our error is that we attempt to employ the Orientalism the West has used against us and use it against other Muslim peoples in the same manner. We don't realize what a strange situation we are in.

A political reality has come into being in northern Iraq regardless of our will. It has certain regional, constitutional, and international support and backing. Most Middle Eastern countries have already accepted this reality. But we still refuse to give it official recognition.

We still tend to view northern Iraq as a purely political and military issue. Paris is close to us while Arbil is distant and foreign. Our media organizations still portray this human geography as the realm of the people living in chaos, terror, and insecurity in a prehistoric era; they are portrayed as threatening us. However, when you fly to Arbil on a one-and-half-hour flight from Istanbul, you will see a calm, tranquil society that is like Urfa or Mardin. Its inhabitants are warm, and they like Turkey. They are eager to establish ties and dialogue with Turkey. But they never intend to be kept from the process they have set in motion.

Turks and Kurds: Pursuing Peace and a Common Future Together[130]

The Abant Platform, affiliated with the Hizmet Movement's Journalists and Writers Foundation (GYV), took up the Kurdish question on July 4–6, 2008 amidst ongoing debates on the closure case against the AK Party and the Ergenekon investigation. During the forum, the issue was discussed in all of its dimensions.

The title of the platform was "The Kurdish Question: Looking for Peace and a Common Future Together." The issue discussed at Abant is an important part of the ongoing crisis. In other words, unless the Kurdish question and other associated issues are resolved, the current crises will remain influential and become perennial. The meeting was supposed to have been held in Diyarbakır a few months ago. However, despite significant progress having been made toward holding this event in the city in Southeastern Turkey, the venue was changed at the last moment, unfortunately. During my attendance at the preliminary work on the meeting, it became clear that some circles and forces did not approve of the discussion of important issues outside of the framework that they had outlined.

There are two common and major questions in the minds of average people in relation to the Kurdish question: First, how sincere are those who advance this question? This question actually implies a doubt as to whether there really is such a question or if the issue was simply part of a plot staged by international forces seeking to undermine Turkey's prestige. Of course, I am aware that this is a simple and naïve

---

[130] First appeared in *Today's Zaman* on Jul. 08, 2008

question. But it should be noted that many disagreements and clashes caused by lack of communication are fostered by such simplistic and naïve factors. The Turkish public keeps these simple and naïve questions in mind while listening to the problems of their Kurdish brothers.

The second question is, "Let us assume that we have overcome the difficulty of facing the problem; then what is the solution?" Undoubtedly, this question is meaningful. It is now time for Kurdish opinion leaders and intellectuals to take concrete action to give a proper response to this question. But I think that, before resolving the issue, it is imperative and important to hold mutual talks and negotiations—I call this, in technical terms, an operation of "negotiation politics." The key to the resolution lies in the wisdom of negotiation politics simply because no solution will be found unless mutual discussions are held. The reason is obvious: Everyone has designed their own "others" based on symbols and images. In this world of constructs and images, it will be impossible for the Kurds and others to get to know each other in the absence of sound dialogue. "Defining" will prevail wherever there is no understanding or dialogue enabling people to get to know each other. At the Abant meeting, I am sure that the vast majority of participants had the opportunity to get to know the people about whom they may have held prejudices from a different perspective. For instance, Turkish people are generally unaware of the facts of Kurdish daily life, which is pretty rich and originated from the same sources as Arab and Persian cultures.

There are even some people who ask whether the Kurds in the region have a profound intellectual or spiritual capacity to take initiative. Those who have seen the TV serials on daily life in the region are particularly doubtful about whether Kurds and Arabs have a sophisticated human mind. But the speech by Abdülmelik Fırat, the greatest living sage of the Kurds, with his arguments and the poetry he recited in Kurdish, Persian, Turkish, and Arabic, left the audience speechless. Of course, people who will make reference to the political, economic, humanitarian, and international dimensions of the problem are strongly needed; but there is also great need for wise Kurds and opinion leaders like Mr. Fırat. The latest Abant meeting also showed us this: We need to speak out on our own behalf and of own our free will. In short, we need negotiation politics.

Chapter 11

The Changing Middle East

What Sort of Change Is Global Modernity?[131]

During his Middle East visit in December 2006, Tony Blair made the following remark in Dubai: "There is an ongoing struggle between the believers and non-believers in democracy and modernity in the world." According to Blair, the invasion of Iraq and the subsequent military operations have sought to force those resisting change and modernity to undergo a process of change and transformation. In other words, the Western world has a mission to change the Islamic world, relying on coercive measures.

It is better to understand the basic argument in these remarks, which make references to upcoming nightmares that will mostly affect the spirit of the modern world and the whole of humanity in the near future:

"Modernization" along with the accompanying notion of "change" has been presented to the Islamic world as a major goal to achieve since Napoleon's arrival in Egypt in 1798. Almost the entire set of policies that the states pursue concerns "change." The other name of change is "modernity" or "modernization." "Change" is both the symbol and political ideology for participation in modern life and the adaptation to modernity. Those who fail to accept the change are ready to be excluded from the modern world; they also become subject to removal from the socio-political system and eligible for punishment based on coercive measures, as recalled by Blair.

---

[131] First appeared in *Today's Zaman* on May 30, 2008

While this is the case, the minds of intellectuals and ordinary people are unclear in regards to the matter. In other words, with the exception of some symbols and a priori assumptions on forms, no one knows what "change" actually means.

Independently of what is associated with modernity, change is actually a cosmic, ontological, and social phenomenon. There is nothing in the universe that does not go through a process of transformation. Not only the symptoms but also the essences are in constant movement. An Arab poet famously remarked, "Change is the only constant that never changes." It is important to talk about movement, even of the essences, because Greek philosophers and Peripatetic philosophers used to think that only the symptoms were in movement. Renowned thinker Molla Sadra proved that change is actually observable in the essence (theory on the movement of the essence), invalidating arguments proposed by Aristotle and Avicenna.

But of course change is not a mere movement. Change represents both a phenomenon of movement and an ethical tendency. In other words, it happens in accordance with certain rules, goals, and meanings. If everything is changed in the universe, this means that nothing has an inherent ability or power to exist or to move. That is to say, everything is perishable, temporal, and limited. Only God is absolute and eternal.

The ethical dimension of change is vertical, which refers to maturity, or horizontal, which refers to backwardness and collapse. In review of social change, we may not ignore these two ethical dimensions. We can all agree that, "yes, we have to change." A process of change naturally affects us; but just in what direction and how should we change? This question is as important as the change itself.

What we have been offered through the last two centuries is a project of transformation. In other words, no demand for change is innocent or free of value and judgment. At the outset, this project was constructed by Europe's traditional modernity. Currently, it is promoted and led by the global modernity under the leadership of the US and used to justify the military operations in the Middle East.

Minds suffer from ambivalence and ambiguity in regards to globalization. All are prone to describe this controversial notion based on their particular interests and priorities. No matter how it is defined, globalization may not be separated from modernity. Globalization may be viewed as the global version of traditional modernity. It is still the sum of processes named, defined, and imposed by the West. Globalization creates beneficiaries and victims. On what side are we and why are we here?

Could globalization—the global version of enlightenment philosophy and modernity—have been different? This is a question that deserves attention. We may respond to this question affirmatively at least on the theoretical level, but we have to pay attention to the reasons it did not happen differently.

Democracy and Modernization[132]

A test is due in order to measure the success of modernity with particular references to its alleged achievements and ideals: liberties and freedoms, welfare and wealth, and security and safety.

1. In essence, modernity inherently involves inequality and injustice. It is quite obvious that the entire world is not able to become as wealthy as the Western world. The striking performance of China causes a rapid exhaustion of natural resources, including oil. As long as there are two major camps—the poor and the rich—in the world, global peace, stability, and serenity are not possible.

2. Wealth and welfare achieved through modernity pose a great danger to the planet and life on it, undermine ecological balances, and make the world an unbearable place. Global warming and climate change are the initial signals of this process.

3. The modern West is based on a perception of the world with no or little intrinsic meaning or goals, and it transforms the human being into an organism focused on production, consumption, and carnal relations. To this end, the basic ideas of this modern world impose nihilism onto the entire world.

---

[132] First appeared in *Today's Zaman* on Jun. 27, 2008

The modern Western world is reluctant to maintain dialogue with other religions and cultures; instead, it opts to distance itself from others. The West will have to either shift to quite a different perspective to create a just and fair world by giving up part of its wealth, or it will remain the source and primary reason of growing inequalities between different regions and classes, of terrorism, violence, ethnic cleansing, and repression.

Western countries rely on 80 percent of the entire world's production while they represent only 15 percent of the globe's total population. Pretty soon this will drop to 10 percent. In other words, they will be a small wealthy island in a sea of poor. This is neither natural nor sustainable.

As long as wars break out to sustain this unequal global order—it should be noted that 95 percent of the 500 wars over the last two centuries were experienced in the Western world or they were caused by the active involvement of Western countries—violence and terror will escalate and this will inevitably prioritize security issues over liberties. As liberties retreat, wealth will diminish and this will trigger even more global crises. Wars have made contributions to the Western world; the current international order guarantees domination and welfare of a part of the world population, but it simply does not care for the others. Today, three Western multinational corporations seek to acquire 75 percent of Iraqi oil for 30 years.

Inequality is causing serious problems and disruption not only on the global level but also on the domestic level because modernization and development plans are inherently based on inequality. Injustice in income distribution leads to social turmoil, blocks positive politics, and causes violence and terror. This is the case not only on the domestic but also on the global level. As long as inequality persists, poverty becomes deeper and more visible and the young and desperate masses in urban areas are alienated; this of course breeds a culture of violence. Current models are unable to control the migration of people from rural to urban areas. Wars and invasions are not the solution to overcome these crises.

Unfortunately, democracies fail to prevent wars because, among others, lobbies, pressure groups, and circles holding the majority of capital strongly influence the decisions of parliaments with their huge financial resources.

Western democracies are the best among the worse, but they have failed to ensure pluralism and justice in the past and today there is no sign that they will achieve these goals because Western democracies are pluralist in a political sense, while they are monist from a cultural and social perspective. They exclude a strong ethical value like justice in the political culture. As terror and wars put an emphasis on security, the sphere of the available and recognized liberties gets narrower. What should be done at this stage is not to blame a certain religion; what should be done now is to seek real solutions to current huge problems.

Whose Democracy Is It?[133]

The West's conception of democracy was tested during the first Tahrir uprising and then again during the 2012 elections in Egypt.

The question was: To what extent would the West's democracy meet the demands of the masses who rushed to the streets demanding democracy? It failed in the first stage. The coup d'état of July 3, 2013 revealed a paradox: On the one hand, the region's most established Islamic movement, the Muslim Brotherhood (MB), voiced democratic demands; on the other hand, the pro-democracy Western world—the US and the EU—supported the coup d'état that suppressed those democratic demands. Not only governments and states backed the coup, but also intellectual and political groups, liberals, secularists, leftists, and nationalists sided with the coup. Ironically enough, Saudis who are governed with a Sharia-based rule have emerged as the financiers of the coup and this has been welcomed by the "democrats."

This paradox signifies a deep, underlying problem: The theory of democracy as formulated by the West has been unable to respond to the intellectual frameworks and social players in Egypt—and partially in Turkey—that differ from the special social and philosophical circumstances that gave birth to it.

---

[133] First appeared in *Today's Zaman* on Oct. 21, 2013

John Esposito, professor and well-known scholar of Islamic studies, says that in the wake of the Egyptian coup, the Western media started to discuss whether Middle Eastern countries are ready for democracy. Actually, they should discuss whether democracy as standardized by the West is capable of internalizing the Muslim world and meeting the demands of Muslims. Otherwise, we should ask, "Is any other implementation of democracy possible?" Indeed, in the Muslim world, the groups who seek to engage in democratic politics tend to take Islam as their reference and enter democratic competition and politically represent the (religious) communities, unlike Western political parties that are generally organized to represent class-based demands. Aware of this, Esposito says:

"By exhibiting an attitude that endorses the Egyptian coup, Europe and the US risk giving the message to the democratic administrations in the Middle East that the West is not ready for democracies that take Islam as their reference. The West has failed to identify the coup as a coup, gave behind-the-scenes support to the coup generals and turned a blind eye to the millions of Egyptians who reject the coup. By doing so, it has adopted the stance, 'We will support democracy as long as it complies with our wishes.'"[134]

In an urge to justify the coup, certain political scientists argue that the MB is actually not a political party, but a pan-Islamic movement that has branches in Arab countries. They further suggest that the MB seeks to rearrange social life and government according to Islamic values. Although they tried to hide the sympathy they felt for the coup perpetrators, academics had engaged in a naive quest to pave the way for the coup after the MB won the elections in 2012 by saying that former Egyptian President Mohammed Morsi was trying to dominate all public institutions and establish a government that wouldn't respect democratic rights. They also maintained that although it was the Freedom and Justice Party that entered the elections, it was the MB that operated behind the scenes and the MB was controlled not by Morsi, but by Supreme Guide Mohammed Badie. In this connection, they argued, Morsi failed to

---

[134] *Zaman*, July 27, 2013

distinguish himself from the MB and so Egyptians—they probably refer to the coup-supporting, liberal, nationalist, leftist, and socialists of the second Tahrir gathering—said to Morsi, "Pardon, but we didn't elect the MB or the Supreme Guide," and when Morsi resisted, they asked for the military's help to save democracy.

If ties with the MB can justify a coup, then all parties should be shut down in all Western countries, given the fact that various lobbyists, interest groups, and civil society organizations (CSOs) can all enjoy an incredible impact on politics, the administration, and decision-making mechanisms. In the final analysis, the MB is a CSO.

Democratic Patience for Egypt[135]

The military's overthrow of democratically elected President Mohammed Morsi ushered in chaos in Egypt.

The attitude Western countries, particularly the United States and the European Union, adopted in the face of this manifest injustice and tyranny has been disgusting. This duplicity and double-dealing attitude of Westerners who market themselves as advocates of democracy creates utter disappointment amongst people.

Morsi did nothing to deserve this tyranny and unfair treatment. During the year he was in office, Morsi faced many immoral and illegal conspiracies and plots, all of which were disgraceful.

The Muslim Brotherhood (MB) is an 85-year-old, vast social movement. It represents one of the best examples of social Islam around the world. It has spread to the entire Muslim world. Its primary goal is to reinforce society's moral, social, and spiritual development. It is a civilian organization. This movement showed occasional interest in politics; some of its political moves proved wrong, while others proved felicitous. But it has never employed hypocritical language; it has never had a secret agenda; it has not become deeply involved with politics while promoting the rhetoric of refraining from politics. When it found an opportunity, it encouraged some of its members to run for parliament. It waited patiently when it didn't have this opportunity. The MB

---

[135] First appeared in *Today's Zaman* on Jul. 08, 2013

never resorted to violence or terrorism. It parted ways with those members who yielded to armed struggle or terrorism. It remained within the legal sphere.

Many of its members were exiled to the Gulf monarchies, but its intellectuals and opinion leaders never endorsed kingdoms, monarchies, or authoritarian regimes. The only exemption to this was Saudi King Faisal (may God have mercy on him). Faisal was a king, but he knew the region could be revived only with Islam and he trusted in the MB in this regard. He ordered the radio broadcasting of the Qur'anic commentary of the late Sayyid Qutb. He nurtured anti-American and anti-imperialist sentiments. When Henry Kissinger wanted to meet him during the oil embargo of 1973, he received him in a tent in the desert, not in his palace in Riyadh. Kissinger was only able to reach the tent after a difficult journey over several days, and asked, "Why did you choose to receive me here?"

Faisal replied, "We came to the cities from the desert. We don't need oil. If necessary, we may return to the desert. But you cannot do without oil." At that moment, Kissinger recorded Faisal's name on the global mafia list. Today's kingdoms, liberals, leftists, nationalists, the world's victorious forces, the financial supporters and backers of the coup, Egypt's Salafis, al-Azhar, and the Coptic Church all performed poorly and disgracefully with regard to the coup.

The ousting of Morsi in a coup is just "a virgule in the historic progress" of the MB, to borrow the words of the late Necmettin Erbakan, who faced the postmodern coup of 1997. In his last statement, Morsi called on the MB and the Egyptian people who side with legitimacy to "resist peacefully." This is a correct and proper call. Egyptians will not accept the coup. And hopefully, they will lend an ear to Morsi and resist peacefully. They will not fall into the mistake of engaging in an armed struggle like the Syrian people. If the Syrian opposition had not submitted to civil war provocations, it could have been successful by now.

Every fair person supports the Egyptian people who resist the coup peacefully. The whole country and even the entire Muslim world will support them if the MB does not engage in armed struggle. The real revolution has just started in Egypt; this will be a moral revolution Muslims will undertake without shedding blood. They will win because they enjoy legitimacy and moral supremacy.

In religions, "patience" is a key notion. Patience is the continuous act of seeking God's help and victory through our actions. In comparison, secular movements act with haste. God is with the patient.

Opponents of Democracy[136]

The coup that occurred in Egypt on July 3, 2013 is proof that democracy in our region is going through hard times. The general tendency in the Muslim world is toward democracy, but this trend is facing "internal and external hardships."

The opponents of democracy in the Muslim world can be listed as follows:

1. The West. With its political and military face, the West is telling us: If you establish governments that act in harmony with my values, the lifestyle I impose on you, and my global interests, then you are free to use democratic means; but if you employ your own values in politics and if you make your religion-oriented lifestyle visible in the public sphere, and if you attempt to establish certain unions among yourselves, then I will not permit this, and I will prefer military dictatorships, coups, and autocratic regimes for you.

2. The Gulf monarchies. We know that this myriad of monarchies enjoying varying power and influence have long been waging propaganda activities against democratic regimes.

3. Military dictatorships. It is no secret that dictatorships in the region are at odds with democracy.

4. Intellectuals and academic circles are inspired by "Eastern despotism," one of the pivotal concepts of the Orientalist perspective. They are convinced that the way the Muslim world joins modern history will not be through democratic means. Profoundly influenced by the 18th century Enlightenment and 19th century

---

[136] First appeared in *Today's Zaman* on Jul. 29, 2013

positivism, all of these intellectuals believe that the state, politics, power, and administration are such important matters that they cannot be left to the public.

5. Minorities. Certain religious, ethnic, sectarian and cryptic groups who lack numerical power are not happy with the way the majority has a say via equal franchise. It is unfair to assert that minorities, as a whole, are categorically opponents of democracy. Some of them, in particular cryptic groups, entertain this perspective. To these we can add "moral marginals."

6. The neocon/Zionist groups, which have always existed in the West and, in particular, in the US, believe that it is easier to work with kings or dictators than with democratically elected rulers who are loyal to their nation. They are mainly in the "democrat/liberal" circles.

7. Certain Islamic groups, movements, and parties that believe democracy is not a legitimate political method when it is assessed against the canons and philosophy of Islam, including its basic philosophic assumptions and its emergence and consequences. Naturally, these groups should be set aside from other groups as their objections to democracy are based on the Islamic creed and philosophy. They can further be grouped as (a) those who radically or categorically object to democracy, and (b) those who believe that democracy can be tamed using Islam's rich theological and jurisprudential legacy, and that proficient scholars and political scientists may be successful in developing a democracy model specific to Muslims.

For many understandable reasons, we can assert that there will be no turning back from democracy for a long time to come. Societies do not wait for theoretical or jurisprudential debates to be settled to everyone's satisfaction. They expect peace. Democracy seems attractive for the masses because people fall for the hope that they can project their will onto the political center, as they are certain that executives will be reshuffled at set intervals.

However, after so many elections, they see that there is no improvement in the situation. This is a dilemma, and societies have yet to make sense of this dilemma. This applies to the West. Democracy suffers from global issues.

The Greater Middle East Project[137]

The borders of the current-day Middle East were drawn in the last quarter of the previous century in order to identify who had governance over which regions. These borders were arbitrary, lacking any consideration for crucial domestic factors.

The main problem was that the key decision-makers were foreign colonialists and imperialists—not the native occupants of the regions themselves. When the Ottoman state was dissolved, the region lost its center, leaving the area weakened and subject to the actions of others.

Now in the first quarter of the 21st century, 100 years since the designations of states that have defined a region, the Middle East is being reshaped. The tensions and disputes of the past still exist, the only difference being that Israel has been installed in the region as a military unit. So the tradition continues: the task of reshaping the region is assumed by those with no concern for the opinions of the region's inhabitants themselves.

During her visit to Tel Aviv in 2006, while the Israeli attacks against Lebanon were still under way, US Secretary of State Condoleezza Rice said it was time for a "new Middle East." She also said, "The operation [the transformation of the Middle East] has started; people of this region will have to submit to this change. Those who have doubts should take a look at Beirut."

Apparently those who would like to build this "new Middle East" will resort to three main instruments:

1. Reliance on military might and invasions (Afghanistan, Iraq, Palestine-Lebanon, Somalia and, most likely, more)
2. Instigating changes in political regimes and to pre-existing borders

---

[137] First appeared in *Today's Zaman* on Mar. 06, 2009

3. Erasing Islam in the Middle East, as proposed by Norman Pod-horetz, one of the masterminds of the neo-conservative move-ment, and implementing projects that will be funded by wom-en's rights movements and NGOs (a variety of institutions and strategic, economic, social, and cultural think tanks supported by Western proponents) aimed to turn Islam into a set of secu-lar rituals

The project to create a "new Middle East"—the title "Greater Middle East" should be avoided because this has been outdated—relies on the implementation of three major ideas:

i) The West represents the core and the center, and the region called "the Middle East" has been defined accordingly. In other words, the West is the center and the Middle East is a periph-eral variable.

ii) The Middle East is a place where Muslims live; it is foreign to the West in both culture and geography.

iii) The region should be kept under control and reshaped con-stantly.

The Middle East is in a straitjacket. The question that the constrained must ask is: will this straitjacket forced upon us be loosened or will we become more comfortable as we conform to its shape? This is the real-ity of the matter, and the people of the region should show their deter-mination to bring about change for themselves, without being config-ured and re-configured according to the whims of others. This can be achieved by establishing a separate, proprietary set of parameters:

1. The region will likely have to deal with a process of change; this change should be ensured by relying on internal dynamics.

2. Negotiation should be relied on during this process of change; a project of change to be imposed via coercion is not democrat-ic and will not bring democracy to the region.

3. Religion is the major source of the political, cultural, internation-al, and socio-political codes of this region. The change that the region needs cannot be brought by marginalizing Islam and lim-iting its sphere to private life.

4. What happened in the 20th century should not be repeated in the 21st century. We need to learn from the past suffering of the region's people and to strive not to repeat past mistakes.

Ethnic groups in the region are all related to each other. If we do not change ourselves, our institutions, and structures on our own, external forces will. This, as witnessed in the suffering and pain of the past, has been proven.

A Way Out[138]

When a region gets reshaped, and while political maps and regimes get changed around, the stones set in place from a previous period of time get resettled and repositioned. But when change does not unfold within a reasonable framework, societal disasters do occur.

When this happens, it is not easy to stay in front of the inevitable floods of anger that are unleashed. Everyone blames everyone else; people become objects of hatred for one another. In order to keep the masses from understanding just what has happened, some provoke them to focus on just one small part of the larger picture. Those who are engaged in this business use platforms like the media to get us all to see just one tree, when what we should really be seeing is the larger forest before us.

A systematic series of events unfolds which then helps elicit hatred from society. The things we see happening around us go beyond the capacity of our consciences to tolerate. Currently, there are four countries in the Middle East which have been engulfed by the language of hatred and enmity. The region as a whole is being pulled into a whirlpool of religious, ethnic, and sectarian violence. We have arrived at the point of defending even the most just and right of cases with the least justifiable ways and types of dialogue. The blood of tens of thousands has been spilt for no reason, and the numbers of those who have been injured and handicapped is expressed in the hundreds of thousands. As for those who have been forced to flee their countries, or even become refugees in their own, these number in the millions.

---

[138] First appeared in *Today's Zaman* on Sept. 10, 2012

Muslims are killing one another; the very same animosity that Muslims are forbidden by the Qur'an to have towards Christians or Jewish people is being expressed by Sunnis, Shiites, Alevis, Turks, Arabs, Kurds, and Moroccans to one another. Nationalism and sectarianism have literally blunted our own sensibilities and knowledge of how to behave. It is the definition of violence steeped in ignorance.

No matter what anyone may say, the truth is that the Greater Middle East Project (GMEP) is in fact being implemented. The main goal of the project is to "leave no county with a Muslim population that is stronger or more influential than Israel" in place in the region. The project began in Iraq, is going through Syria, and will eventually arrive at both Iran and Turkey. This is indeed the story of the black, white, and yellow cow (to be sacrificed).

In the first stage of the project, [Turkey as] "the soft power" is employed to show deep-rooted political and societal changes take place. Here is what Colin Powell said in Morocco in 2004: "We will not impose change from the outside in countries that head into the Greater Middle East Project. These changes will be started internally alongside social and economic advances, and we will see that political and economic reforms take place hand in hand with more developed countries; we will encourage the people of these countries!"

However, when "soft power" does not work, the method (i.e. the second stage of the project) to be applied—in order that things do not happen too late—is "creative chaos." Through this method, all the stones are overturned, and countries of the region are thrown into complete chaos. Look at what occurred in Iraq; not only was it divided into three parts, the main center of Islamic civilization was torn apart, the substructure was destroyed, and ethnic and sectarian groups were turned into each others' sworn enemies.

Now we see that Damascus is on the same route. Let us recall that Condoleezza Rice once stated quite openly: "We will change the political maps and regimes in 22 Islamic countries." Amongst these 22, Turkey was included.

There can be no question of course that we did not draw the lines of these countries, nor did we build their current facilities. But we could have used our volition and some shared decisions to define them again. The trap into which we have fallen, combined with the way we have been divided up, does not allow us this opportunity though. My personal conviction and belief is that, until the year 2011, Turkey had a great opportunity. Unfortunately though, when it came to both the Kurdish issue and the events in Syria, Turkey stumbled on a basic set of mistakes, and changed its 10-year course of reading events around, instead turning to hawkish policies.

If hands other than our own are to once again shape this region, there is no country, nation, or sect which will emerge the better for it. We will instead be stepping into a very painful and remorse-filled century before us. Muslim people and nations must set aside the meaningless competition between one another and instead move and act in harmony with one another.

Muslims are killing one another. It will be said later that Islam was unable to stop the clashes and to unite. But no, this is not Islam; this is the crime and sin of some Muslims. Muslims who take religion seriously know that it is a great sin to fight against other Muslims and to nourish hatred in the name of ethnic roots or sects.

Those who know this have great duties and responsibilities. Let us not fall into this trap. There is no other way out, except acting with conscience and justice in brotherhood and union.

Breaking Free of the Straitjacket with Internal Dynamics[139]

Muslim countries gained their independence within the framework set up by two big colonial states, Great Britain and France, in the aftermath of the Ottoman state's withdrawal from the Middle East.

In these countries, whose boundaries were drawn without paying attention to the historical past and social fabric of the region, the void left by the Ottomans' withdrawal was never filled.

The problem was basically this: Western countries designed the region, but this design turned the entire region into a chaotic environ-

---

[139] First appeared in *Today's Zaman* on Feb. 13, 2009

ment. Ironically, the same Western countries now argue that the region cannot be fixed or civilized. They are not only spreading this Orientalist view, but are also stressing that they alone could achieve stability in the region. This is what the US, which plans to rule the Middle East relying on a strategy employed by the Ottoman state, has been doing since 2003.

After all these developments, there is this question on everyone's mind: Will the Middle East, which includes Turkey as well, become a stable region via interventions by outside powers? In other words, is it possible for a region, as well as its people, to continue marching towards the future relying on projects imposed and promoted by external forces without using its own dynamics?

Democracy is the most popular political regime of the current age. It is the best among the worst regimes, and Middle Eastern peoples have no argument with that. I may even argue that in comparison to Turkey and Iran, Arab Middle Eastern nations are closer to a democratic system in terms of their sociopolitical culture. At least the homogeneity of the nation-state has not yet determined the core structure of the society in them. Civil rights still recognize different options of individuals and social groups. Besides, the major demands of Muslim communities in the Muslim world include democratic participation, education, health, and the removal of the barriers before a freer civil society. The autocratic regimes should not mislead us; just because the political regimes in these countries are autocratic does not means that the sociopolitical culture is of an autocratic and totalitarian character.

The reason I am recalling all this is that the neo-conservatives did not consider the social demands and tendencies in these communities when they decided to take democracy and freedom to the Middle East. Influenced by interest groups, lobbies, and the broader view of Orientalism, they concluded that only coercive measures would work to stabilize and democratize the region; consequently, they presented their intention of bringing democracy and freedom to the region as justification for their military invasion.

The only concrete model that the US has to offer is the fact that Germany and Italy were democratized by means of violence and coercion after they lost World War II. Fascism was defeated in these countries via war and military means. This told Westerners that the same path could be followed with respect to the Middle East. However, in addition to the sociocultural characteristics of the Middle East, there is something else that justifies our inquiry into the validity of this approach: that Germany and Italy were a natural part of the political culture and history of Europe. Just as postmodernism inevitably followed modernism, the arrival of democracy after fascism was not surprising. Besides, democracy was not a popular regime in Europe until World War II. De Gaulle's commitment to democracy is controversial. In short, World War II brought democracy to Europe, but what made this possible was internal social dynamics.

The overall picture at the present time is as follows:

The US military invasions and their subsequent failures show that the methods employed during this process have failed to take democracy to the region. If the same methods are used, people will continue dying. The region has its own dynamics. They should be respected, and artificial barriers before these dynamics should be removed.

And there is another point: that Islam is the greatest source of legitimacy and motivation for a transition to democracy in the region. Any project not justified by Islam will not be permanent, nor will it be endorsed by the peoples in the region.

The Discourse of "Barbarians in the Middle East"[140]

Rudolf Bkouche, a member of the National Bureau of the French Jewish Union for Peace, in an article where he commented on Israel's attacks against Lebanon in August 2006, said there was only one thing left behind from Zionism: "A Jewish state serving as an outpost of civilization against barbarism."

The West does not admit that the real problem stems from the fact that the Palestinian people have become refugees in their own territories and that Israel has constantly expanded its territories in an attempt to make room for additional Jewish migration from different parts of the world. What's more, Western countries argue that Israel exercises

---

[140] First appeared in *Today's Zaman* on Jan. 09, 2009

its right to defense, alleging that every country is entitled to this right; however, they fail to accept the right of resistance of the people whose territories are under occupation. More importantly, civilians are murdered; mosques, hospitals, schools, UN-controlled buildings, and ambulances carrying casualties are bombed; and children attending graduation ceremonies and traffic police officers on the streets are killed, but the West still ignores that all these massacres are actually war crimes.

Bkouche, a man of reason and conscience, explains this as follows: "No measure is taken against a state which considers itself entitled to do anything it wants because this country is part of a larger family of European countries. We say barbarity against civility; yes, this is true if we admit that all civilizations have contributed to barbarity to some degree and that Western civilization has made its contribution during the period of colonialism and the two world wars in the 20th century. The Israeli state joins this barbarity as an outpost of civilization."[141]

Contrary to popular belief, the Western public is naïve. Despite a high rate of literacy and school attendance, the people are easily manipulated by certain institutions and actors. What the American and European people are told by these actors is this: "Israel represents Western values in a region where savages and barbarians from the Middle Ages live. It pays the heavy bill of Western civilization." Benny Morris makes an interesting analysis on the functional value of Israel for the Western world: "Of course, we cannot leave Palestine to Hamas. If we do not stop Hamas, we will keep watching scenes where the women walk a few steps behind their husbands."

This Orientalist depiction has a strong influence. A Westerner may tolerate the killing of babies held by women who walk a few steps behind their husbands by Israeli troops if they look at this picture alone. Civilian massacres are not committed secretly. A high-level Israeli commander made this statement during the Israeli assault against Lebanon: "We dropped 1,800 cluster bombs in Lebanon....They told us that this is a

---

[141] *Zaman* daily, Aug. 21, 2006.

good time because people are coming out of the mosques and the rockets would deter them."[142]

For the public, this is nothing but a mere reflection of the clash of civilizations. Yes, Israel kills civilians and tries out new weaponry on the Palestinian people in each new assault. But in the end, this is a war between the civilized and the barbarians, and if they are not stopped, the Middle Eastern barbarians will destroy Western civilization. Did Bernard Lewis, who knew the region well, not advance this along with supportive arguments?

When communism was defeated and the Soviet Union—the Evil Empire—collapsed, former Israeli Military Intelligence Directorate head Shlomo Gazit added a new mission to Israel's fight against the barbarians. According to Gazit, Israel's mission after this historical milestone would be to keep the anti-democratic regimes in the region alive; it was necessary to protect these autocratic and dictatorial states against Hamas or Islam.

The Political Destiny of the Middle East[143]

According to American Islamologist John Esposito, there is a strong demand in the Middle East in general and in Turkey in particular for democratization, civil initiatives, and individual freedom; meanwhile existing political regimes are trying to survive by oppressing this demand.

What makes these regimes legitimate in the international arena is the possibility that one day "the threat of Islam" may replace these oppressive regimes. The phenomenon that the legality of oppressive regimes is based on the probable, potential, and fictitious threats of oppression is an ironic fact of contemporary times. I think the priorities of the international system and its "strategic" approach regarding the region should also be added to this fact.

The way son Abdullah became the king of Jordan after the death of his father King Hussein shows a concrete example of who really desired

---

[142] *Haaretz* daily (on Sept. 13, 2006), quoted in Tamer Korkmaz, *Zaman* daily, Nov. 14, 2006.

[143] First appeared in *Today's Zaman* on Apr. 30, 2012

democracy and liberty in and for the region. As is known, for almost thirty years King Hussein's brother, Prince Hassan, was considered the heir to the throne. Prince Hassan is an intellectual person who is known for his idea that democratic priorities joined with Islam would make a proper environment for a participative political culture and he thought that if it happened, then it would lead to further democratic initiatives in the Middle East. He reached out to social groups that were ostracized from the system in Jordan and he believed that a common formula for social cohesion could be developed with them.

While everybody expected that Prince Hassan was going to come to the fore after the death of King Hussein, there was an abrupt development and King Abdullah came to the fore. If Prince Hassan, who had been known as heir apparent for a long time, had come to the lead, maybe there would be a hope for a real change. However, "the great will" that raised King Hussein from his deathbed, brought him to the Capital Amman, and made him enthrone his son didn't want such a change.

The extent and the depth of this will's profound impact on the political system of the Middle East haven't become apparent yet. On the one hand, the strategic approach of this determinant will and the status quo that it projected for the region drags the people of the Middle East into a deep state of schizophrenia; on the other hand, it pushes them outside of the realm of history.

Whether in terms of "global modernization" that is led by America or in terms of "traditional modernization" still defended by Europe, the three major factors that are required for both are "democracy, human rights, and the free market economy." In the case that existing political regimes in the Middle East are criticized, the main criteria of this criticism are these three factors. But whenever steps are taken in the Middle East to implement changes towards these ends, these attempts are thwarted, primarily by Europe and America, which have political, military and economic plans in the region.

This isn't only an illogical paradox or a moral hypocrisy, but also a direct expression of the deep distrust towards the people of the region due to energy sources and the geostrategic situation of the region. The West (Europe and the USA) apparently didn't want these assets that it offered to the entire world by means of international contracts and obligatory texts about human rights to be controlled by the initiative of civil and social powers in the Middle East. It considered that such a development would create a threat in terms of their interests. It has been so at least so far.

Here is the question: In spite of many social explosions, is the Middle East still under the tight control of the great will? What do the powers that didn't consider even Prince Hassan to be trustworthy think of the administrative changes in which the Muslim Brotherhood is actively taking part? One of the most stereotypical of these oppressive regimes is surely the Baath regime. And the Committee of Union and Progress (CUP) has been able to protect its existence in the government thus far.

Syria was headed by [the mentality of] Talat Pasha [of the CUP] and Iraq was headed by Enver Pasha [of the CUP]; I wonder if the supporters of the CUP will leave with the departure of Saddam Hussein and former Syrian President Hafiz Assad? Or just as it happened in our country, will the rulers change but the basics of the regime remain the same? Will apparent legal oligarchical dictatorships and autocratic structures collapse and republicans that go on being in the driver's seat with deep supporters of the Committee of Union and Progress (CUP) replace them?

Occupation Forces Left a Legacy of Crisis[144]

The US has finally conceded that they have lost the war in Iraq. Richard Perle, known as the Prince of Darkness, said invading Iraq was a mistake.

How should his words be interpreted? Even if Perle apologized after admitting the mistake, would that mean everything is over and done with? The US devastated a country that was one of the essential centers of [Mesopotamian and Islamic] civilization in the world, seized thousands of its historical works, destroyed its infrastructure, killed more than a million people, forced 4.5 million to emigrate, smuggled the country's oil, and now they are saying, "It was a mistake." This is a declaration not of the end of the occupation, the legitimacy of which was doubtful from the very beginning, but of the end of ethical values. The war lobby

---

[144] First appeared in *Today's Zaman* on Jun. 02, 2009

is falling apart. Authorities in the pro-war "civilian wing" of the Pentagon and the White House have already boxed their personal belongings and vacated their offices. Former US President George W. Bush said he would not withdraw US troops from Iraq and lost public support. Current US President Barack Obama's vow to gradually withdraw troops was the Anglo-Saxon alliance's last step before their final maneuver.

But there is still uncertainty. When and how the occupying forces will withdraw from Iraq will continue to be an important item on the agenda. There are some conclusions that can be made about the recent developments. Iraq as a whole is not completely satisfied with America's realization of having lost the war, or with the certainty that troops will leave. There are some groups that are unhappy with this development. Among these groups, the most important one is the Kurds, who believe this period has offered them an unprecedented opportunity. If the US withdraws from Iraq and leaves the Kurds on their own, this will not only hinder the program the Kurds have prepared, but also leave countries in the region to themselves. While the right thing is to leave regional countries alone and allow them to conduct negotiations and search for a common solution without the help of third parties, for one reason or another, non-regional forces have intervened in regional issues at every level. The Sufis have a great saying that goes "Sorrow gives birth to a blessing." Leaving the Kurds to themselves forced them to move closer to Turkey, and this is a rather good development.

Along with the Kurdish group, there are some countries in the region that are not joyful about the US withdrawing from Iraq, at least not at this point. According to the threat assessment of these countries, the region has fallen under Iranian domination. Shiites have realized their own strength and have become political. The occupation of Afghanistan and Iraq, Israel's bloody attack on Lebanon, and the developments in Palestine in recent years have done nothing more than bring Iran to the forefront. Iran was disturbing the Taliban in the east and Saddam Hussein's Baath regime in the west. The Shiites were not expecting to be able to take political initiative this early. But everything changes quickly. The region embarked on a different course, and Iran declared that it was the only force that could resist Israel and that it would not allow the

US to make arrangements in the region all by itself. Certainly this challenge by Iran forced not only the US, but also the UK and Israel, to think long and hard. The one point we can say about Iran at the moment is that it appears to be very successful with its policies.

There is a new picture before us. The UK, which had aligned with the US in the beginning, is no longer appearing in the front of the line. Those with sharp vision can see that this country, which has a 300-year experience of colonialism, is a shadow in the very front of this picture. The failure of the US's estimations, which lacked depth and elaboration, proves that it has not been able to fully succeed in its efforts. What the US benefited from in the expensive Vietnam War, which caused great grief, is still unclear. Now let's look at what's happening in Iraq one more time.

The US entered Iraq like an elephant entering a glassworks shop and destroyed and broke everything. It suffered cuts and injuries to itself and now wants to get out of the situation. Its strategic ally, the UK, is preparing a "remodeling and repairing" plan. The US, not having learned a lesson from Vietnam and Iraq, is now making the same mistakes in Afghanistan and Pakistan. Who is controlling the US's mind?

Does Anybody Really Know?[145]

The US occupation of Iraq that started in March 2003 has ended. It should be noted that the occupation is only over in military terms. With its embassies, consulates, military attachés, advisors, private companies, new bases, and small but powerful military equipment, the US will continue to keep Iraq under its control. Civilians will have replaced military servicemen to oversee nearly 200 assignments, jobs, and duties. Therefore, reports or analyses saying that the US has withdrawn and Iran filled the vacuum hold no truth. But, of course, Iran is trying to gain an edge by demonstrating initiative in Iraq; that is true.

At this point, there are four questions that we need to ask: What happened in Iraq? Why did it happen? What could happen next? And what should actually happen? The answer to the first question offers a dramatic and tragic picture. Everything relevant to this question is heart-

---

[145] First appeared in *Today's Zaman* on May 14, 2012

breaking. The overall picture pertains to the kind of Iraq that the occupying forces have left behind following a complete US military withdrawal from Iraq.

There are different reports and figures. According to reports by independent agencies and institutions in 2008, the occupation claimed 1 million lives in Iraq. Back then, there were reports of some 2 million refugees. However, US sources argued in December 2011 that the number of Iraqis killed during the occupation was 100,000. The number of internationally displaced persons and refugees is 4 million.

According to French researcher Geraldine Chatelard, more than 1.5 million Iraqi people have left their country. It is not an exaggeration to say that 4 million people have left Iraq since the start of the invasion, in 2003.

Thirty-thousand Iraqi women, including 12-year-old girls, were raped; there is a visible rise in the number of blond babies in Iraq's southern regions. Like in Bosnia, some mothers have committed suicide.

There have been 550 scientists and intellectuals deliberately killed. This number nears 3,000 when academics of all different disciplines are added to the equation. Based on witness accounts, the Iraqis hold MOSSAD agents and Pentagon staff responsible for the killings. According to journalist Layla Anwar, there were 45,000 scientists in Iraq before the occupation; now, they are gone.

There were 18,900 people put behind bars and tortured for being insurgents. The WikiLeaks cables published in 2010 showed that extreme methods of torture were employed to intimidate thousands of Iraqis between 2004 and 2009, just because they defended their homeland. The Abu Ghraib prison has become notorious because of the tortures committed there. There are 16,000 civilians still missing. A number of museums in Baghdad and other cities have been looted. Approximately 170,000 pieces have been stolen from the Iraq Museum alone.

The infrastructure of Iraq has totally collapsed. There is no potable water; the unemployment rate is around 70 percent. Seven million people live below the poverty line; they are struggling to survive on $2.20 a day. There are 1.5 million people who are homeless. During the period between 1990 and 2002, 1.5 million people died from the inhumane embargo imposed by the US. The number of deaths in connection with the embargo is on rise. According to a report by the Turkish Association of Physicians in 2005, 12 percent of the hospitals in Iraq were not suitable for use. Measures are falling short on addressing infant mortality. Twenty-seven percent of infants under the age of 5 are malnourished. The literacy rate was 80 percent in the past; now, it is down to around 50 percent. In short, Iraq is devastated and dilapidated.

_ In fact, nobody cares about the Muslim people who were killed. The US government does not keep records of Iraqi deaths; only statistics for the occupying forces are kept. These statistics show that 4,747 American, 179 British and 139 soldiers of other nationalities have been killed in Iraq. The number of wounded soldiers is around 32,000.

It should be noted that the ongoing tragedy in Afghanistan is no less grave than the one in Iraq. A short note: While hundreds of thousands of people were being killed in Iraq and cities were being destroyed, the warplanes of the occupying forces were taking off from the Gulf countries, the Arab brothers of the Iraqis, and the base in Adana, Turkey.

But what did the US and other occupying forces want? The argument about weapons of mass destruction was a lie; the American media admitted it. Saddam never had a relationship with al-Qaeda. What did the US want from Iraq? Does anybody know?

Whose Turn Is Next after Syria?[146]

The oppressive Baath regime would have been gone by now had things gone well, as we desired. But almost all have committed mistakes in Syria, which include the following:

1. The Syrian opposition, which asked for a regime change with justifiable reasons, should not have resorted to counter violence and armed struggle. We have two concrete examples on this matter: First, the shah regime murdered 60,000 people during the revolution in Iran (1978-1979) according to Ayatollah Khomeini, but the Muslims did not use guns on his orders. The Hosni Mubarak regime was toppled and nearly 1,000 demonstrators died during the turmoil, but the Tahrir Square revolu-

---

[146] First appeared in *Today's Zaman* on Dec. 01, 2011

tionaries did not resort to arms. The Egyptian army, which does not want to transfer the power to the people, is now killing demonstrators; its goal is to terrorize the people and make them use guns, as in Syria. The Syrian opposition should have refrained from a violent response and given assurances that it would not take revenge, that it would take the necessary measures to protect the rights of non-Muslims, and that the Kurds who have been deprived of their fundamental rights under the Assad regime would be recognized as equal citizens.

2. Iran repeated the most dramatic mistake of its revolutionary history, standing by the bloody Assad regime for mere reasons of realpolitik, just as it did in 1982. What would have best suited the Iranians, who endured a despotic and repressive regime, would have been to stand against the brutal repression of the civilian demonstrations in Syria and tell the Assad regime that this would be the end of their rule before taking measures to end the bloodshed. The ambivalence of the Lebanese Hezbollah also deserves criticism in this regard.

3. Over the last year, I have stated that Turkey's Syrian policy is wrong. Today, Turkey's foreign policy has moved from the point of "zero problems with neighbors" to zero problems with the Western world. The most obvious reflection of this is Syria. Turkey was pretty successful when it was pursuing its own agenda in the region; the current tragic outlook was, however, created after American pressure and involvement.

Arabs say you should not cry and mourn the dead and that you should not regret what happened. So we should focus on what happens from now on.

The current regime in Syria will eventually be changed. It is hard to estimate when this will happen. But it is certain that the process is irreversible. Unfortunately, the whole situation may become bloodier. From my standpoint, I am trying to look at the events through "ideal politics" by taking the realpolitik into consideration. It is the job of the policymakers and administrators to devise the strategies and tactics that would accommodate both approaches. It is not my business.

The world, the region, and the country have different realities. But the solution that would be best for the region could be attained if the nations in the region showed a determination to take ownership of their own future.

The argument I have been defending for years is this: Unity in the region will be achieved through the initiative and leadership of Turkey, Iran, and Egypt. The roadmap for the future of Syria could be drawn by these three countries, which should gather together to discuss this matter. Like I wrote during the Iraqi invasion and prior to the initiation of the NATO campaign in Libya, an Islamic Peace Mission should be created under the auspices of these three countries; and, if necessary, this mission should intervene where brutal rulers spill blood.

There is no need to be pessimistic or overly-optimistic. The Western-Jewish alliance focuses on the Muslim world as a global power. This alliance takes action to invade or bomb countries. It completely destroys the infrastructure of residential areas; and in the meantime, it kills despots and replaces the ones left behind. What it wants in response is as follows:

1. Pay me for the guns and weapons I used; this can be either in oil or other means of payment;
2. I will reconstruct the destroyed cities;
3. I saved you from the despotic regimes, so behave and comply with my orders; clear the way for the rule of groups aligned with my worldview.

Syria is now under the spotlight; Iran will be next if conditions become ripe. No one can argue that Turkey is not on the list.

The Iranian Threat?[147]

Recently the Anatolia news agency featured an interesting report: Murat Mercan, the chairman of Parliament's Foreign Affairs Commission, told Israel's *Haaretz* daily, "A nuclear Iran is a threat also to Turkey and sanctions against Iran will be effective if they are applied efficiently."

Murat Mercan, who is a senior member of the ruling Justice and Development Party (AK Party), made this statement while visiting Israel as a

---

[147] First appeared in *Today's Zaman* on Dec. 16, 2008

guest of the Shalem Center's Adelson Institute for Strategic Studies, headed by Israeli State Minister Natan Sharansky. He also said Turkey believes the entire region should be free of nuclear weapons. When asked whether Israel should also be free of nuclear weapons, Mercan replied quite ironically: "I wish Israel would not feel threatened; then it, too, could disarm from nuclear weapons."

For Mercan, Israel is not the only country that feels threatened by Iran's nuclear plans because Iran is also a threat to Turkey. Naturally, one is inclined to ask what the recent projects Turkey has undertaken in cooperation with Iran mean. If Turkey perceives Iran as a threat, why did it sign a memorandum of understanding (MoU) with Iran last month for the development of natural gas reserves in the south of Iran? Mercan gave an interesting answer to this question: "Because a memorandum of understanding does not mean that anything has actually been done. In general, Turkey will not deviate from any policy that is accepted by the United Nations Security Council with regard to Iran."

We are living in a country of really weird things. Since the beginning, Turkey has reiterated that it has no intention of allowing its territory to be used in any attack against Iran. One of the basic parameters of the foreign policy pursued by the AK Party government is "zero disputes and close cooperation with neighbors." It is obvious that the country has made great progress in achieving these targets. Moreover, Turkey takes care to reinforce its prestige in the eyes of Western countries by emphasizing its weight on its neighbors and Muslim countries. For instance, a few weeks ago Turkey declared that it might act as a mediator between Iran and the US.

What could be more natural than Turkey improving its trade with its neighbors? The fact that its economy has been integrated with the global system and that about 70 percent of its exports are to European countries is not a big advantage, contrary to what is commonly thought. It is actually a disadvantage, as the recent global economic crisis has clearly shown. If Turkey can rearrange its commercial and economic relations with its nearby neighbors, it may find a big market awaiting it. The economic crisis has shown that regional integration is a smarter strategy than uncontrolled globalization. Turkey should not disturb its relations with Iran just because the US and Israel are not at peace with Tehran. US Secretary of Defense Robert Gates, who will keep his office in Barack Obama's administration, says any attack on Iran would end in disaster. Why should Turkey be more imperialist than the emperor? The European countries do not act in this way. Germany and Switzerland have made comprehensive trade agreements with Iran.

There is another important point in Mercan's statement that should be emphasized. "Yes, any attack on civilians is terror," he said, with regard to the attacks on the city of Sderot from the Gaza Strip. "I visited Sderot, and I saw how its residents were being attacked, but I also know the tragedy and sorrow in Gaza well. I advise Hamas to stop attacking civilians and propose that Israel stop imposing sanctions on Gaza," he said.

What fair advice he is giving! On one hand, there is a country that invaded and continues to invade the land and denies international rights and legal norms to that land's inhabitants and, on the other hand, there are oppressed people striving to survive in the small piece of land left to them. A century ago, Turkey owned these lands, but now, as an irony of fate, an indifferent politician talking on behalf of Turkey is uttering words about this place as if he were a third person.

Between the Merciful Tent of Empathy and the Brutal Antipathy[148]

Ehud Barak, one of Israel's leading politicians, once said, "If had been born to a Palestinian family, I would throw stones at Israeli soldiers just like Palestinian children are currently doing. We must get rid of this Palestine burden. Palestinians have been living in these lands for thousands of years."

Just like other Israeli administrators and politicians, Barak, too, fought against Palestinians for years. He is the former Israeli chief of General Staff, i.e., a high-ranking Israeli who personally attended and commanded many military operations. He eventually came to a point where he understood the Palestinians and their struggle.

---

[148] First appeared in *Today's Zaman* on May 23, 2008

Apparently, Barak felt empathy toward the Palestinians. Empathy can be briefly defined as one person's effort to understand the other person by putting himself in the shoes of this other person. Prophet Muhammad, peace and blessings be upon him, said, "You should seek for your brother what you seek for yourself." In the Islamic faith, "all human beings, i.e., the children of Adam and Eve, are equal in terms of their value as human beings and their ontological essences." Being a Muslim does not give one the right to do injustice to a non-Muslim.

Everyone needs to understand others by feeling empathy toward them. If we can do this even occasionally, many social conflicts may be avoided. On the 60th anniversary of the establishment of their state, how many Israelis can feel such empathy toward Palestinians? Public opinion polls suggest that about two-thirds of Israelis defend the cruelty the Israeli state has inflicted upon the Palestinians in the lands it has occupied as justified.

If we are supposed to understand and be tolerant of the occupation of a land by a people, based on a claim that dates back hundreds of years, and the violent seizure of houses, gardens, and other property in this process, and if this is accepted as a valid convention in the international arena, then there will not be a single piece of land around the world that is not claimed by someone else. For instance, Muslims, noting that they ruled Spain for eight-and-a-half centuries and Sicily for over two centuries, may claim to be the rightful owners of Spain and Sicily, and may attempt to occupy them.

Likewise, if a state claims to bring together everyone whom they consider to be of their race—a race considered to be the founding reason for the state—in Israel, wherever they are around the world, then the question of how this will be distinguished from racism will remain ambiguous.

There is also another important point. The world is progressing toward a certain point. Humanity has gone through great pain. Democracy, human rights, rule of law, the equal right to vote, nondiscrimination of people based on religious, racial, regional, or class differences, everyone being bound by law, and other criteria have evolved into universal ideals. Terrorism is a condemned crime. The most prominent characteristic of terrorism is the killing of innocent people for whatever purpose. Whether terrorism is committed by people, organizations, or states does not change anything; when all is said and done, innocent people die. Even so, one cannot understand or accept why these criteria are not applied to the Israeli state and why Israeli administrators and politicians are seen exempt from these criteria.

For sixty years, Palestine has been suffering a great tragedy. Millions of Palestinians have been displaced and about five million Palestinians are living as refugees. Seventy-eight percent of the historical Palestinian lands are under occupation, and the Palestinians living in the remaining twenty-two percent are fragmented. What's most tragic of all is that today about two million Palestinians are living in the open prison of Gaza, which is like the Nazi concentration camps. Hundreds of thousands of children, women, the old, and the innocent die, but Israel uses its international influence to silence everyone. This does not bring sympathy for the Israeli people. Instead, it breeds antipathy. Israelis should feel empathy, and if they have decided to be a country in the region, they should understand they that cannot find peace and solace through occupation, tyranny, and fighting against the people in the region.

Call for Reason[149]

The author of these lines has never leaned toward anti-Semitism because a Muslim who is aware of the authentic sources of his faith knows that anti-Semitism is a sin, or a crime prohibited by his religion.

The problem arises from the confusion stemming from efforts to portray any criticism against Israel's policies as anti-Semitism. Israeli politicians do not want to hear criticism when they engage in actions that hurt the conscience and sense of fairness and justice of ordinary people. They accuse critics of the Zionist ideology of pursuing anti-Semitism.

Anti-Semitism can be described as feeling hostility toward, and humiliating, Jews just because of their religion and/or ethnic roots. It is a crime irrespectively of its target. However, it is also a crime to violate

---

[149] First appeared in *Today's Zaman* on May 07, 2010

other people's rights, occupy their territories, banish innocent people from their homes, and conduct ethnic cleansing on local people in order to create space for people they bring from around the world. No religion, ethnicity, or state ideology can be used to justify this. Carried out by Jews, Muslims, or Christians, it is the same crime. No religion or ethnic group can be privileged to commit persecution. Just as we shouldn't question the religious or other identity markers of victims, we should also not ask it when it comes to the persecutors.

Another note is that critics of Israel deserve to be perceived as "friends of Jews," not as "enemies of Jews," because no political power, state, or empire can persist by relying on tyranny. The wails and cries of the oppressed will eventually invite divine destruction upon the oppressors.

As a matter of fact, we see that similar criticisms are also voiced by sane, conscientious, and wise Jews. Recently, several Jewish intellectuals from Europe issued a statement calling on Israel to withdraw from the settlements in the West Bank and East Jerusalem. Underlining also that Israel is risking itself by pursuing immoral and irrational policies, they wanted the Western world to intervene in the problem. For them, it was morally and politically wrong for Israel to occupy the Palestinian territories and launch the construction of new settlements; they also found the systematic support of Israeli policies dangerous.

Billing themselves as citizens of European countries, JCall consists of more than 3,700 Jewish intellectuals, including EP Greens group co-chairman Daniel Cohn-Bendit and famous Jewish philosopher Bernard-Henri Levy.[150]

Intellectuals stress an important point: The Netanyahu government's immoral and irrational policies have made Israel's legitimacy questionable in the Western world. These policies are risking the existence of Jews in the Middle East. The solution to the question can only be made rationally. This implies that an independent Palestinian state must be established for the survival of a democratic Jewish state.

Israeli politicians failed to see beyond the tunnel vision of Zionism the naked truth that the world, and particularly the West, is losing

---

[150] *Zaman*, May 3-4, 2010

interest in Israel. "Many moderate Jews living in Europe do not endorse Israel's illegitimate and irrational policies," says former Israeli Ambassador to France Elie Barnavi. Noting that with its settlement policy Israel has triggered questions about its own legitimacy, Cohn-Bendit cautions, "If Israel does not withdraw from the occupied areas, then Jews will run the risk of being a minority in Israel." Bureau Nationnal de Vigilance Contre l'Antisémitsme (BNVCA) President Sammy Ghozlan argues that the statement advocates Palestine's theses, saying, "The duty of European Jews is not to criticize the decisions of the Israeli people, but offer solidarity with them." However, famed French intellectual Levy, who signed the petition, says, "European Jews should stop giving unconditional support to the Israeli government."

Interesting statistics justify these warnings. "Israel has become the most dangerous country for Jews," wrote the *Yediot Ahronoth* newspaper. The rate of immigration to Israel is continually decreasing even though Israel is building new settlements for new arrivals. For instance, only 946 Jews have immigrated to Israel in 2010 thus far, as compared to a figure of 10,000 the previous year. Israel should take heed of the European Jews' call for reason.

Why Are We in Conflict with Each Other?[151]

A "war of religions" can be defined as the efforts by clerics and practitioners of one faith to destroy those of another faith, believing that the other faith is false. Islam does not approve of or encourage such wars. Islam further admonishes a "faith-based" attack against another religion as well as wars among sects or groups of the same religion. A faith-based war is, however, allowed only if it seeks to avert an open and imminent threat or an actual attack from the outside, that is, if it is for self-defense. This is understandable in that Islam recognizes a legal right to life for the religions it deems as false or superstitious.

The main factors for the wars among Christians were largely about the basic tenets of faith. The disputes or conflicts between Sunni and Shiite sects or among Sunni sects or groups cannot be considered legit-

---

[151] First appeared in *Today's Zaman* on Jan. 19, 2015

imate justification for war, as the common characteristics among these sects or groups are "maximal," not "minimal."

"Common grounds" constitute the very reference for peaceful coexistence of diverse religions or the sects or groups that are considered "heterodoxies." As Islam—which is capable of acting like a big umbrella extending over all religions, sects and groups—is not taken as reference, but used as an instrument for political and military strategies, Muslims cannot benefit from it properly.

Even if it is false or superstitious, a religion, sect or group may have tens of thousands or millions of followers. Is it possible to destroy a sect or group with millions of followers in a country? Most importantly, the religion of Islam is not a killing machine; rather, it makes people live and it enhances their lives. With its particular rules and regulations on the issue, Islam provides non-Muslims with security of life and property, it establishes sound and reliable communication with them and it delineates the very framework of their fundamental rights and freedoms. For Islam, any person who follows a false or superstitious faith has the potential to be guided to the right path; therefore, a person's right or opportunity to be guided cannot be taken away from them.

Although we have the potential for conflict, as seen in various cases in history, the main triggering factor for this potential has been external, particularly after the early 21st century.

Speaking about the Iran-Iraq war, former US Secretary of State Henry Kissinger said that their goal was to make them kill each other, and they attained their goal. Today, in line with their goal, the chaos in Iraq has a tendency to spread to Syria and the rest of the region. The strategy developed regarding our region is based on conflicts between countries, sects or ethnic groups.

Religious, sectarian and ethnic differences are potential areas of conflict. However, this potentiality cannot be triggered out of the blue. Rather, external factors play a role in this. In the wake of the 9/11 attacks, Kissinger ominously announced that Muslims would fight with each other. In line with Kissinger's prophecy, Muslims are mindlessly spilling each other's blood. Moreover, conflicts among religious communities and groups have also been added to the mix.

The bloody conflicts are masterminded by a doctrine called "creative chaos." This chaos seeks to destroy the Muslim world's potential to emerge as an alternative and subjugate it to the global system. According to the doctrine, societies will be decomposed into their constituents and these constituents will be made autonomous and led to conflict with others. For instance, Sunnis will start to see themselves as the representatives of the absolute truth, and, in this context, deny Shiites and Alevis the right to exist.

On the other hand, Shiites will embark on the mission of taking revenge for the members of the Prophet's Family (Ahl al-Bayt) who were killed 1,400 years ago. Likewise, Kurds will not respect the rights of other nations, but focus on their national interests. Each religious community will believe itself to be the only group that will be saved, and see others as being in error.

When society is fragmented in this way, it will be open to all sorts of attacks or intervention. But the main bulk of responsibility lies with Muslims, inside or outside. Whatever is happening to us is the result of our own acts and deeds.

The Region at a Critical Juncture[152]

There are four major problems the Middle East has been unable to resolve:

1. Despite rapidly changing internal dynamics, democratization has not been achieved and the people are still not effective and influential in decision-making mechanisms and processes.

2. Economic resources are being wasted; no effective measures have been taken to deal with the problem of equitable distribution of income.

3. Islam and the civilian and political institutions of Muslims are ignored by the global system. When Muslims are asked to integrate with the modern world, they are expected to wholly accept the Western lifestyle, resulting in a war against their traditions that blames their religion for their lack of assimilation. This is simply cultural colonialism that will be followed by a military, political, and economic one.

---

[152] First appeared in *Today's Zaman* on Mar. 10, 2009

During a recent visit to Saudi Arabia, President Abdullah Gül mentioned a secret enmity against Islam in the West. This should be taken into account. After the dissolution of the Soviet bloc, the global system replaced the Soviets with Islam and Muslims, defining the religion as its enemy. From a historical perspective, Muslims and their Prophet were satanic people in the subconscious of Westerners. The West pursues a deliberate policy by which it seeks to keep Islam out of the political system because if it is allowed in, the external threat—or the demon that needs to be dealt with—will be within the system.

4. The Palestinian question, the source of many problems in the region, is not fairly and justly addressed. Unless this question is resolved, there will be no peace and stability in the region and the world. Resolution is possible only if Israel complies with the UN resolutions, withdraws its troops from the occupied territories, and establishes good ties with the countries in the region.

There is one thing that Israel should know: It may not keep the territories it occupied under its control simply by making references to Prophets Abraham, Isaac, and Jacob (peace be upon them all). It may not claim any right over the area stretching from the Nile River to the Euphrates, arguing that it is the "promised land." This will mean that wars and conflicts in the region will continue forever.

And another point that remains ignored is this: The international powers that established domination in the region leave a legacy of crisis in the region when they withdraw. They leave many issues unresolved so that the future of the region struggles with chronic crises and problems.

There is not a single country in the region that does not have problems with its neighbors. The projects imposed by external actors will cause further disagreements, disputes, and conflicts in the region.

It seems the vast majority of the problems in the region have been imposed by the West. The political map of the Middle East, its repressive regimes, and its pathological problems are not ours; they are neither the property of Islam, nor are they the legacy of Islamic history. They were created by the Westerners who left these problems unresolved. To this end, it could be said that the Middle East is a straitjacket that the Western world put on the Islamic world.

Our region has been ruled by big states and empires throughout history; different religions, sects, and ethnic groups have coexisted in these vast political entities. People and groups from different ethnicities, religions and races still live together without any problem in the region. Creating pure ethnic or sectarian worlds may lead to great suffering.

We are going through a critical juncture. There is one fact that we should be aware of while the region is being reshaped: No single nation-state, ethnic group, or sect will survive this crisis by acting on its interests alone.

Turks, Kurds, Arabs, Turkmens, Persians, Sunnis, Shiites, Christians, and Jews should have a broader imagination for a new world. Without imposing values, restricting the rights and freedoms of others, or denying the identities of others, we may end the suffering by relying on mutual dialogue, tolerance, solidarity, and common interest.

We can make the Middle East our common house where everybody is allowed to speak their own language by converting it from a Tower of Babel.

Chapter 12

Human Rights

West, Islam, and Human Rights[153]

Muslims have found themselves greatly deceived in the modern world as they tried to lead a social life in compliance with their religious sources and develop a vision about man, society, and the world. They hoped this would be an alternative to the nation-states that oppressed them as well as to the "Enlightenment" on which their political and administrative philosophies were based.

Muslims wrongly assumed that they would continue to exist by sharing the principle of equality with the modern man and enjoy fundamental rights and freedoms freely. This was their illusion.

They are only now starting to realize that this assumption was wrong. There were two reasons for their failing to realize this in a timely manner. First, severe pressure from political regimes urged Muslims to adopt easy escape routes, particularly including the "rights and freedoms mentality" whose philosophical bases Muslims were not completely aware of. Second, they further presumed that the concepts of human rights and freedoms defined along the basic philosophical assumptions of the Enlightenment could be reconciled with Islam's theology (*kalam*) and basic religious premises. They now increasingly realize that this was too optimistic.

"Man"—granted certain rights and freedoms by the Enlightenment, which emerged on the historical scene to be guided by reason to defy "God and Lord," i.e., the religious doctrine, the Church's dogmas, and

---

[153] First appeared in *Today's Zaman* on Nov. 05, 2010

absolutist rules—is defined by its "own philosophical assumptions." In other words, the philosophical and cultural climate in which human rights and freedoms were formulated is outside the religious sphere, and it opposes religious doctrines and challenges religion's role to guide man. Thus, the concept of human rights is based on human reason, not on any religious resource—say, the Qur'an or the Sunnah in the Islamic setting. Reason, which the Enlightenment glorifies or takes as its basis, is free from all sorts of religious teachings or guidance, and it follows that the man who has rights and freedoms is a "secular" man. To paraphrase, a man who accepts religious guidance has no rights or freedoms.

If human reason instead of any religious, metaphysical, or theological resource has the final say in defining human rights and freedoms, and if entitlement to these rights and freedoms is decided based on "being a man," then this is indicated not by man's "compliance to religious duties" but his omission of them. What defines these rights and freedoms then are constitutions and laws, not religious provisions. Constitutions and laws are drafted by human beings, not by religious resources. So it is not God, or His Prophets or His Books that describe what rights and freedoms are, but the secular man. This man arbitrarily calls rights and freedoms what he did not consider as such in the past; he might expand or contract their sphere, or add or omit rights and freedoms.

Freedom of religion and conscience, which forms the basis of many Western values, emphatically recognized by Western democracies in general and EU acquis in particular, sits on the principle of the separation of church and state, religion jettisoning its claim to regulate the public sphere, and increasingly that it must survive in a marginal, private, and relative sphere vis-à-vis the larger cultural and political system. Thus, religion's claim to regulate social life is a demand that falls outside Western democracies and the system of Western values as delineated by the EU.

Accordingly, any demand for rights or freedoms that is based on religion as well as religion's visibility in the social and public sphere has no place in this system. This is the main reason why the European Court of Human Rights (ECtHR) rejects almost all religious demands. All applications concerning the headscarf, claims by the second wives and their children, and employment of headscarved women at public institutions and so on are rejected. This is because the urge to wear a headscarf does not come from the value of a human being who is guided by secular reason but from the religious injunctions of Islam and its associated system of behavioral norms.

Because the Western paradigm does not consider religion-oriented rights and freedoms as proper "human rights," the only option left is to treat them with "tolerance." If a headscarf demand is not a "human right" but a matter of tolerance, this demand will only exist in a restricted sphere and to the extent that it is tolerated by secular people.

Human Rights: Common Definitions and Varying Attitudes[154]

The UN's Universal Declaration of Human Rights was adopted in December 1948. It was an important declaration because it concerned every community in the world. Other international agreements have been declared as well.

While the applicability of these agreements is controversial in some countries, the UN's declaration is not. Even though just about every country has signed the UN declaration over time, human rights have not essentially improved over the last 60 some years. After millions of people lost their lives for petty reasons due to the dust clouds of World War II and fascism caused tremendous distress in Europe, the declaration sparked much hope. However, the current circumstances are not all that pleasant.

The following question is still valid: Is the concept of human rights an ideal that is acceptable for the whole of humanity in terms of its content and ultimate goals? My answer is yes, but with four reservations. My four reservations are:

1. It is a great shortcoming that the West and particularly the Enlightenment period's intellectual and cultural resources are the only source of reference for the definition of basic human rights and freedoms. The

---

[154] First appeared in *Today's Zaman* on Jul. 16, 2010

outlook of other cultures—as well as Islam, which has a critical perspective on this matter—should be adequately taken into consideration and the criticisms and recommendations of Muslims should be considered when developing a universal definition. The West cares about the rights of people who fit its description of what a person should be like and does not really care about the rights of those who don't fit this description.

2. Since the West is the only one that developed the definition and made it universal, the West decides how to apply it. The problem which arises is that this subject, which in the final analysis represents a moral attitude, has double standards. It's evident that subconsciously the West believes that concepts such as democracy and human rights apply only to the West.

There is the conviction that it's not a big deal when human rights are violated in non-Western societies and particularly in the Muslim world because it doesn't deserve them anyway. In every circumstance where the West's political, economic, and strategic interests are in question, the West does not lash out when democracy is postponed or human rights are disgracefully violated in the Muslim world; in fact it even encourages it.

3. Similarly, depending on the situation, the West does not hesitate to use a moral value such as human rights as a political tool to advance its national interests, hinder countries with which it has a dispute, and even to cause division in these countries. The West only defends these rights when it comes to groups that represent its values.

4. If human rights are a package that needs to be approved universally, then some countries and governments should not be exempt from this. However, Israel does not feel that it has the responsibility to uphold human rights, just like how it does not feel bound to international agreements or to decisions taken by the UN Security Council. Israel is exempt from all rules and sanctions, and the Palestinians that are being oppressed by Israel are not being regarded as human beings.

As long as these substantial and understandable reservations remain, human rights will not be culturally adopted and will not evolve into universal values that are protected and defended by everyone. As a result, the West should stop acting like a chief teacher that feels compelled to teach everyone else everything and develop the moral maturity to "want for others what it wants for itself."

Yet these reservations are no excuse for states and political powers in countries that are in the same or worse situation than us to violate rights. Intervening in religious, intellectual, and economic freedom still happens in many parts of the world.

There are people who still live under covert and openly authoritarian and totalitarian regimes and suffer great pains.

If we do not like the West's definition of human rights and freedoms, then let's try and determine an outline for ourselves. If the West is adopting a double-standard attitude on this matter due to moral weaknesses, then we should adopt a universal attitude that thrives on ethical and moral virtues.

Majority and Minority[155]

"Minorities" are those with lower numbers. The groups whose members are lower in number in a country differ from the members of the majority from a political and sociological perspective and cannot dominate sociopolitical life. The legal consequence of this is that minorities have to bear with deprivations.

According to a definition prepared by Francesco Capotorti, UN rapporteur for the Sub-Commission on the Prevention of Discrimination and Protection of Minorities, concerning Article 27 of the International Covenant on Civil and Political Rights, a minority is a "group numerically inferior to the rest of the population of a State, in a non-dominant position, whose members—being nationals of the State—possess ethnic, religious or linguistic characteristics differing from those of the rest of the population and show, if only implicitly, a sense of solidarity, directed towards preserving their culture, traditions, religion or language."

In this context, a minority can be defined as a religious, ethnic, or political group which is numerically inferior to the rest of the population and which is supposed to suffer from certain deprivations.

---

[155] First appeared in *Today's Zaman* on Mar. 30, 2014

This definition framework is problematic from an Islamic perspective. From an Islamic perspective and historic experience, there is no designation of "minority." The term "minority" (*aqalliyyat*) was borrowed from Western jurisprudence in the 19th century when we started redesigning our social and political lives according to the modern viewpoint. From what I gather from the practices of Prophet Muhammad (peace and blessings be upon him) in Medina, specifically the Charter of Medina—an agreement drafted by Prophet Muhammad as a formal agreement between him and all the significant tribes and families of Medina, including Muslims, Jews, and polytheists—as well as from established practices in history, Muslims' relations with non-Muslims are defined by two terms: *muahid* and *dhimmi*.

A *muahid* is a non-Muslim who does not fight Muslim for a religious cause, does not collaborate with the enemies of Muslims, and does not force Muslims away from their homeland (see Surah al-Mumtahanah 60: 8-9). *Muahids* are entitled to participate in the establishment of the political community and can be a member of the political union. A *dhimmi* is a non-Muslim person who fights against Muslims and has been vanquished by them. *Dhimmis* are not entitled to participate in the central administration of the state, but their sociocultural rights are guaranteed under laws and in principle. Their rights to perform their rituals, establish places of worship, and teach their religion are safeguarded. Moreover, they are entitled to regulate their civil spheres and lifestyles according to the dictates of their religions and they do so with their autonomous laws and courts. The rights granted by Islam to *dhimmis* are not granted by modern democracies to the citizens. *Jizya*, or a per capita tax, is a special tax imposed on non-Muslims in return for their participation in the general financing of social and public life; it is not a special form of punishment. *Jizya* is similar to "paid-for military service" in today's practice, so the state's *dhimmis* are like the hundreds of thousands of Turkish citizens who are eager to benefit from this service by payment.

This framework is shaped according to the governing provisions of Islamic law and is dictated by the Qur'an and the Sunnah. Yet it is impossible to say that Muslim countries are beds of roses for non-Muslims.

Historically speaking, non-Muslims at times suffered from unfair treatment which was imposed on them in breach of Islamic law.

Liberal democracies fail to properly resolve the problems of minorities. Various religious and ethnic groups are given a "minority" status if they are numerically low. Moreover, marginal groups with diverse lifestyles or heterodox moral values compared to the majority of society are also described as minorities. This creates several problems in terms of their participation in political processes and decision-making mechanisms. Liberal democracies treat "minority rights" as superior to laws and constitutions, but this practice poses problems to relations between the majority and minorities, whose lifestyles are in conflict with the majority. Decisions are taken by majority vote but the rights of minorities, which are closed to the majority's votes, are protected. This in fact paves the way for conflict between the majority and minorities.

Kurds and Their Rights[156]

The first generation of "human rights," considered the most fundamental rights, was developed when the West lost hope in the church and the absolutist monarchies that garnered all the powers and authorities. Then, the second and third generation rights were also made into laws. The West couldn't rely on religion as the source of these rights. This was because the church, which was identified with religion, was part of the problem. Necessarily, the West headed for "secular" references. Here the intellectuals, scientists, and philosophers who opted for reason as the basis of their inquiries played a crucial role. Currently, powerful lobbies, states, and vocal marginal groups can ensure that the crimes, sins, and wrongdoings—which deteriorate the very spirit of law and morality— are treated as part of "human rights." As this rights theory goes beyond limits, it starts to give way to unintended consequences.

There is clearly a rights issue in the Muslim world. Not only governments, but also groups (sects, factions, communities, and so on.) violate rights of each other. They comply neither with the injunctions of their religions nor with the West's human rights.

---

[156] First appeared in *Today's Zaman* on Oct. 27, 2014

The Kurdish armed insurgency that has been going on for about 40 years is justified—apart from its regional and global repercussions—based on three factors. Kurds rightly argue that their ethnic identities are ignored by the socio-political system and they are deprived of their right to use their mother tongue. The role Kurds, as a nation, played or play or may play in past, current, or future political formations are of secondary importance. The matter has three components:

First, all legal and constitutional obstacles to Kurds' articulation of their ethnic identities within the system. Second, Kurds should be allowed to use their mother tongue freely in education and other areas in addition to Turkish as the official language. Third, the social and economic welfare level of the region where Kurds predominantly live should be improved.

Anyone who reads and correctly understands the Holy Qur'an should champion these rights. The following verse defines the main framework of ethnicities and rights to use mother tongues: *"And among His signs is the creation of the heavens and the earth, and the diversity of your languages and colors. Surely in this are signs indeed for people who have knowledge (of the facts in creation, and who are free of prejudices)"* (ar-Rum 30:22).

This verse indicates that racial, national, and ethnic differences are the works of God. The Earth is like a garden teeming with all sorts of colors, languages, and other diversities. Diverse creatures were created in the heavens and on Earth. Human beings live on Earth and have different colors and languages. These colors and languages are divine. Therefore, they cannot be taken as a source of discrimination. Whoever takes them as a source of discrimination is indulging in racism.

Every linguistic and color group has its unique characteristics, names, and tendencies. But they do not constitute legitimate justifications for one group's dominating others. In his Farewell Sermon, Prophet Muhammad (pbuh), made this final point: "All humankind is from Adam and Eve; an Arab has no superiority over a non-Arab nor a non-Arab has any superiority over an Arab; also a white has no superiority over black nor a black has any superiority over white."

The linguistic or color groups and naturally formed nations and communities have equal rights. None of them can be granted fewer rights.

Islamic Rights of Non-Muslims[157]

At the beginning of the last century, the population of non-Muslims in Istanbul was 40 percent and 25-30 percent in Anatolia. Today, their total population can hardly reach 100,000 due to the infamous policies pursued by the Unionist (Ittihatçı) and Republican politicians: 60,000 Armenians, 25,000 Jews, and 3,000-4,000 Greeks. Even after adding Syriacs and others, their population can hardly number 100,000.

Problems non-Muslims face in Turkey are never-ending. In the first place, they are still treated as "minorities" under the law we imported from Europe 150 years ago. They are neither considered "autonomous *dhimmi*" (protected people) within the *millet* system of the Ottoman Empire nor are they allowed to enjoy the rights of "modern" minorities. Moreover, non-Muslims are the first to be used for provocation or for kindling a political crisis; their priests, writers, or missionaries are easily slaughtered. The "ecumenical" title of the patriarch of the Greek Patriarchate in Fener, one of the world's two largest churches, is denied. Their community properties can be readily confiscated via court orders. Halki Seminary on the island of Heybeliada near Istanbul is not allowed to provide education. The word "Armenian" is regarded as an insult. Calling a Turk an "Armenian" is one of the worst swearwords you can use. When Israel kills Palestinians, the Jews in Turkey are held responsible for the killings. Anti-Semitism is running amok. The case of Syriacs is the worst of the minority population. They are neither considered as a minority proper nor are treated as reputable citizens. The law concerning their rights to elect or be elected to the foundations they have established was annulled in 2012. Since then, they have been unable to elect executives to these foundations.

That the centuries-old problems continue during this period under a "religious conservative ruling party" gives the impression that these problems stem from Islam. All of these problematic practices are the result of the Turkish Republic's conception of non-Muslims. They have nothing to do with Islam or Islamism.

---

[157] First appeared in *Today's Zaman* on Oct. 20, 2014

The status of non-Muslims should be discussed at two levels: within the Islamic perspective and from the perspective of Islamist policies. Given the fact that Islamism consists of efforts to develop a mentality, perspective, and social solutions—or more broadly, socio-economic, cultural, administrative, and inter-state policies—that rely heavily on Islam, it is wise to distinguish Islam from Islamism. Islam relies on divine revelations, while Islamism is the product of the human mind. Still, Islam and Islamism overlap to a large extent. If there are shortcomings of Islamism, they have nothing to do with Islam, but can be attributable to Islamists.

As I noted elsewhere, the Holy Qur'an puts non-Muslims into two distinct categories: *muahid* and *muharrib*. *Muahids* are non-Muslims who do not fight Muslims, but opt to coexist with them, and they enjoy equal rights and freedoms at the socio-economic and public level when they make a political contract with Muslims. If they choose to fight Muslims as *muharribs*, and are defeated, these non-Muslims become "dhimmi." *Dhimmis* enjoy broader rights and freedoms than "minority rights" from a social and economic perspective, except for prohibitions from certain administrative duties.

The non-Muslims of Turkey should be "equal" with Muslims until everyone can cherish their private, civil, and civic diversities in autonomous spheres. Thus, all non-Muslims, regardless of their religions or sects, should enjoy the same rights with any Muslim Turkish citizen. In this context, we should recognize the ecumenical title of the Patriarch. We should immediately open the Halki Seminary. We should abandon the principle of reciprocity, which can be hardly justified in terms of Islamic or humanitarian principles and which has turned into a tool of oppression between Turkey and Greece. The community foundations and their properties should be freed from all sorts of encumbrances. Their rights to hold administrative positions should be recognized. The media outlets that employ disheartening or discriminatory language against non-Muslims should be closely monitored. False information about non-Muslims in textbooks should be removed.

This is what I personally believe to be the set of rights Islam grants to non-Muslims. An Islamist policy that rejects the "nationalism of new Turkey" must champion these rights and freedoms.

Chapter 13

Clash or Dialogue of Civilizations

Have the Clashes Ended?[158]

Last December, Samuel Huntington died. But does his theory about the "clash of civilizations," which he introduced in the mid-1990s, endure? Here's how we can ask this question: Do we still think that Huntington—who asserted that "clashes between civilizations" would fill the vacuum left in the wake of the end of the Cold War—was right?

Much time has passed since his theory was first broached, so the questions about it are even more meaningful now.

"Civilization" in itself is a troublesome concept these days. All talk of "culture" and "civilization" is relatively new to the world; these are concepts gifted to us by the modern age we inhabit. "Culture" seems to elicit abstract ideas, while "civilization" elicits more concrete ones. In fact, when we think of civilization, we often tend to think about the institutions on which our societies depend, such as political, military, and economic organizations. Yes, these are all closely linked to our conception of civilization.

But if the above is true, then which civilizations that exist on earth are we really talking about these days? And, thus, which civilizations are we expecting will actually "clash"? After all, the whole world is now the West! There are many people who believe the borders of the West can no longer be determined. There are, of course, geographical borders that determine where Europe lies. In fact, we can even point to the cul-

---
[158] First appeared in *Today's Zaman* on Jun. 19, 2009

tural geography that defines Europe. But the West is very different in this respect.

From the very start, I never thought that any useful theory of clashes could be elicited using the concept of "civilizations." Some choose to replace the word "civilization" with "religion," so that what we are talking about becomes a "clash between religions." The Sept. 11 attacks did nothing to weaken this idea. But despite George W. Bush and the neocons, this idea was rejected by respected thinkers and religious authorities in both the Christian and Islamic worlds. And almost ignoring the very tough religious foundation that had been set, they decided to swivel their attention to "dialogue between religions."

The dialogue that ensued between religions basically underscored just how shaky Huntington's theory really was. While many thought about the topic only in terms of "civilization," there was clearly another reality: When looking at the general flow of our daily lives, we noted that there really was not more than one civilization at hand, or that the "civilizations" Huntington was talking about just were not there. In truth, we have left the era of plural civilizations behind us. As modernity spreads across the face of the earth, civilizations die. And with no more than one civilization, who exactly is going to clash? From methods of production to models of organization, from media to transportation, from building styles to sitting styles, everything and everyone in the world is becoming more and more alike. Asians get aesthetic operations to achieve more rounded eyes, while Turks from the Black Sea region busy themselves with rhinoplasty, trying to achieve the perky "ski-jump" style of nose associated with the West. On another level, police all over the world, from London to Paris, from Istanbul to Tehran, all work the same way, using the same batons to disperse crowds of students in the same manner. Political slogans, ideals, concepts... all seem the same. A law is formed in the arena of international politics and deemed a "universal law." For the most part, people aren't protesting these developments. This appears to indicate that when we are talking about the humans of this world, there are no longer multiple civilizations at hand. After all, who can oppose the hegemonic civilization surrounding us? Whoever dares to immediately becomes the "other." At the same time, though, many things are on the wrong track.

It has always seemed to me that the proponents of this theory of "clash of civilizations" were people who really wanted to see these clashes take place. There really are many factions rooting for clashes to occur. And it is terror that is the most effective instrument used in seeing this theory of clashes turned into reality. After every act of terror, there is always a period of trauma. And two things emerge from this trauma. One is a tightening and tension that occurs in the West and in democracy itself. Certain restrictions are placed on civil liberties and rights. From the perspective of democracy, of course, this isn't good at all. The second thing that emerges after terror is that, from a cultural angle, Islam is pushed further and further out of the global system. Neither of these reactions augurs well for humanity, though.

Islam and Terror[159]

As soon as reports came of Yemeni al-Qaeda's claim of responsibility for the 2015 Paris attacks, a familiar mechanism was set in motion. The attacks were encoded as "Islamic terror" and defined as the "9/11 of France." Even though there was scanty information about the details of the attacks, those who know everything passed judgment: "Islam should be reformed." Of course, as was the case with the 9/11 attacks, calls were made with a bossy attitude on the Muslim world to "condemn terror" and "keep a distance from terrorists."

Any sane Muslim who is informed about their religion will not defend terror. The attacks on Charlie Hebdo, which disgracefully published cartoons denigrating the Prophet Muhammad, peace and blessing be upon him, cannot be met with approval. But whether this attack can be described as "Islamic terror" deserves discussion.

Indeed, many European leaders, in particular the French president, asserted that it is wrong to blame Islam or Muslims for this attack. This was the right move given the fact that if it had been portrayed as "Islamic terror," some people in the Muslim world—which are already

---

[159] First appeared in *Today's Zaman* on Jan. 26, 2015

going through a pathological phase—would have lent increased support to the perpetrators of this attack, and about 15 million Muslims in Europe would have become the target of racists throughout Europe.

For the last 25 years, we have been trying to get rid of the label "Islamic terror" the West had glued on us. Western Orientalism has evolved into "Islamophobia" and "Islamic terror." This has been so deeply engraved in people's minds that it is virtually impossible to remove it.

This new Orientalist perspective defines "Islam" as the "absolute evil." This evil is like a sinister virus that quickly transforms the body into evil, making it produce evil acts. This is what they advise us to do: "The road to getting rid of this evil is to create a form of ‹protestant' Islam, as was the case with Christianity." The next step to follow would be to spread the West's military and political domination over the Muslim world, which does not have power of disposition over its own sources of information and knowledge as well as natural and physical resources.

Unrestrained attacks on the part of Israel, repressive regimes, military coups (backed by the West) and autocratic regimes that are secretly encouraged warrant the continuation of the status quo. It is for this reason that al-Qaeda-like organizations may pop up to wreak havoc around the world with different views and methods. Here is an amazing academic hypocrisy: Western social sciences draw attention to the fact that no social incident occurs out of the blue, but rather that certain factors determine or influence it. But in the face of any deviation in the Muslim world, Westerners tend to conceal their decisive roles in that pathology, but still refer to evil factors that somehow derive from Islam.

The Paris attacks do not constitute Islamic terror. For us to refer to them as "Islamic," the Muslim world would have to actually endorse this attack. These attacks were condemned in virtually all of the Muslim world. This attack is not "Islamist terror" either. If it were, Islamist movements and parties would endorse it. But virtually all movements and parties, including Hezbollah and Hamas, condemned it. This attack cannot be depicted as "Salafi terror" either. If it were, Salafis would consider this attack legitimate.

Yemeni al-Qaeda claimed responsibility for the attack. So it was an act by al-Qaeda. Just as no one can depict the acts of terror by the Kurdistan Workers' Party (PKK) as "Kurdish terrorism," or acts by Israel as "Jewish terror," this incident cannot be described as "Islamic terror." Those who claim responsibility for it should explain its legitimacy, benefits and disadvantages. Al-Qaeda does not seek permission from anyone for its acts.

A Carefully Orchestrated Fear: Islamophobia[160]

US President George W. Bush says he was misled about the Iraq issue. Allegations about weapons of mass destruction and terror connections were all lies. Likewise, Islamophobia was and still is a lie.

The notion of Islamophobia is widely referenced. Phobia refers to irrational fear. In actuality, such a fear is empty and baseless. There is nothing to justify such a fear. But the individual still fears something— an object, entity, or event. A famous example is the fear of mice. We know that a mouse cannot hurt us, but most of us are afraid of them.

But the intention and goals of those who describe Islam as a cause for fear are different. We may say that the notion of fear of Islam was first formulated by the famous Orientalist Bernard Lewis in the 1990s. He discussed this even before the publication of Samuel Huntington's famous "clash of civilizations" thesis. He asserted that Western civilization was based on Greco-Roman and Judeo-Christian heritage, that it has made visible progress, and that some nations, particularly Muslims in the Middle East, are jealous of this progress because they have failed to make similar achievements. He holds that Muslims pose a threat to Western heritage and civilization. Therefore, he concludes that there is a growing threat spreading from the Islamic world toward the West and that this should be taken seriously.

Before the American invasion of Afghanistan in 2001, Bush gave a speech in which he made reference to ideas like those of Bernard Lewis. The title of his speech was, "Why do they hate us?" Bush gave the following answer to this question: "Americans are asking: 'Why do they hate

---

[160] First appeared in *Today's Zaman* on Dec. 05, 2008

us?' They hate what we see right here in this chamber—a democratically elected government. Their leaders are self-appointed. They hate our freedoms—our freedom of religion, our freedom of speech, our freedom to vote and assemble and disagree with each other." Of course, the "they" in Bush's address refers to Muslims who hate Americans. According to Bush, what drove the terrorists to carry out such a grave attack against the Twin Towers was this hatred.

When the twin towers were hit, this terror assault should have been explained by the West. Why did such a thing happen? Some theories were advanced to address this question. Some asserted that this can be a provocation of secret services. Others have argued that al-Qaeda was responsible for this. Because of the longstanding presence of the American military in the Muslims' sacred lands, its invasion in the region during the Gulf War, and its killings of Muslims, al-Qaeda decided to launch an attack. This suggests that al-Qaeda and its militants all planned and executed the whole incident. Therefore, it is not possible to talk about the involvement of secret services in this.

The explanation of the American president in his speech was important. He attempted to give this message to his nation and to the whole world: "We are good. We are achievers. We are brave. We are smart. We are strong. We are rich. And they are not. They are cowards. They are weak. They are poor. They are less smart. They get jealous of us instead of making progress and working to get better and achieve liberation and wealth. They envy us and eventually they start to hate us."

This was Bush's explanation. Western people partially believed this explanation due to extensive support by the media. What was injected into the minds of the masses was the idea that Islam poses a threat to the world, particularly to Western civilization, wealth, and progress.

"Islamic Terror" – a Smokescreen of Interventions[161]

The 2008 Mumbai terrorist attacks killed 195 people, wounding 295. A never-before-heard-of terrorist organization named Deccan Mujahidin assumed responsibility for the attacks.

---

[161] First appeared in *Today's Zaman* on Nov. 02, 2008

What national or international strategic and political purposes these bloody attacks serve is a topic for another article. But, immediately after the attacks, their connection to Pakistan was suggested. It seems that these attacks will be used for attaining particular targets. We can already predict what the main justification for whatever is done or proposed under the pretext of these attacks will be: "Islamic terror."

The term Islamic terror was coined by neocons. When the Bush administration decided to conduct military operations in strategic countries and oil-rich locations within the Islamic world, these operations were justified by manufactured reasons that would later be denied by US officials. One of these manufactured lies was Islamic terror.

Since then, the unreasonable foundations of this Islamic terror classification have repeatedly been questioned: Why should there be a necessary connection between "Islam" and "terror"? If there is a necessary tie between Islam as a "religion" and terror, shouldn't we be able to propose similar associations between terror and other religions? If we know the religious identity or religious affiliations of a terrorist, will we be sufficiently justified in establishing a connection between their act and their religion? If so, we are supposed to attribute the acts of terrorists to their religions. For instance, is the terrorist act by a fanatic Jew who raided a mosque in al-Khalil and killed 50 Muslims his own personal action or should we attribute it to Judaism? If we take the logic that produced the "Islamic terror" classification, then we should describe the attack in al-Khalil as "Jewish terror." However, neither this nor the collective killings of civilians by Israeli soldiers are treated under this category. Similarly, for many years, Catholics and Protestants fought each other, and there were terror attacks on civilians in Ireland. But no one talked about "Christian terrorism," which is perfectly justified.

In reality, when we closely examine the profiles of terrorists whose Muslim identities are always emphasized, we see that there is no necessary connection between Islam and their terrorist acts.

Indeed, the British intelligence service MI5 published a report in August 2008 stressing that the majority of the people who are prone to terrorism tend not to know their religion well or tend not to perform the basic religious duties. The report, titled "Understanding radicalization and violent extremism in the UK," also clarifies the "Islamic terror" classification and contains interesting observations: (1) Radicalism may be seen in every group in society; it is difficult to categorize these people. (2) The people who engage in terrorism are ignorant about their religions. (3) A well-established religious organization within society may protect people against terror.

The report was prepared based on the findings of studies conducted on hundreds of thousands of people. "[T]he majority of those over 30 have steady relationships, and most have children. The majority are British nationals and the remainder, with a few exceptions, are here legally. Around half were born in the UK, with others migrating here later in life. Far from being religious zealots, a large number of those involved in terrorism do not practice their faith regularly. Many lack religious literacy and could actually be regarded as religious novices. Very few have been brought up in strongly religious households, and there is a higher than average proportion of converts," the report says. The report also stresses that the majority of terrorists tend to be radicalized after traumatic experiences or economic troubles.

It is wrong to pursue political goals through the use of Islam as a vehicle. This is clearly unfair to Islam and Muslims. As evidently shown by the MI5 report, terror is a different category, and it has nothing to do with Islam or Muslims, who regard life as a divine gift.

The Arguments and Goals of "Islamophobia"[162]

Islamophobia, as produced by certain circles of the world, seems to be based on two arguments: "Islam threatens modern culture and civilization" and "Islam generates terror and terrorists."

As outlined in his "clash of civilizations" theory, itself inspired by Bernard Lewis, Samuel Huntington implied that the West represents the peak of human development in this "clash." Lewis had already argued that, with the continual influx of immigrants, Islam would disrupt the "traditional" demographics and cultural texture of the West. If Islam threatens human development, it should be feared.

---

[162] First appeared in *Today's Zaman* on Dec. 02, 2013

Lewis argued that it's wrong to refer to Islamic terrorism, but that all terrorists are Muslims. That is to say that Islam mentally paves the way for terrorism, and those who are born into this mental universe can express themselves only through terrorism. Those who believe that terrorism is in the very nature of Islam think the basic tenets of Islamic theology argue that a Muslim must become a terrorist because the only religion acceptable to God is Islam and a believer is superior to a non-believer.

Furthermore, there is no generally accepted definition of terrorism. The main component of all definitions is the targeting of civilians. Thus, all attacks that target innocent civilians for any reason (religious, political, economic, strategic, ethnic, or regional) can be considered terrorism. So acts that target civilians are terrorist acts, whether they are conducted by individuals, organizations, or states. In this context, if an Islamic organization conducts a suicide attack against a target, killing dozens of innocent civilians, this is a terrorist attack. Likewise, if a state shells the cities of another country, killing thousands of civilians, this too can be defined as terrorism. Modern warfare that targets civilian settlements falls into the category of state terror.

The question is: If a terrorist act is performed by a member of any specific religion, does this change the nature of this act? Of course not. If so, why is such an evil act attributed insistently to the faith of the evil-doer when the person in question is "Muslim" (as a true Muslim cannot be a terrorist)? More importantly, why is any resistance by Muslims defined as "Islamic terrorism," while similar acts by others are not related to their religion? For instance, the civil war in Ireland lasted for 25 years. About 3,600 people, mostly civilians, died in violent attacks between Catholics and Protestants. Why wasn't this described as "Christian," "Catholic," or "Protestant" terrorism? The Armenian Secret Army for the Liberation of Armenia (ASALA) killed dozens of Turkish diplomats, but no-one referred to its acts as "Christian" terrorism. No-one refers to Israel's killing of innocent civilians as "Jewish" terrorism.

As a matter of fact, these definitions are aptly made; no righteous religion or nation would engage in terrorism. Terrorism is conducted by individuals, organizations and states. If this is the case, excluding Islam and Muslims from this general rule and depicting resistance by Muslims defending their homeland, along with some seemingly "terrorist" and genuinely "terrorist" acts by certain organizations as "Islamic terror" is actually part of the process of turning Islam and Muslims into objects of hate.

Identifying Islam with terrorism is not a simple slip of the tongue. It promotes Islamophobia across the globe, lending legitimacy to the machinery of domination and exploitation in the region, used by the global powers that be.

Can Obama Defeat Islamophobia?[163]

In the speeches delivered in Cairo and Ankara, US President Barack Obama sent strong messages that his administration "is not—and never will be—at war with Islam" and that it wants to "seek a new beginning."

But when it comes to how much we can believe these messages, questions remain among the Muslim public. At this point, before losing all hope, we simply need to wait and see. If there are some truly concrete steps taken to tackle the fear of Islam, everyone will stand behind Obama. And at the top of the list of concrete steps to be taken is the removal of Islamophobia from the world's agenda.

The current wave of "fear of Islam," formulated in America and spread from there rapidly throughout the world, aims to achieve a range of economic, political and strategic military goals. According to Samuel Huntington's ("Clash of Civilizations") formula, which sought to restructure and firm up the American national identity in the wake of the end of the Cold War, there was a search for an "other that exists both internally and externally." The "internal others" pointed to by Huntington are the "Hispanics and blacks," while the "external others" are Islam and the Muslim world. America, pursuing hegemony on a global scale, in fact managed to project this fear of the "external other" onto a global level, within the framework of George W. Bush's understanding of the "foreign other." And so it was that Islam began to be defined as a "threat" that elicited fear on the global level.

One of the underlying factors in efforts in America to spread the fear of Islam is the significant Evangelical movement, which is deeply

---

[163] First appeared in *Today's Zaman* on Jun. 09, 2009

influenced by Jewish lobbies and neocons, who controlled the administration under Bush. Thus, depictions of Arabs as "terrorists" and of Islam as a "religion of terror" began to be used in both Jewish and Christian Zionism in order to legitimize Israel's illegal stances, which both of these factions perceive as being part of "God's plan."

Despite all of the above, things are not completely without hope these days. Eliminating the "fear of Islam" in America may be difficult, but it is not impossible. Historically speaking, Muslims have not fought with America. It was developments which occurred in the wake of the 1979 Iranian revolution that first sparked clashes between the Muslim world and America. In fact, if we exclude Protestant missionary activity in the 19th century—looking back for a moment to recall that certain Protestant missionaries caused enormous problems for the Ottoman Empire, bringing Muslims and Armenians face-to-face in clashes despite the fact that these two groups had lived together in friendship for centuries—the fact is that Islam and the Protestant world really had not faced one another earlier. To the contrary of models of modernization being developed in Europe, these two worlds—the Islamic and the Protestant—had cultures of politics which were neither primitive nor institutionalized. In fact, America resembled in this sense the Ottoman Empire much more than it did the European continent.

In short, America possesses the qualities necessary to neutralize—even if through some difficulty—preconceptions formed as the result of economic, military, and political factors. Of course, when preconceptions and predetermined views become based on long-lived clashes and basic paradigms, overcoming them is more difficult than, as Einstein noted, splitting the atom.

It is precisely from this perspective then that it should be noted that there is an important difference which separates the "hostility toward Islam" developed in Europe and the "hostility toward Islam" developed in the US. When it comes to Islam, the handicaps possessed by Europe are multidimensional:

1. The problematic relationship between Europe and religion now and throughout history means that Europeans' views of other religions and the general reality of religion is impaired. Europeans tend to not

see their own religions in a good light, so their view of Islam is automatically cast in a more difficult light.

2. The effects and traces of the Crusades—and all of the clashes experienced with the Islamic world and the Ottomans—are deeply ingrained in the collective memories and sub-consciousness of Europeans. These effects persist, and the deep scars left from these periods have still not been erased.

3. Orientalism and the West's general me-oriented vanity should be added to all this. Of course, Europe does have a self-examining humanist face, but it tends to turn everyone who is not from Europe into the other, depicting these "others" in a one-sided fashion.

4. As a fourth factor here, we could add Europe's relationship with the Islamic world, based as it is on conflict, and the multi-dimensional differences in interests and motivations that divide Europe and the Islamic world.

This subject is one which should be discussed and kept alive in the eyes of Muslims who are looking for solutions these days. This is also a topic that should be considered by Turkey, which wants to become a full member of the EU. The primary expectation of the Muslim world from Obama is for this new leader to take a firm stance against the baseless fear of Islam created by America.

Europe Should Give up Isolating Itself[164]

Early in September 2009, French Interior Minister Brice Hortefeux made fun of the Muslims in his country. Opposition parties raised hell about it, demanding that he resign, but all these events were important in that they served to bring a truth to the surface. The minister made racist remarks.

Le Monde published video footage on its official Web site about the incident. In the footage, Hortefeux was standing next to a young party member of North African descent and who wanted to pose with the minister for a photo. The crowd around them began making jokes about "integration" and a woman from the party, referring to the young Amine

---

[164] First appeared in *Today's Zaman* on Sept. 18, 2009

Benalia-Brouch, says, "He's our little Arab." Another person tells the minister that he eats pork and drinks beer, and Hortefeux responds: "Ah, well that's no good then, he doesn't fit the stereotype at all, then. Not at all like that. All the better. You should always have one. When there's one of them, that's OK. It's when there's lots of them that you get problems. OK, good luck..."[165]

There was a similar incident in Austria in June 2009. Interior Minister Maria Fekter had said, "All refugees in the country should be kept under control in a camp and they should be banned from leaving the boundaries set for them. Otherwise, they commit crimes."[166]

While the reactions of the French and Austrian interior ministers may seem different, they are essentially the same. The French minister's reaction is "cultural" while the Austrian minister's is "criminologic." Yet, both ministers imply that the problems they are referring to are basically caused by the failure of foreigners who came to Europe from outside—these include those coming from colonies, immigrant workers, and refugees—to integrate with the Western society in addition to their behavior, which disturbs this society.

The cultures of societies consist of value judgments, the reference framework they adopt, and their historical experiences. In this process, religion plays a major role. According to a study conducted on Turkish workers in Germany, the first thing that made the Turkish workers who went to this country in the 1960s become aware of their own identities was their encounter with pork. When they saw meals made from pork, they remembered that they were Muslims, and whether devoutly religious or not, they refrained from eating pork. Here we observe the important role played by religion.

Of course, societies influence each other, a natural and expected phenomenon. The current status of some African clans, which seem primitive to us, is mostly attributed to their isolation from the external world. There are several reasons for this. Sometimes extreme self-confidence or a sense of self-sufficiency may cause societies to sever their ties with the external world.

---

[165] Quoted in *Milliyet*, Sept. 12, 2009
[166] Quoted in *Radikal*, Jun. 22, 2009

There are important reasons behind the tension Europe is experiencing with foreigners. Some relate to historical and religious factors while others are connected to the level of socioeconomic welfare. Political and military factors that cause conflict and tension, too, can be added to this list. Yet there is a plain truth: In the past, European countries failed to develop multi-religious, multi-ethnic political structures—contrary to what Muslim states did. When Protestantism emerged as an interpretation of Christianity different from Catholicism, wars and massacres followed. One-third of the continent's population lost its life in this process. During that time, there existed not only different sects of Islam, but also different religions under the rule of Muslim states. In a sense, what gave Islam its dynamism in history was its ability to develop multi-religious, multi-ethnic social models.

Today, there are two major problems facing the West: First, the West is extremely self-confident of its culture—therefore enjoying the false belief that there is nothing it can learn from other societies; and second, the West does not care for the problems, famines, or poverty in other parts of the world as it tries to preserve its standard of life. Europe and more generally the West have responsibilities toward the non-Western world. They have to fulfill these responsibilities by opening themselves to the external world and treating them as their equals.

Reasons Not to Trust the EU[167]

Turkey shaped its foreign policy during the 1950s according to the Cold War conditions in place at the time. Shouldering a role within the Western alliance, Turkey both helped protect Europe's security and found itself delivered from the responsibility of developing its own defense strategy.

This was a level of comfort that a lethargic mindset could only dream of. No doubt those who made Turkey into a NATO member thought that the struggles between the two main polarized blocs would last forever.

In 1990 though, a polarized world suddenly collapsed. It was as though Turkey fell into a vacuum, splitting off—if not officially, at least

---

[167] First appeared in *Today's Zaman* on Dec. 10, 2012

practically—from the center to which it was connected. One inevitable result of this was to elicit questions in the minds of many of what its "new foreign policy preferences" were going to be. Making a new choice in foreign policy was not slated to be easy for Turkey, as the new choice was going to both force it to emerge from its listless state of the past, as well as force it to find some new defense resources.

And in fact, neither Turkey's intellectual stock nor its economic strength ended up being sufficient to meet its new demands and situation.

The leaders who came later did not learn the necessary lessons from the many decades between1950-1990; they thought that Turkey could overcome the new problems it was facing by becoming a full member of the EU. They pointed to the EU as being a gateway to hope in front of Turkey. This is despite the truth that, even if Turkey were to become a full EU member, it is doubtful whether Europe would really be interested in protecting Turkey's real interests.

A decline in support for the EU among Turkish citizens—from around 78 percent in 2002 to around 30 percent in 2012—is the result of a lack of trust in the EU on the societal level. As new developments in the Balkans, the Caucuses, and the Middle East continue to unfold to the detriment of Turkey, the growing difference between Turkey and the EU emerges with more clarity. As the public sees it, trusting Europe was, from the very beginning, a mistake.

At this point, it might be appropriate to remind those of you who find my comments biased of some words from historian Fernand Braudel. In his book "The Mediterranean and the Ancient World," this French historian talks about the three civilizations formed in and around the Mediterranean up until today. According to Braudel, these are the Catholic Christian, the Christian Orthodox, and the Islamic civilizations. Despite some support shown by Orthodox Slavs for the Muslims against the Catholics during the first Crusades, the fact is that in the Balkan Wars—which occurred at the start of the 20th century—these two arms of the Christian world united to fight the Ottoman state and Islamic civilization. What is clear from Braudel's analysis herein is that the Balkan Wars were a reawakening of the spirit of the Crusades, with cooperative efforts aimed at dealing a deadly blow to the Islamic world.

Can we really say now that this "spirit of the Crusades" has disappeared? For as long as right and fair reasons justifying the invasions and occupations of Iraq and Afghanistan are not found, this question will continue to be asked.

Another significant development is this:

No one can allege that the whole "clash of civilizations" idea has really disappeared from the global agenda. Whether it is Bernard Lewis or Samuel Huntington, those who throw this theory out for people to think about are really talking about religions, not civilizations. Despite the spread of nihilism produced by modernity, the factor of religion looks set to play a stronger and stronger role in international political relations every day.

This being the situation, Turkey must turn to its essential and genuine axis, and find ways to create healthy and sustainable alliances with partners-in-fate traversing the same axis. And this enterprise is one which will—in an era when regionalization and new regional integration is occurring parallel to globalization—happen only through putting the dynamics of an Islamic union into motion.

Varying Stances on Islam Bear the Potential to Dissociate Europe[168]

The main theme of the referendum in Switzerland was "No to minarets, no to Sharia, no to the burqa, and therefore no to Muslims and the religion of Islam." Swiss Minister of Justice Eveline Widmer-Schlumpf said it was not "a referendum against Islam...but a vote directed against fundamentalist developments."

According to this view, minarets are an "Islamic demand" and Islamism means fundamentalism. This is called making matters worse when trying to be helpful. Which part of this error should be fixed? Minarets have been around for much longer than pan-Islamism. There is no relation between these honest Islamic symbols and the fundamentalism people are trying, incorrectly, to connect to Islam.

---

[168] First appeared in *Today's Zaman* on Dec. 08, 2009

The campaign was led by right-wing, racist, xenophobic groups and those who don't want immigrants in the country. But more and more people are paying more attention to "Islamic opposition." The arguments rightists and racists are using in their campaigns are very important. The head of the Party for Freedom (PVV) in the Netherlands, Geert Wilders, compared the Qur'an to Hitler's book "Mein Kampf" and said it was just as fascist a book. The PVV is not a marginal party; it received the second largest number of votes from the Dutch in the European Parliament elections.

This individual, who is also the maker of the film "Fitna" (Strife), is openly saying "no to mosques" because he is "tired of the worship of God and Muhammad in the Netherlands." This racist is so ignorant that he does not know that Muslims believe Muhammad (pbuh) is solely a Prophet and do not worship him.

According to whites-only British National Party (BNP) leader Nick Griffin, Islam is a "wicked and vicious faith." The party has two members in the European Parliament. Griffin is bringing a new meaning to racism and the freedom of expression. He describes former Ku Klux Klan leader David Duke as "always totally non-violent." He expressed his views before 8.2 million viewers on the BBC program "Question Time."

The point we have reached is thought provoking. One out of every six members of the European Parliament is racist and xenophobic. By all means it may be said that these views are expressed by the members of certain parties. Of course it is that way. The important point is that those who spread hatred, racist thoughts, and xenophobia emphasize "liberal thinking and freedom of expression." How much liberalism this view philosophically allows is another issue. The point in question is protecting hatred, racism, insults, and enmity with freedom of expression. Whenever Muslims and Islamic opposition are in question in particular, liberal politicians immediately bring up "freedom of expression."

These racist tendencies, which are on the rise, are related to Europe's process of defining its own identity. Multiculturalism, which envisioned that everyone would be able to coexist whilst retaining their own unique identities and sharing the same rights as others, did not find the support expected in Europe. "Europeanism and European Union ideals" are insufficient in building a common and unifying identity. Europe will either return to its Christian roots like the pope said and define its identity in that way or resort to racism and xenophobia-driven nationalism. We should bear in mind that this is a dangerous, conflict-prone, and destructive identity fostered by Western secularism, which leads to nihilism. Those who are attempting to build a new identity are factionalizing Muslims and Islam by presenting them as "an imminent and ready danger."

European racists are going to want to spread more hatred toward Muslims and try to demonize Muslims living in Europe as well as the global Muslim world. But the main conflict will emerge and continue in Europe. On the one side there will be those who defend building Europe's new identity on the basis of Christianity and those who are in the "democratic bloc" (liberals, Greens, socialists, Christian Social Democrats) who argue that racist fanaticism, racism, and xenophobia will harm Europe— and on the other hand there will be racists and fascists.

After the attack on the twin towers on Sept. 11, 2001, Henry Kissinger said the real conflict would continue within Islam between the radicals and moderates. Today we can say the same for Europe and the West in general. The basic problem that is dividing Europe is the disagreement over the stance against Islam and Muslims. This disagreement is dividing different European ideologies. The question is will the West choose to live peacefully with Islam or choose to clash?

Islam is helping Europe remember God and enabling it to face itself in the mirror. Of course we as Muslims are going to stand beside sincere Christians, non-Zionist Jews, and the democrat bloc that defends living together.

Dialogue of People from Various Religions[169]

The part of efforts launched in the name of fostering inter-religious dialogue that seems most meaningful to me is that in a world where so many things are said and done about religions, the need for mutual visits and the exchange of ideas between people from different religions clearly stands out. The subject of "inter-religious dialogue," frequently

---

[169] First appeared in *Today's Zaman* on Jan. 11, 2008

pronounced at the international level, is a result of this need for mutual visits and the exchange of ideas. Some (biased) people assess mutual visits between different religions as part of conspiracy theories and either interpret them as an attempt to serve a dubious purpose such as "combining all the religions" or try to portray these meetings as the Christian world's efforts to fool the Muslim world. Both theories are incorrect because except for the quintessential unity of the true Abrahamic religions, it is impossible to unify all religions given their current forms, teachings, and sacraments, and to establish a new religion that would be a mixture of all of them; only naive humanists or deists can believe this may happen. On the other hand, Muslims are not credulous people who will take such bait.

The ethnic and religious conflicts in certain crisis-prone regions of the world are getting deeper by the day. And unfortunately, the legitimacy of an important part of these conflicts is based on religions. Many fascist leaders and murderers claim that they kill their enemies in the name of their religion. The most recent and horrific example of this is Serb ethnic cleansing of Muslims in Bosnia and Kosovo in the 1990s. But on the other hand, we know that some sincere clerics from the Orthodox Church did oppose the massacres perpetrated by those abusing Christianity. Some priests openly declared that the war in Bosnia was in no way tolerable or legitimate according to Christianity and declared their churches as against the war in Bosnia. What harm could it ever bring upon anyone for Muslim scholars to exchange views and ideas with such Christian clerics?

In addition, many clerics from the Catholic world want all religions to adopt a common stance against atheism, pornography, prostitution, the dissolution of the family, homosexuality, drugs, alcoholism, the culture of consumption, and nihilism into which people are rapidly sliding. Undoubtedly, this cultural and moral degeneration is dangerous also for the religion of Islam. Islam does not aim for the sole salvation of Muslims; it is a message of salvation for the entire humanity.

We should, on the other hand, bear in mind that the Christian Church in the past helped colonialists and played a great role in the establishment of the deeply rooted prejudice against the Islamic world by inciting the Crusades. However, as some Christian theologians put it, bringing up this historical fact over and over again does not serve any purpose except to create further enmity and more rifts. The process we, as humanity, are going through threatens all religions and beliefs and causes humankind to decay.

Looking from this angle—and in terms of the attacks made on all religions and the subjects that are of concern to all religions—inter-religious dialogue and cooperation are initiatives that point to the spirit of the new times.

There is something that has recently caught my attention: When we take a close look at the identity of the people who launch such sincere initiatives and who make painstaking endeavors in this great cause, all are, regardless of their religious identity, people who take their religion seriously and firmly believe that their religion is a means of salvation. And the underlying reason for people from secular segments to be against such initiatives is that they are disturbed to see religion being taken seriously. And without a doubt, the idea that religions can be saviors is one that can never be taken into regard by people feeding on traditional French secularism. However, nowadays, strangely enough, the Catholic Church claims that secularism, with extreme practices and borders, is causing social values—and the family in particular—to collapse. Leaders such as French President Nicolas Sarkozy confirm this. Moreover, Sarkozy also says that secularism will not be able to efface France's Christian identity.

The Pro-active Asset of Global Peace: Religious Diversity[170]

It is true that among the European public and particularly among elitist circles, "Islam" and the Islamic identity of Turkey—a candidate for full membership in the EU—has led to questions as to whether this would bring reconciliation between Islam and the modern world, and whether Muslims are able to coexist with Europeans in peace.

---

[170] First appeared in *Today's Zaman* on Sept. 19, 2008

In terms of religion, Muslims have extensive experience of coexisting with others. Throughout history, Muslims have lived together with Christians and Jews. Muslims have also coexisted peacefully with the followers of other religions, such as the Kurdish minority of Yazidis. Currently living in the province of Mardin in Southeastern Turkey and in northern Iraq, Yazidis follow an ancient religion derived from Zoroastrianism.

The tolerant Ottoman experience has not yet been adequately explored. Without making exaggerations or excessive claims, it could be said that our experience and art of coexistence is rich enough to make us understand the deep crisis that the modern world is going through—and to help overcome that crisis.

Another point that needs to be underlined is that currently, the major religions have entered a process by which they take a critical look at their histories, adopt a stance to understand each other, and make interfaith dialogue efforts acceptable to all. For the present time, it does not seem possible to point to a potential clash between religions or their followers. Politicians, military decision-making circles, economic interest groups, and other lobbies may seek to provoke such a clash by exploiting religions. But there is no such clash in reality. Quite the contrary, religious leaders are looking for possibilities to assume roles in solving the common problems of all humanity.

Undoubtedly, assuming common roles and responsibilities vis-à-vis common global problems and entering a process of mutual understanding does not mean ignoring the fundamental theological principles of religions, neglecting religious diversity, or inventing a new religion out of existing ones. This is neither possible nor desirable.

However, no one can ignore the importance of the factor religion plays in the solutions to the problems facing the world. God created us for a wise reason and asked us to coexist based on peace and mutual understanding. Maybe we used to live far away from each other or on isolated islands in the middle of the sea in the past; in those times, staying away from each other was possible to some extent. Our mutual relations were based on deadly and bloody wars. But today, we have entered a new world and a new era.

Global mobility, interdependence, and transformation in the movement and flow of goods, services, information, and transportation make the isolation of geographies and local cultures impossible. The EU cannot isolate itself. There are about 20 million Muslims living in EU countries, even if Turkey is not admitted. Admitting Turkey as a member with its own cultural and historical identity will make the EU more diverse and rich, aborting the infamous clash of civilizations thesis.

Giving a precise date to Turkey for a start of negotiations is not the assurance of full membership. However, starting the negotiation process is important in terms of rapprochement between two different cultures and two diverse lifestyles. The Prophet Muhammad (pbuh) said, "People are enemies of what they do not know." Today, what we define as "the other" and a threat is actually who we do not know. The best way to prevent greater tragedies is to develop processes by which we understand each other and improve our relations and dialogue. Turks seem to be ready for this.

To this end, it is possible to say that religion is an opportunity and asset rather than an obstacle to Turkey's membership in the EU. If dialogue is further improved between religions and if the followers of these religions express their willingness to coexist, this will reduce the legitimacy and justification of a number of conflicts.

Mardin Model: The Peaceful Coexistence of Diverse Identities[171]

As the modern nation-states go through tremors, the question of how diverse constituents can live together emerges as a fundamental question.

When the Soviet Union disintegrated, it was said that the doors of the building in which different religions and ethnicities were imprisoned were opened to let them go free. Yes, the Soviet Union was a big prison that kept diverse identities under tight control; however, before long, it was understood that the Western world and other geographies were in a similar situation.

---

[171] First appeared in *Today's Zaman* on Jul. 03, 2009

Localization on one hand and regionalization and globalization on the other are dealing big blows to the nation-state. The nation-state would propose that individuals should have a singular identity defined from high above. Actually, it would not only propose it, but also impose this endorsed identity and repress other identities. People might not be raising their voices, but this would not mean that they were perfectly satisfied with this repressive identity. Indeed, at the first opportunity, they acted to make what they thought to be their primary identity more visible.

While the nation state was being battered by the above-mentioned factors, modern society entered a process of disintegration in the postmodern era. The question is how to make sure diverse religious, ethnic, and cultural communities can live together peacefully. This is one of several questions which are the most taxing in the postmodern period.

In parallel to the weakening of multiculturalism in the West, right-wing parties and racist and xenophobic movements grew stronger, which implies that there are grave problems with respect to the coexistence of diverse identities in Western countries. If things go on in this manner, we can say that differentiation among different groups will become more salient in near future.

There is no doubt that the people who have respect for diverse religions, cultures, and ethnicities are trying to find solutions to this issue of coexistence. As the positivism of the 19th century and the idea of a Western-oriented process of modernization are left behind, people are turning their eyes to different resources. At this point, authentic referential sources of religions and historic experiences of different human geographies gain importance.

We have a concrete example at hand: Mardin. Located in southeastern Anatolia near the northern border with Syria, this city is considered "unlucky" as it is economically "underdeveloped" and it has not been "modernized." However, this very quality can also be regarded as its luck. Indeed, the city has a past dating back several thousands of years, and one can see the concrete architectural traces of this ancient history that date back 850 to 5,000 years ago. Moreover, these building are not derelict but are currently being used as mosques, inns, and churches. In addition, there are several religious groups living side by side: Muslims, Syriacs—with its three different sects—and Yazidis, whose numbers are considerably small now. From an ethnic point of view, we can discern Arabs, Kurds, and Turks. There are even Arabized Circassian and Chechen people. The houses of the people who migrated from Hungary to this city are still there.

After the 1960s, there was a sizable decrease in the number of Syriacs, from 70,000 to 3,500 today. The Syriac Orthodox Patriarchate moved from Mardin to Damascus in 1932. Nowadays, Syriac families are returning to Mardin from metropolitan areas and from Europe. Except for places of worship and cemeteries, we see that Syriacs and Muslims use the same markets, neighborhoods, and streets. In other words, diverse religious and ethnic groups do not live in isolated ghettos but can intermingle with each other at any time of day.

Last week, several Turkish journalists and writers were invited to Mardin. For two days they discussed the "rehabilitation of the social texture and the perspective for a democratic future." They all agreed on this conclusion: everyone must come to Mardin in order to see in actuality how differences can coexist peacefully in this great center of civilization. Another point that everyone emphasized was that Mardin Governor Hasan Duruer, Mardin Mayor Mehmet Beşir Ayanoğlu, and Artuklu University Rector Serdar Bedii Omay are working in harmony to make this city a model city of modern times.

Diversity Is Our Richness[172]

It is commonly agreed that we need greater tolerance in an era where crisis, conflict, and uncertainties are regarded as the spirit of our time.

The entire world—and not just certain parts of it—is in desperate need of greater tolerance. In terms of recent developments, we can conclude that the world has never been in a state of such extreme crisis and chaos.

There are now a number of crisis regions; new conflict zones emerge on a constant basis. Nobody would expect 15 years ago that a small African country, Rwanda, would become an area of bloodshed and mas-

---

[172] First appeared in *Today's Zaman* on May 23, 2011

sacre. Nearly one million men and women were slaughtered over a two-week period.

We are currently dealing with a situation and phenomenon that influences the entire globe. These tragedies may be given different titles or diagnoses. However, there is one reality: It is now a great risk for people to lead their lives in a time viewed as the peak of the civilizational journey. Tribal habits and intolerance are kept alive in such a time of great civilizational progress. The ideology of macro nationalism that defines the other as a harmful, threatening, and dangerous enemy that needs to be destroyed can transform into mass hysteria. At every popular gathering, say a soccer game, these hysteric sentiments turn into war calls that urge people to join the crusade against their foes.

However, from an alternate point of view, our world is comparable to a rich garden adorned with colorful flowers. *"And among His Signs are the creation of the heavens and the earth, and the difference of your languages and colors. Verily, in that are indeed signs for men of sound knowledge"* (Surah ar-Rum 30:22). Every religion, culture, philosophy, and belief adds different colors to the richness in this garden. We cannot all possibly think the same way. God has created us different. Had He wished, He would have created us one single nation; but instead He bestowed on us different methods and paths. These differences become apparent in behaviors, norms, traditions, and customs. This does not necessarily mean that there is no single truth, that every religion represents a different truth, and that Islam as the final revelation of God's will and preference will not promote its call among others. Multiplicity among unity is the result of respect for the One and the assurance for coexistence along with diversities and differences.

Every group and every nation contributes to this diversity and beauty by acting in reference to the legacy it inherited from its unique history. In this case, there is no other way than maintaining an environment of tolerance between the different religions, cultures, and traditions. We may hold different points of views; however, tolerance and respect for others, as well as other similar fundamental notions, have to be commonly endorsed and adopted by all.

Maybe it is time to reconsider different thoughts as well as traditions that have been ignored from a different perspective. To start with, the UN should change its stance vis-à-vis different thoughts and cultures. An organization arguing that it has a mission to represent the nations of the world and address their problems is supposed to pay attention to other traditions and appreciate their values. This should be underlined: If the ongoing problems are trans-boundary in nature, in this case, we have to find solutions that will be based upon common cultural inquiries and efforts.

We are inheritors of a cultural legacy and tradition that teaches us to live together with different religious and ethnic groups in peace and harmony. In our rich history with diverse experiences, no coercive policies such as assimilation or integration with the dominant culture have been pursued. Quite the contrary, as the diversities of different religious and cultural groups were legally protected.

In our culture, a human being is invaluable. For this reason, his fundamental rights—regardless of whether they are inherent by birth or acquired later—are sacred. The preservation of diversity is one of these fundamental rights. The preservation of diversity is the duty of the state as a result of respect for God's will. In the end, God has created all of us different and asked us to rush to goodness. In this case, we all have a responsibility to protect the human being and help him improve himself; this is inevitably related to tolerance.

Interview

They Have Gained Access to the Secrets of the AK Party's Cosmic Chamber[173]

Ali Bulaç, who served Recep Tayyip Erdoğan as an advisor between 1995 and 1998, says, "A Unionist team[174] infiltrated the Turkish foreign ministry and the cosmic chamber[175] of the AK Party in 2011. This Unionist team convinced Erdoğan that he would construct anew the Ottoman Empire and would become the leader of the Middle East."

Did you ever guess that the Middle East would become this turbulent?

I should first note that the prevailing situation in the region is mainly the result of the faulty policies that Iran and Turkey followed. There is also the reality of China and India rising in Asia. While the USA is focusing now on the Far East, it does not want the Middle East to remain as a region of military engagement.

---

[173] "AK Parti'nin Kozmik Odasına Girdiler" (They Have Gained Access to the Secrets of the AK Party's Cosmic Chamber), interview by Fatih Vural, *Bugün* daily, June 15, 2014.

[174] The secretive Unionists (or *İttihatçıs* in Turkish) are regarded as the successor elites of "the Committee of Union and Progress" (CUP), who have worked to achieve their common goal of grabbing power, overthrowing governments, or changing the administration by relying on pressure, coercion and anti-democratic methods. They've been active since the late Ottoman period.

[175] The term "cosmic chamber" does not necessarily refer to a special top secret place where the plans of a power structure are decided upon or where their top secrets are archived. It is more of the dirty laundries or innermost secrets of a power structure, which is generally referred to as, or rather dubbed, "the cosmic chamber," especially by the Turkish press.

So, there was a need for a regional power to play a role here. The three most important actors in the region are Turkey, Iran, and Egypt. However, Egypt has heavily been influenced by the oppressive regime of Mubarak, and Iran has been clashing with the West since the Islamic revolution. Turkey, on the other hand, is a Nato country. It is continuing the EU accession process, and has been undergoing a process of westernization for over two centuries. It lays claim to practicing both democracy and Islam together.

All this gave Turkey a head start, but there were three things that the global powers demanded from Turkey. The first was to keep Israel within safe borders and to make it a state accepted in the region. The second was to prevent any damage to petroleum wells and energy power lines. The third was to prevent radical groups, of the al Qaida sorts, from coming to power. They told Turkey, "If you accept this, we are going to make you the Japan of the Western world." And Turkey agreed to all of this.

When did they ask all this?

During the negotiations taking place between the years of 2000 and 2002. This is how they paved the way for the AK Party.[176] President Clinton publically instructed the European Union from his plane: "Lift the barriers in front of Turkey." When he came to Turkey, he further said, "Turkey is going to construct the 21st century."

This was not just lip service, but a strategy. They said, "If what is preventing you is the army, then we are going to sideline all those members of the military." Accordingly, the Erdoğan government passed the democratic reforms, and the direct foreign investment increased. The synergy of Turkey also became a source of inspiration for the Arab Spring.

---

[176] In December 2002, Erdoğan finally achieved to walk up the steps of the White House and was welcomed in the Oval Office by President Bush, though the politically banned Erdoğan was not even holding the prime minister's office at the time. Thus, Washington gave him full support, to the extent of according Erdoğan a presidential reception at the White House when he was only the head of the AK Party, but not yet elected to the Parliament.

Turkey Fell into the Trap of the Saudis

How did Turkey become a source of inspiration?

There were three important elements involved. One was the reaction against the oppressive regimes in the region. The second was the reaction against income inequality, poverty, and unemployment. And the third was the reaction against Israel. When the democratic transformation of Turkey is considered together with the revolution in Iran and the awakening among the Arabs, this transformation is something which would save their honor as well. But a fundamental change took place in Turkish foreign policy in the year 2011.

What was that change?

When demonstrations began in Syria like the ones in Tunisia and Egypt, Turkey made a strategy change and supported the armed groups there instead of persuading Bashar al-Assad to introduce more reforms over a long period of time. It thus caused the militarization of the Syrian civilian opposition. Here, Turkey fell into the trap of the Saudis, who persuaded Turkey to support the armed struggle in the first place. As such, a good number of people flew into Syria across the Turkish border in places like Iskenderun, Hatay and Kilis. Turkish hospitals gave medical treatment to the people brought from Libya and some other parts of Africa, and they were given safe harbor. These people were financed, and sent to Syria to fight in an armed struggle. Of course, Turkey wasn't the only country allowing this. A multitude of people entered Syria from Jordan, Lebanon and Iraq, and the civil war began.

Iran, on the other hand, is giving logistic support, money and weapons to Syria, Hamas, and Hezbollah. Iran saw that Assad's Syria was about to fall, and that this would be a blow to Hezbollah. All this would chop off its Shiite arms and legs; thus, it has also intervened in the civil war in Syria.

If Turkey did not militarize the Syrian opposition in that period, and if Iran had persuaded Syrian President Assad to negotiate, then Assad's relationship with Turkey would be much better now. Assad was indeed listening to Turkey at the time and whatever reforms he was carrying out, he used Turkey as a model. For instance, he had made the reform regulations concerning the local administrations according to Turkey's legislation in this area. Every time I visited Syria during this period, I could see that the country had leapt forward ten years.

The Erdoğan Government Wanted to Dominate the Middle East over Syria

Prime Minister Erdoğan said, "I told Assad to expedite the reforms, but he did not do it."

The truth is that Turkey asked Assad to accomplish in three months what it couldn't do in thirty years. Even if Assad launched more radical reforms, Turkey would not have accepted it. The Erdoğan government's strategy was this: "We were late in Libya. Let us not be late in Syria. Let us act together with Saudi Arabia. Let us establish a regime in Syria, favorable to us. And then let us dominate the Middle East over Syria." But Turkey misread three things.

What were they?

The first was the fact that Assad was not someone to be overthrown in three months, as they had assumed. 45 percent of the Syrian population is behind Assad. All of the Nusayris and Christians, some of the Kurds, secular Arab nationalists and secular Sunnis, many scholars, and many in the business world, especially the business market of Aleppo, are supporting Assad. In this case, the Arab nationalists are the only ones the Erdoğan government could rely on. But the Arab nationalists would never accept Turkey as a leader.

The second mistake was Turkey's misreading of the region. According to a treaty of strategic alliance signed by Iran and Syria in 2006, if one of them were attacked, the other was going to provide support.

We Cannot Overpower Syria

Before the civil war, Assad publically said, "I am willing to become the 82nd province of Turkey. The only thing I ask of you is that you will not disturb our relationship with Iran."

However, the policy of the Turkish government was based on detaching Syria from Iran and bringing it closer to the West; the hope was that, through this, Turkey could dominate the Arab world. Syria detected this and became apprehensive. The Turkish foreign ministry interpreted this as, "Iran, Iraq, and Lebanon are now together with Syria. If we intervene in Syria militarily, we will have to fight the other three, as well. We are not up to the task. We cannot even handle Syria."

Why did they think that Turkey can't handle Syria?
Militarily speaking, the air force of Syria is, for instance, four times superior to that of Turkey. But Turkey has committed a third mistake. It has established the NATO radar system in Kurecik, Malatya. In return, Russia greatly modernized its own military facilities in the Syrian port of Tartus. Indeed, no one knows what the new Russian weapons are. In order to find out, Turkey flew reconnaissance planes over them. But they downed this plane over Iskenderun. Strangely enough, the thing which downed the plane was not a rocket, but the heat spread by a rocket. This advanced technology intimidated the USA, too. It understood that Turkey cannot overthrow Assad on its own.

Al Qaida Is in the Service of the Saudis

Who imported al Qaida into the region?
My personal opinion is that there is no direct involvement of any state behind al Qaida, but petroleum-rich princes. Al Qaida is one of the strongest terrorist organizations of all time. It was established upon a certain doctrine, but without an organizational structure. Therefore, it is not that easy to figure it out or control it. Those who established it are usually well-educated engineers, lawyers, and so on. They have graduate degrees and are very proficient in advanced technology. A large segment of the organization has entered into politics as Arab nationalists or Marxists. In the final analysis, this organization is serving the Saudi's regional strategies.

What is the Saudi's regional strategy?
It is the patronage ideology, centered on the Saudi's Wahhabi and Salafi ideologies. They do not want Turkey to revive the Ottomans. They do not

want the Muslim Brotherhood, centered in Egypt, to dominate the region, either. They hate the Shia, too. Therefore, these Saudis are competing with Turkey, Iran, and Egypt. They have established links with the Islamic groups and fighters throughout the world, especially after the Afghan war.

The Sunnis in both Iraq and Syria are left to their fate. Turkey could not have anticipated this, but the Saudis were entrenched in this zone. On top of al Qaida, first al Nusra and then ISIL appeared.

There Is a Danger of Irreligiosity Spreading

*How did the etatist Islamists influence
the secular man's perception of religion in Turkey?*

They have proved the emptiness of their religiosity, lacking the very essence of religion. They emerged as the new-rich, which have turned to consumption and vanity and which have escaped into their luxurious complex settlements, forgetting their humble past.

*Has this rich class, backed up by the AK Party,
become the new elite of the Turkish state?*

Yes, they have, and they have been growing in the state's greenhouse. They are not producers, but commission agents. They open the green space in cities to development and simply act as the middle men. They suddenly acquire enormous amounts of money (while turning all the green space into housing developments and shopping malls). But they do not transform this big money into investments. This is because they do not know how to produce. They simply buy for themselves a luxurious SUV like a "Beast of the Earth," (*Dabbatu'l-Ard*) or they buy the most expensive clothes and headscarves for their spouses. Leaving their former neighborhoods in Beykoz, Fatih, Uskudar, or Cengelkoy, they escape to the new settlements with high security on the shores of the Bosporus. The people they left behind are now saying, "Their Islam serves but to fatten their pockets," and they are developing a hatred against or opposition to the religion itself. Can there be a catastrophe greater than this?

What is the religious consequence of this?

It's very serious, indeed. It is, however, an obligation for all those who are well-aware of the true value of the religion to develop a critical attitude and oppose such degeneration and decay. Otherwise, without being aware of it, this society could become full of non-believers or materialists. When people lose their hope in religion, nihilism could take its place. Throughout its history, this society has never been so fractured. It is, therefore, necessary for all, including and especially the believing leftists and Islamists, to come together and re-assess the situation.

Would the end of the AK Party also mean the end of political Islam in Turkey?

No. But I don't agree, first, with the claim that the AK Party is Islamist. The party members have stuck to the arguments of religion just to legitimize what they have been doing, especially after 2011. In reality, however, they have revoked the *muamalat*—the practical, legal aspect of religion regarding all of the transactions between people. These are, indeed, the people who have given up Islamism. But all these wrongdoings will make it difficult for any new party having an Islamic background to come to power in the future.

Iran and Turkey Can Stop ISIL

What is the goal of ISIL?

Its goal is to take the historic land of Sham (*bilad as-Sham*)—which includes the entire region of Syria, Lebanon, Jordan, Palestine, and Iraq— under its control. As such, a new Salafi state is emerging with the Wahhabi Saudi support in the south of Turkey. It has already taken over Mosul and it is advancing fast. Turkey is now in a miserable and desperate situation.

How far can ISIL advance in the fragmented Iraq?

It should first be noted that after the affairs of Egypt and Syria, the relationship between Turkey and Saudi Arabia went sour. The advance of ISIL is not in favor of Turkey or Iran. If they cooperate, however, they would stop ISIL. If not, ISIL will advance as long as the civil war continues in Syria. In Iraq, there is a weak administration anyway. Prime Minister Maliki is not in control of everything, and he has serious troubles with the Kurds of Iraq.

In that case, can we say that the probability for Iran
to make Turkey retreat in Syria is quite high?
Turkey has already lost the war in Syria. At this moment, it is in need of Iran in all respects. Turkey's influence on the Syrian opposition is also weakening. Two years ago, Turkey had a much better chance of success: it could persuade the Syrian opposition, and Iran could persuade Assad. In this way, the opposition would get out of the country, and Iran would make Hezbollah leave Syria. A road map could have been drawn.

However, Turkey and Iran are both misreading the region. The time of a nation state dominating the entire region is already over. The Kurds are unfortunately committing the same mistake. If Turkey, cooperating with Iran and Egypt, had gone into the region with a soft, democratizing power, it could have had a patronage to bring order in the region. This opportunity was there for the taking.

They Were Carried away with the Lust of Reviving the Ottomans

Why could not Turkey make use of this opportunity?
Because some adventurous Unionist team members seized control of Turkish foreign policy in 2011.

But don't you think that the backbone of this Unionist team
was already crushed through the Ergenekon case at that time?
These Unionists themselves are the secretive Ergenekon members who seemingly are against the clandestine Ergenekon organization! In a systematic fashion, they infiltrated the AK Party, and they seized control of the party's foreign policy. Just like Enver Pasha of the late Ottoman period, they started to entertain the lust of establishing a new Ottoman empire! In the beginning of 2012, in the Central Anatolian city of Kayseri, [Foreign Affairs Minister] Ahmet Davutoğlu said, "We are going to return to the pre-1911 borders. We are going to re-acquire all the land we lost. Without us, not a leaf can move in the region." What this sort of discourse means is that we are to annex 50 states across a vast territory of 20 million square kilometers from Bosnia to Yemen, from Crimea to central Africa. As you can see, the ultra-nationalist (*ulusalcı*) and

Islamist minds of Turkey are sick. Here is what they have in their minds: "An Islamic union or a regional union will be established. And this will be realized under the leadership of Turkey."

Have the Unionists also taken Erdoğan under its influence?

They have convinced Mr. Erdoğan by saying, "Mr. Erdoğan! You are going to be the leader of the Islamic world. With God's will, we are re-establishing the Ottoman empire from the Balkans to the Caucasus and from there down to central Africa!" And when they said this, the regional countries of Egypt, Iran, Jordan, and Syria stood up. One would normally expect these people to have taken a lesson at least from our near past, from the case of the late President Özal.

Özal once got Turkey into hot water by saying, "The 21st century will be the Turkish century." Even the Turkic republics in Central Asia did not endorse this kind of discourse. Once, the governor of Almaty, then the capital of Kazakhstan, had said to me, "You have come to us with a manner as if you were Canadians or someone from the First World. You keep giving us advice as if you have solved all of your problems."

Arabs Have Understood the Intentions of the Turkish Government

You have described 2011 as the year in which the Unionists seized the control of Turkish foreign policy. It is also considered as the year of Erdoğan's drastic change in domestic policies. Are these transformations in both domestic and foreign affairs concurrent?

Yes, I see them as simultaneous, concurrent. For Erdoğan, there is a rational reason for this drastic change both within and without Turkey. While his government was saying, "We are going to dominate the entire region once again," they also named the new Bosporus bridge after Yavuz Sultan Selim, the sultan who took the entire region under Ottoman control. This was sending a message to Iran: "We are going to stop you." They were also telling the Kurds: "You will be our dear ranger in charge of our farm."

In addition, they were saying to the Arabs: "We are coming. Like the four-century long rule following Yavuz Sultan Selim, we are going to dominate you for another 400 years." They even said, "Turkey must develop rapidly. The European Union is an obstacle in front of us. Turkey must have an authoritarian regime if it wants to develop more rapidly, like China. Therefore, let us detach ourselves from the EU accession proceedings."

When all these things in their agenda became clear, the Arab intellectuals and Islamists were awakened, saying: "Their intention is very bad. They wish to become neo-Ottomans." What is still alive in the minds of today's Arabs is the Committee of Union and Progress (CUP) of the late Ottoman period.

Arabs experienced nothing but oppression throughout the rule of the Committee of Union and Progress (which came after the CUP overthrew Sultan Abdülhamid II). They rightly wonder: "Why should we be under your control now?" In addition, there are about 300 million Arabs, a huge population that is much larger than the population of Turkey. In terms of natural resources, the Arab lands are much richer than Turkey. What's more, Islam emerged there. So, there is really no reason for Turkey's dominance over the region.

December 17, 2013: State Restoraton

Why did the suppression of plurality arise in the country in 2011?

The general public did not approve of Turkey's Syria policy. Our Alevi citizens were rightfully concerned. As the reactions grew, the AK Party government became increasingly authoritarian to suppress them. Here, it is important to point to the fact that the AK Party government was a coalition.

Who were included in this one-party coalition!?

AK Party originally came from the National View (Milli Gorus) tradition. The voting potential of this Islamist tradition is around 20 percent. Another significant part of this coalition is formed of center-right voters. In addition, the Kurds, the poor, and the traditionally conservative segments of Turkish society are the large voting blocks of this coalition. All religious orders and communities, fundamentalists, and moderate Islamists were also part of this one-party coalition.

In year 2011, however, the AK Party said: "This is not the sum of all voting constituents but our own vote, and we do not recognize any alliance or partnership with anyone."

However, the powerful will residing within the state was irritated by the very existence of the religious people within the state apparatus. This iron will deemed their presence to be totally against the establishment philosophy of this laicist state! Thus, they said, "Let's clear the state of them." This reflex is well-established within the state!

What kind of reflex is this?

An unrelenting one. The military interventions of May 27, 1960, March 12, 1971, September 12, 1980, the postmodern coup of February 28, 1997, and finally December 17, 2013 are all the continuation of this reflex. This time, on December 17th, and unlike the earlier events, the state is restoring itself through the ruling AK Party. They said, "Let's start the restoration by clearing out the strongest actor!"

The State Is Going to Make Use of the AK Party to the Full Extent, Then Throw It Away!

You mean they have started this process with the Hizmet Movement?

Exactly. It is because the Hizmet Movement (or "the Community" as it is popularly referred to in Turkey) is very strong. It has a universal global vision. It establishes dialogue with people from all walks of life and in all languages through the world, and it is very successful in developing these relationships. It has an internationally-accepted etiquette and societal support. It addresses the vast majority of the middle class; therefore, when it demands further democratization, you cannot disregard or suppress it. It is independent of the government and is not sustained through the financial resources of the state, either.

But the AK Party has been involved in widespread corruption. When the secretive Unionists gained access to the innermost secrets of the party's cosmic chamber and the foreign affairs ministry, they made Erdoğan accept this doctrine: "The governmental power normally belongs to the Republican People's Party (CHP) backed up by the military. But, we have now taken CHP's place. Therefore, we need to reconcile with the 'deep state'."[177]

---

[177] The "deep state" has a specific meaning and origin in Turkey where a small oligarchical elite cadre retains a stranglehold on democratic politics. With its entrenched,

Then the only thing that changed is the actors of the tutelage.

Exactly. They persuaded the AK Party by saying, "There is a populous Turkish army, one of the biggest in the world. There is a huge Turkey behind you. We are going to start peace negotiations with the Kurds. We are going to be a power in the Middle East. Beware! Never rely on your supporting partners. They would cheat you, or sell you out." So, they have begun with the Hizmet Movement.

First, they have begun a major operation on the Nur Movement (from which the Hizmet Movement originated). They have also started closing down the dormitories of the Suleyman Efendi community. They are threatening the Mahmut Efendi community as well.

The other religious communities' turn will also come, because this is a major operation, or rather the project of the state. After using the AK Party to the full extent, it is going to throw it away. Similar to how they imprisoned the people after they made use during the postmodern coup of February 28, they are going to do the same to the people of the AK Party when they are completely finished with them. This is how it works all the time. This state is like a spirit migrating from one body to another, thus reincarnating itself endlessly. At this moment it is living in the body of the AK Party.

The Civic Religious Communities Have Turned into State Organizations

Ironically, the AK Party has still been getting the support of many religious orders and communities even after all this. How did it win them over?

The religious orders and communities [that are supposed to be independent of the government] have first been obliged to the help of the municipalities since 1995, and then to the financial resources directly controlled by the central administration since 2002. Cutting these financial resources would result in the extinction of their activities. This net-

---

hidden existence deep within the state, this dual, or deep, state forms the backbone of power intervening whenever they deem it necessary, and is ever-able to calibrate or manipulate the policies of the "democratic state."

work of relationships that is based upon mutual interest has even made them legally guilty.

Then, many of the religious orders and communities in Turkey are not NGOs, are they?

For something to be counted as a [non-governmental] civic society organization, it has to be volunteer-based and independent of the government. Beginning with the rule of the Welfare Party (RP), when money started to be transferred from the state funds to these religious organizations, they were no longer civic society organizations: they have become "state establishments."

The AK Party: The Greatest Catasrophe since the Gallipoli War

Can we also talk about the concept of "the state's ulama" in this period?

The most important reason for Mustafa Kemal and his colleagues to be able to establish the Republic in the way they did was the war of Gallipoli. In that war, 50,000 Islamic scholars (*ulama*) died. Leaving their books and classes in the religious schools of the time, they were martyred at the front. The entire stock of these religious scholars was exterminated in the war. And now, the AK Party is the greatest catastrophe that has befallen us since that war! It has transformed the scholars into those who are paid for and thus controlled by the government!

It virtually numbed their minds, making them unable to think reasonably. While they were supposed to continue their struggles in civic life along the line of the great Islamic jurist Abu Hanifa, they have helped sustain post-Kemalism. At this moment, it is mainly the Islamists building upon and giving strength to post-Kemalism.

So, it is kind of a post-Kemalism cursing Kemalism itself.

That's right. It is just like post-modernism, criticizing modernism: in the final analysis, it is the continuation of it.